Starting Points for Your Internet Exploration

The Web is like thousands of TV channels or 10,000 New York Public Libraries—it includes hours of entertainment and volumes and volumes of information. Here's a brief list of good starting places that will make it easy for you to find your way to the stuff you find intriguing or useful.

AltaVista: a big, fast, searchable database

http://www.altavista.digital.com

AudioNet: a guide to audio broadcasts on the Net

http://www.AudioNet.com

CNET's search.com: a one-stop starting point

http://www.search.com

Excite: more than just a directory

http://www.excite.com

Gamelan: Java applications sorted by category

http://www.gamelan.com

HotBot: a search tool from HotWired and Inktomi

http://www.hotbot.com

Infoseek: a search service with broad coverage

http://www.infoseek.com

Inktomi: a search tool using parallel computing

http://inktomi.berkeley.edu

Lycos: an enormous searchable database

http://www.lycos.com

100Hot: the most popular Web sites by category

http://www.hot100.com

Talk.com: a space to chat with celebs and regular folks

http://www.talk.com

Yahoo: a subject-oriented index to the Web

http://www.yahoo.com

Surfing the Internet with Netscape Communicator 4

Surfing the Internet with Netscape® Communicator 4

**Daniel A. Tauber and Brenda Kienan
with J. Tarin Towers**

SYBEX

San Francisco • Paris • Düsseldorf • Soest

Associate Publisher: Roger Stewart
Acquisitions Manager: Kristine Plachy
Acquisitions & Developmental Editor: Sherry Schmitt
Editors: Bonnie Bills, Anamary Ehlen, and Lee Ann Pickrell
Permissions Editor: Dana Dubinsky
Technical Editor: Dale Wright
Book Designer: Suzanne Albertson
Graphic Illustrator: Lucka Zivny
Desktop Publisher: Maureen Forys
Production Coordinators: Grey Magauran and Anton Reut
Proofreader: Charles Mathews
Indexer: Ted Laux
Cover Designer: Design Site
Cover Illustrator: Sergie Loobkoff
Cover Image: PhotoDisc™

Screen reproductions produced with Collage Complete.
Collage Complete is a trademark of Inner Media Inc.

SYBEX is a registered trademark of SYBEX Inc.

TRADEMARKS: SYBEX has attempted throughout this book to distinguish proprietary trademarks from descriptive terms by following the capitalization style used by the manufacturer.

Netscape Communications, the Netscape Communications logo, Netscape, and Netscape Navigator are trademarks of Netscape Communications Corporation.

The author and publisher have made their best efforts to prepare this book, and the content is based upon final release software whenever possible. Portions of the manuscript may be based upon pre-release versions supplied by software manufacturer(s). The author and the publisher make no representation or warranties of any kind with regard to the completeness or accuracy of the contents herein and accept no liability of any kind including but not limited to performance, merchantability, fitness for any particular purpose, or any losses or damages of any kind caused or alleged to be caused directly or indirectly from this book.

Photographs and illustrations used in this book have been downloaded from publicly accessible file archives and are used in this book for news reportage purposes only to demonstrate the variety of graphics resources available via electronic access. Text and images available over the Internet may be subject to copyright and other rights owned by third parties. Online availability of text and images does not imply that they may be reused without the permission of rights holders, although the Copyright Act does permit certain unauthorized reuse as fair use under 17 U.S.C. Section 107.

An earlier version of this book was published under the title *Surfing the Internet with Netscape® Navigator 3*, copyright ©1996 SYBEX Inc.

Library of Congress Card Number: 97-65909
ISBN: 0-7821-2055-5

Manufactured in the United States of America

10 9 8 7 6 5 4 3 2 1

Still, and always

To Lonnie Moseley—sister, mother, friend

And to her mother and family, with gratitude

Acknowledgments

A book is always a collaborative effort; this one has been especially so both in this edition and in all its past incarnations. We are indebted to the many people who have helped to make this book happen.

Our thanks go to contributing writers Peter Stokes and Sofia Marchant for their cheerful work under very tight deadlines.

At Sybex, thanks as always to Sybex heroines Barbara Gordon, Chris Meredith, and Kristine Plachy; to Sherry Schmitt, who got us all going; to Bonnie Bills, who kept us on track; to Anamary Ehlen and Lee Ann Pickrell, who checked our p's and q's; to Dan Brodnitz, who smoothed some rough bumps; to Ellen Bliss and Dale Wright, who saw to it that technical details were checked and correct; to Dana Dubinsky, who pursued screen-shot permissions like nobody's business; to the production team of Grey Magauran, Anton Reut, Charles Mathews, and Maureen Forys, who transformed manuscript and screen shots into an actual book; to Jane Dalisay, who tracked down answers to tough questions; to Heather O'Connor, who obtained permissions for the software on the CD; to Lucka Zivny, who translated our scribbles into the charming line drawings; and to indexer Ted Laux, master of his craft, who compiled references with admirable compulsion. Thanks also to Tarin's pals Brian Matheson and Sean Porter, who helped with both the WOT page and some generally sticky questions, and her brother Matthew, who did a newbie tech edit of Chapters 5 and 7.

At Netscape, we are thankful for the long-awaited arrival of Suzanne Anthony, and for her answers to all those urgent beta questions.

As always, Dan and Brenda are profoundly grateful for the support and understanding of family and friends, who somehow remain our family and friends despite our choice of career and its demands. For the record, we name Joani and Jessica Buehrle; Sharon Crawford and Charlie Russel; Kevin, Caitlin, and Kevin Cunningham; Jerry Doty; Rion Dugan; Fred Frumberg; Jessica, Martin, and Lori Grant; Carol Heller; Mai Le Bazner, Katri Foster, and Peter Bazner; the McArdle and Undercoffer families; Carolyn Miller; Lonnie Moseley and Cordell Sloan; Wynn Moseley and her family; Freeman Ng; Gino Reynoso; Margaret Tauber; Ron and Frances Tauber; Savitha Varadan; Femmes Who Feast; and Robert E. Williams III.

Contents at a Glance

Table of Contents

Part Two:
Navigating, Communicating, and Publishing
45

Chapter 3
Navigating via Navigator

47

Chapter 4

Been There, Going Back

87

Chapter 5

Discussion Groups and E-Mail the Collabra Way

113

Chapter 6

Communicating via Conference

171

Chapter 7
Experiencing Live Content

193

Chapter 8
Starting Places and Search Tools

225

Chapter 9

Composer: You Too Can Be a Web Publisher

279

Part Three:
Getting Started with Communicator
345

Chapter 10

Laying the Groundwork for Installing Communicator

347

Chapter 11

Getting Communicator Going

399

Appendix A
What's on the CD

419

Index

433

Introduction

Since its nascent moment, Netscape Navigator has been the browser of choice for millions of in-the-know Internet users. Now, in Netscape Communicator, the widely anticipated Navigator 4 has become a key component in an innovative new suite of programs.

Netscape Communicator is not simply a Web browser—it's a whole suite of tools that open doors to Internet and intranet collaboration on a previously unheard-of scale. Using them, you won't just be surfing the Internet, you'll be learning how to use the Internet to communicate and how to create your own little piece of the Web. Everything you've imagined doing online, from chatting to experiencing live content with Java and plug-ins, is available inside Communicator. Let's look at the pieces in the package:

◆ Netscape Navigator, the award-winning Web browser, is where the action is. You'll use Navigator to look at all the sights and sounds of the Web, including live content that incorporates Java, JavaScript, ActiveX, VRML, and multimedia plug-ins.

◆ Communicator's Message Center combines Messenger, a full-fledged e-mail program, and Collabra, an easy-to-use Usenet news reader. Messenger's functionality allows you to embed links, images, and even entire Web pages into your e-mail messages, while Collabra helps you sort through and participate in online discussion groups.

◆ Composer, the Web-page editing tool, makes creating your own Web pages as easy as word processing—no need to know HTML.

◆ Conference lets you "talk" to other people in real time on the Internet. Conference includes an Internet phone, a file-sharing utility, a chat tool, a collaborative browsing tool, and a shared whiteboard for drawing and painting.

◆ Netcaster delivers Web content when you want it, on your terms and schedule.

Netcaster was only available in beta form when this book went to press. For updated information on further releases of Netcaster, point your browser to the Sybex Web site, http://www.sybex.com, and click on Updates.

Building upon the sweeping success of Netscape Navigator, Communicator's components are integrated into one easy-to-use package. Communicator takes communication and collaboration, the founding principles of the World Wide Web, into a new dimension.

◆ What's New in Navigator 4

Netscape Navigator 4 adds many new and improved features to an already successful product, now integrated as a cornerstone into the larger suite of programs called Netscape Communicator. Netscape is always pushing the envelope—some of the new features in Navigator 4 further enhance navigation and the layout options available to those who publish on the Web. With Netscape Navigator 4 you'll get

- ◆ Sophisticated new page layout options, like absolute positioning, layering, Web fonts, and style sheets
- ◆ Increased security through digital signatures that identify users, companies, software, or even applets
- ◆ Automatic installation and signing of plug-ins
- ◆ Enhanced access for Java applets
- ◆ Enhanced support for VRML and VRML 2.0, with seamless integration of 3-D environments into Web pages
- ◆ Compatibility with ActiveX/Active Platform to bring even more live content to Web pages
- ◆ New, improved integration with OLE objects, allowing you to view and edit Microsoft Office documents from within your browser window

This keeps Navigator (and Netscape) way ahead of the pack, still setting the standards in the Web browser race toward new technologies.

 Netscape regularly improves and updates the look of its products. The contents of this book reflect the state of Communicator as of our publication date. Although the functionality we describe should not differ from the way your software works, some of our screen captures may not match exactly what you see on your screen.

◆ Is This Book for You?

This book, written in plain English and filled with how-to know-how, will get you started in no time using all of the components of Communicator—exploring the World Wide Web, e-mail, online discussion groups or chat sessions, collaborating with the folks at work or new friends around the world, and creating Web pages with no trouble. If you already have the basics under your belt, you'll find that this book will help you learn tips and tricks that the geeks on the block won't slow down to tell you about. You'll learn how to use the Communicator software and how to track down new add-ons, plug-ins, and helpers to enhance Communicator's abilities even more. Plus, you'll be armed with hundreds of starting places for your Web exploration. After all, what good is the Internet if you can't find anything?

Getting and installing Communicator involves setting up a connection that is able to "introduce" your Internet service provider to Communicator each and every time you access the Internet using Communicator. Setting up this connection was quite a tricky procedure in days gone by, but don't worry. This book covers connecting via Windows 95 or Windows NT, both of which include all the software you need to make a Communicator connection through your own Internet service provider. This book also covers making your connection via some other very popular options: NETCOM's NETCOMplete software, America Online, and CompuServe. And it covers connecting via a LAN or RAS (*remote access server*). Whatever your preferred method, you'll learn how to get Netscape from the Internet itself and how to set up a working, reliable connection. With this book, you'll be up and running in no time.

 Instructions for setting up a connection and getting Communicator are in Part Three, along with information on service providers, commercial online services, and other online connection options.

Throughout this book, you'll find the Internet addresses of hundreds of Internet sites of all kinds. These sites will provide you with additional information on every topic in this book, from getting connected and getting tech support to publishing a bang-up Web page to announcing your Web page and more. You'll also find the Internet addresses of fascinating sites that will get you started and keep you going in your Web travels—

these sites cover topics like art, education, personal finance, reference, sports, and travel, with lots of useful or entertaining stuff in between.

◆ What's on the CD

On the CD that comes with this book, you'll find and easy-to-use Web site with links to all the URLs featured in this book. You'll also find the software you need to get connected to the Internet with America Online or NETCOMplete. You'll also find a number of handy tools for making the most of your Internet or intranet experience, including

◆ JetEffects, for developing quick Java applets without needing to be a programmer; and Bongo, for creating Web presentations to deliver live content

◆ Intermind Communicator and Castanet Tuner, for tuning into custom Web channels; and Castanet Transmitter, for delivering your own channels

◆ Peak Technologies' PeakJet, for enhancing your Web experience by accelerating your browser's performance

◆ WebPrinter, which greatly simplifies printing stuff off the Web

The Appendix describes this stuff in more detail and shows you how to install it.

◆ How This Book Is Organized

This book is organized into 11 chapters, beginning, logically enough, with Chapter 1, a brief introduction to the Internet. Chapter 2 goes into more detail about the World Wide Web and how Communicator can help you use the whole Internet. Chapter 3 shows you the basic Navigator how-tos, while Chapter 4 tells you in basic terms how to stay organized by using bookmarks and other tools to track your travels. Chapter 5 describes communicating with others via Messenger (for e-mail) and Collabra (for discussion groups). Chapter 6 offers even more communication options through its coverage of Conference, Communicator's chat, Internet phone, file-sharing, synchronized browsing, and whiteboarding program (whew!). Chapter 7 introduces you to live content, including "push" channels (which you can experience via Netcaster) the three-dimensional worlds enabled by VRML, as well as Java, JavaScript, Active Platform and other interactive and animated content.

With basic navigation skills under your belt, you might want to focus your Web travels. Chapter 8 describes some good launch points for your Web travels along with how to use the new search technologies that are such an important part of maximizing your Internet experience.

Chapter 9 shows how you too can be a Web publisher—it includes a primer on designing Web pages with Composer, Communicator's easy-as-pie Web page creation program, along with tips for successful Web page design and even information on how to publicize your Web page.

Chapter 10 makes clear how you can get connected using various popular options for Internet connectivity and then how to get Communicator from the Internet itself. Chapter 11 follows up by providing step-by-step instructions for setting up Communicator to work with your Internet service.

You'll also find an Appendix, which, as mentioned previously, describes what's on the CD that comes with this book.

◆ Conventions Used in This Book

Surfing the Internet with Netscape Communicator 4 uses various conventions to help you find the information you need quickly and effortlessly. Tips, Notes, and Warnings, shown here, are placed strategically throughout the book to help you zero in on important information in a snap.

 Here you'll find insider tips and shortcuts—quick information meant to help you use Communicator more adeptly.

 Here you'll find reminders, asides, and bits of important information that should be emphasized.

 Here you'll find cautionary information describing trouble spots you may encounter in using the software or the Internet.

A simple kind of shorthand used in this book helps to save space so more crucial matters can be discussed; in this system, directions to "pull down the File menu and choose Save" will appear as "select File ➤ Save," and the phrase "press Enter" appears as "press ↵."

Long but important or interesting digressions are set aside as boxed text, called *sidebars*.

This Is a Sidebar

In boxed text like this you'll find background information and side issues—anything that merits attention or adds to your knowledge of what's going on behind the scenes.

And throughout the book you'll find special "What's Out There" sidebars telling you exactly where on the World Wide Web you can find out more about whatever's being discussed or where to find the Web page being described.

What's Out There

The URL for the home page of interest at the moment will appear in a different font, for example, `http://www.dnai.com/~vox/`.

◆ Let's Get This Show on the Road...

Enough about what's in the book and on the CD—to start your Internet exploration using Communicator, turn to Chapter 1; to find out how to get and install the software, turn to Chapters 10 and 11.

If You Need Assistance

For answers to your questions about Communicator or its components, call 800/320-2099. Make sure you have your credit card handy if you have yet to purchase your copy of Netscape Communicator. You can also get help via e-mail at client@netscape.com. If you received your licensed copy of Communicator from your Internet service provider or another third party, you may want to contact them for support.

◆ Technical support for Windows 95 Dial-Up Networking is available at 800/936-4200 or 206/635-7000.

◆ Help with NETCOM's NETCOMplete is available at 408/881-1810 or support@ix.netcom.com.

◆ Help with America Online is available at 800/827-3338, and help with CompuServe is available at 800/848-8900.

Part One:

The Internet, the Web, and Communicator

The Big Picture

You'd have to live in a vacuum these days not to have heard of the Internet. Scarcely a day goes by without some mention of it on the nightly news or in the local paper. Internet addresses have become as common in advertisements as 800 numbers. Millions of people—inspired by excited talk and armed with spanking new accounts with Internet service providers—are taking to the Internet, with visions of adventure.

A few short years ago, the Internet (which is actually 25 years old) was trafficked mainly by academicians and researchers, who used it via text-based interfaces that left a lot to be desired in terms of aesthetics and ease of use. Compare DOS to Windows and you can see the difference between the Internet then and the Internet now. With the advent of graphical Web browsers like Netscape Navigator (see Figure 1.1), the Internet exploded, and the World Wide Web—the portion of the Internet that Web browsers brought into focus—became the hottest new medium since television.

If you know all about the Internet and the World Wide Web, turn to Chapter 3 to delve into using Netscape Communicator. For a brief introduction to the whole Internet and the World Wide Web, read on.

```
                                          NASA Jet Propulsion Laboratory (p1 of 2)
        [LINK]
        [INLINE]
        [LINK]
        [INLINE]
        [LINK]
        [INLINE]
        [LINK]
        [INLINE]
        [LINK]
        [INLINE]

                                    [LINK]

        [INLINE]
        News Flashes
        Extra! Extra! The latest announcements, image releases and mission
        updates
        JPL Missions [INLINE]
        An online guide to JPL's missions, instruments and programs
        About JPL [INLINE]
        Basic information on the Laboratory
        Spotlight [INLINE]
        The new, the unique, the memorable among the Laboratory's net
        offerings [INLINE] [INLINE]
        Pictures & Video
        Space images, artist's conceptions, animations and more
        Information [INLINE]
        News releases, fact sheets, status reports and JPL's newspaper
        Web Directory [INLINE]
        A comprehensive, alphabetical index to JPL public web pages
     -- press space for next page --
        Arrow keys: Up and Down to move. Right to follow a link; Left to go back.
      H)elp O)ptions P)rint G)o M)ain screen Q)uit /=search [delete]=history list
```

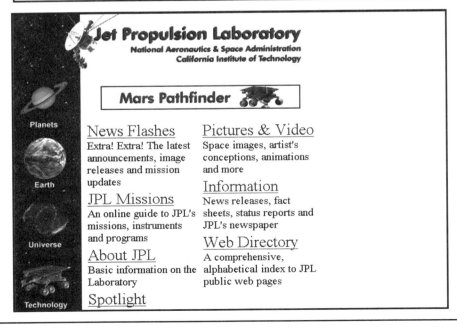

Figure 1.1: Here you can see the difference between a text-based view of the Internet (top) and an easy-to-use, graphically pleasing Netscape Navigator view (bottom).

◆ A Communicator View of the Internet

Leave it to Netscape to build upon the success of Netscape Navigator by bringing together an entire suite of tools for using the Internet. That suite, Netscape Communicator, offers an elegant point-and-click interface to guide you through the Internet's best resources. It includes not only Navigator, the terrifically popular *Web browser* (a program with which you can view graphically intriguing, linked documents all over the world and search and access information in a few quick mouse-clicks), but also a powerful e-mail program, advanced tools for online conferencing and collaboration, a publishing tool that's as easy to use as a word processor, and more.

Communicator is available for all popular computers—PCs running Windows, Macintoshes, even Unix workstations. Communicator, on any of these machines, looks just about the same, too. (In this book, we focus on Communicator for Windows 95 and NT, although many of the principles we discuss apply as well to the Unix and Mac versions.)

Let's take a quick look at the Internet before we move on. Then, in the next chapter, we'll investigate how the Web fits into the Internet and just what kinds of stuff you can look at out there.

What's Out There

As we go along, we're going to tell you what you can find using Communicator and where that stuff is located. You'll see notes like this describing an item of interest and giving you the item's *URL* (its *Uniform Resource Locator,* or address on the Web). Don't worry if you don't understand this URL business yet—you will soon, and then you can look for the stuff we've described.

◆ What the Internet Is All About

So what is this Internet thing we're hearing so much about? At its most basic level, you can think of the Internet as a vast collection of even vaster libraries of information, all available online for you to look at or retrieve and use. At another level, the Internet might be thought of as the computers that store the information and the networks that allow you to access the information on the computers. And finally (lest we forget who made the Internet what it is today), it is a collection of people—people who act as resources themselves, willing to share their knowledge with the world. This means, of course, that when you interact with the Internet—particularly when you make yourself a resource by communicating and sharing information with others—you become a part of this vast network.

 The Internet is a global network of networks. When your stand-alone machine gets connected to the Internet, special software on your machine "tricks" the Internet into accepting your machine as one of the networks that make up the Internet. Your machine—and you—become literally part of the Internet.

The idea of the Information Superhighway, made so popular a couple of years ago, is still a convenient metaphor: information flowing great distances at incredible speeds, with many on-ramps of access and many potential destinations. High-speed data paths, called *backbones*, connect the major networks; these actually do function much like an electronic version of the interstate highways. Through lower-speed links, local networks tie in to the Internet, much as city streets feed onto highways (see Figure 1.2). The beauty of the Internet system is that not all networks are, or even need to be, directly connected, because the Internet structure is one of interconnection. You can, in effect, hop from network to network to get where you want and what you want without having to access any central point to do so. (In fact, there is no central point to a network of networks.)

The highway metaphor begins to break down, however, when you realize that the Internet transcends geography. It's a global system, that's true, but when you use the Net, you probably won't be very conscious that the material you're viewing on your screen at one moment is actually located on a machine in Switzerland, and that what you see the next moment is actually on a machine in Japan. Perhaps a more accurate metaphor for the Internet would be having a global remote control at your fingertips, able to switch to just about any topic (or channel if you prefer) of your choosing.

In the Information Superhighway of the future, we might expect an electronic replacement for the everyday postal system (this has already begun to happen in Germany, we're told) and convergence of our cable TV, phone, and newspapers into online information and entertainment services. These possibilities come closer to reality every day.

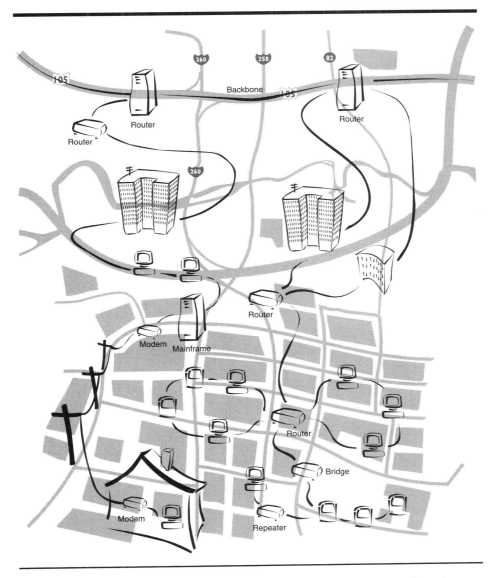

Figure 1.2: The Internet can be imagined as a system of highways and roadways, although it has no actual geography.

What's Out There

The Electronic Frontier Foundation (EFF) is active in lobbying to ensure that the Information Superhighway of the future includes protections for individual rights. You can find out about the EFF and what it is up to at `http://www.eff.org`. Other information about the government's initiative for building the Information Superhighway is available at `http://far.mit.edu/diig`.

While we're not quite up to the fully integrated superhighway envisioned by futurists yet, the Internet as it exists today delivers plenty of power. The resources and information you find are available for use on the job, as part of personal or professional research, or for just plain fun. No matter how you view the Internet, the idea that individuals as well as corporations can access information around the world has a particular appeal that borders on the irresistible.

The Internet may have begun as a government and academic project, but there is no single system or governing body in control—especially when you consider that anyone, in any country, has the potential not only to access the Internet, but to serve data to the world.

What's Out There

You can get a good idea about how long all of this Internet-building stuff took by reading Hobbes' Internet Timeline, a concise guide to what happened when in Internet history. Take a look at `http://info.isoc.org/guest/zakon/Internet/History/HIT.html`. For a little more depth, try the Internet Society's Brief History of the Internet, at `http://www.isoc.org/internet-history`.

◆ Where It All Began

To understand how the Internet came into being, you'd have to go back 30 years or so, to the height of the Cold War era. The think-tank military planners of that age were concerned not only with surviving a nuclear war, but also with communicating in its aftermath if one should occur. They envisioned a control network, linking bases and command posts from state to state, that would remain operational despite direct attacks. With this in mind, the U.S. Defense Department's Advanced Research Projects Agency began work on a computer network called ARPAnet during the 1960s.

The principles of the network were simple. It had to operate from the outset as if it were "unreliable"—to adjust up-front for the possibility of downed communication links. Control, therefore, would be decentralized to further minimize any single point of failure. Data would be split up and sent on the network in individual Internet Protocol (IP) *packets*. (A packet can be thought of as being similar to an envelope; see Figure 1.3.) Each packet of data would carry within it the address of its destination and the return address, and any individual packet could reach its endpoint by the most efficient route. If part of the network became unavailable, the packets would still get to their destinations via an alternate route and would be reassembled with their full content intact.

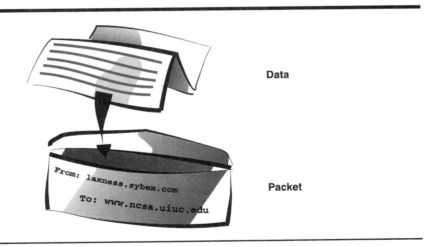

Data

From: laxness.sybex.com

To: www.ncsa.uiuc.edu

Packet

Figure 1.3:   Data (e-mail, documents, video, whatever) travels across the Internet in packets.

Though at first this may sound inefficient, it put the burden of communicating on the computers themselves, rather than on the communications network. That was the foremost issue on the minds of the planners: that the system did not rely on a central *server* (a machine on the network that holds or processes data for the other machines on the network). This proposal linked the computers together as peers instead, giving each computer equal status on the network and allowing for different types of computers to communicate, de-emphasizing the communications infrastructure. Thus, even if large pieces of the network were destroyed, the data itself could still reach its destination because it was not concerned with using any given route to get there. Therefore, the Department of Defense commissioned the initial implementation of ARPAnet in 1969.

 Perhaps you work in a business where a lot of machines are cabled together as a LAN (*local area network*) or an *intranet.* Each of these networks is like a smaller version of the Internet, in that a bunch of machines are linked together; but they are not necessarily linked to other networks via phone lines. LANs also usually have a central *server*—a machine that holds data and processes communications between the linked machines, which is unlike the Internet in that if your LAN server goes down, your network goes down.

Throughout the '70s and early '80s, the ARPAnet continued to grow, and more developments occurred to spur interest in networking and the Internet. Other services and big networks came into being (such as Usenet and BITnet), and e-mail began to gain wide use as a communications tool. Local area networks (LANs) became increasingly common in business and academic use, until users no longer wanted to connect just select computers to the Internet but entire local networks (which might mean all the computers in the organization).

The original Internet, the ARPAnet, was replaced in 1986 by a new backbone, the National Science Foundation (NSFnet) network. NSFnet forever changed the scope of the Internet in that it permitted more than just a few lucky people in the military, academia, and large corporations to conduct research and access super-computer centers (see Figure 1.4).

With the good, however, came the bad as well. More people using the Internet meant more network traffic, which meant slower response, which meant better connectivity solutions would have to be implemented. Which brings us to where we are today, with many companies (AT&T, Sprint, Netcom, UUNet, and more) running national backbones, and demand increasing exponentially as more and more people want to connect to the Internet and discover the online riches of the '90s (see Figure 1.4). Eventually, NSF's 56K backbone was shut down. Today most traffic on the Internet is conducted over backbones maintained by private companies, including the major telephone networks (AT&T Worldnet, MCINet, and Sprintlink are the names of their Internet divisions).

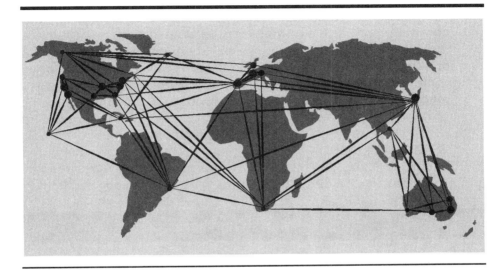

Figure 1.4:   The Internet is a global resource, with servers on every continent.

What's Out There

Editor Win Treese has been compiling an extraordinary set of Internet figures and statistics in the style of Harper's Index. For a closer look, go to `http://www.openmarket.com/intindex`. And the Web site for PBS's "Life on the Internet" documentary is a great place to learn about the people and story of the Internet. Find it at `http://www.pbs.org/internet/topics.html`.

◆ The Burning Issues of Control, Funding, and Use

Perhaps you've begun to wonder who runs this thing and who pays for it.

Who Runs the Internet?

As odd as it may sound, no one person or organization has overall authority for running the Internet. Despite this—or perhaps because of it—the Internet runs just fine, in the opinion of many people who use it. Although there is no governing body that controls every function or machine on the Internet, there are several organizations who make decisions about the overall structure the Internet generally follows. A group called the Internet Society (ISOC), composed of volunteers, directs the Internet. ISOC appoints a subcouncil, the Internet Architecture Board (IAB), and the members of this board work out issues of standards, network resources, network addresses, and the like. Another volunteer group, the Internet Engineering Task Force (IETF), tackles the more day-to-day issues of Internet operations. These Internet caretakers, if you will, have proven quite ably that success does not depend on your typical top-down management approach.

What's Out There

Join the Internet Society at `http://www.isoc.org`. Their subcommittee, the Internet Architecture Board, sets the standards at `http://www.isi.edu/iab`. The Internet Engineering Task Force (`http://www.ietf.cnri.reston.va.us`) tackles day-to-day issues online.

The Fuss about Government Regulation

As this book goes to press, there has been a lot of talk about the U.S. government regulating the Internet. Legislation has been discussed, proposed, voted on, and is being considered by Federal courts. The issues involved in this are many, most notable perhaps is the conflict between the international nature of the Net and the non-international nature of the legislation. Here's the dilemma: If a Web site produced in the Netherlands is acceptable by Dutch standards of "decency," but is then viewed by, say, a minor in Biloxi, Mississippi, the minor's community might not agree with the Dutch definition of decency, particularly for children. What to do?

Another issue involves whether Internet service providers should be treated as *common carriers*. Common carriers are companies in governmentally recognized businesses, like phone companies and mail delivery services, that offer service to anyone without taking responsibility for content. You may think because phone companies cooperate in catching obscene callers and because mail delivery services cooperate in discouraging use of their services for transporting illegal substances that they are responsible. But notice that in fact they are cooperating with authorities but incur no liability themselves if a user of their service breaks the law. The question in this case is whether Internet service providers fall into that category or whether they are liable for the content that is delivered via their services.

What's Out There

You can find out more about these and other issues by visiting the Voters' Technology Watch at http://www.vtw.org and the Center for Democracy and Technology at http://www.cdt.org.

Who Pays?

A common misconception has been that the Internet, by its very nature, is free, but this is certainly not the case. It costs a pretty penny to maintain a machine that can serve up stuff on the Internet, and someone has to pay those costs. Individual groups and institutions—such as the federal government, the National Center for Supercomputing Applications at UIUC, and MIT's Media Lab—do indeed pay to provide the information they serve on the Internet. Companies like AT&T, MCI, Sprint, Netcom, and UUNet incur costs in providing the backbones that they now maintain. And all those companies and organizations (and even just plain folks) who are offering increasing amounts of Internet content are paying for content development, design, technical infrastructure, and maintenance of their sites, along with the use of high-speed communications lines of one sort or another. All this is not cheap.

At the other end, new users quickly find out that connecting to the Internet through a service provider (such as Netcom, WorldNet, or PSI) or a commercial online service (such as America Online or CompuServe) requires a monthly usage fee; and because it is necessary to connect through a phone line, telephone charges may also be involved.

Additionally, all these companies and people providing Internet content have now begun to look for ways to recoup their costs and perhaps even make a few bucks along the way. There are currently a few business models these content providers are trying on for size—for example, advertising on their sites, licensing their content to other companies or groups, getting paid sponsorship, and selling access via subscriptions or usage fees. Eventually they'll probably hit upon something that works and stick with it.

As you can see, the Internet is by no means free, although it is a great value. For content providers, it is an enormously successful new mass medium that takes their message out into a big world. For users, it is entrance into a universe of easy access to information, entertainment, and connection to other like-minded people.

What's Out There

You can find a lot out about how the Internet is run by reading *Boardwatch* magazine, at http://www.boardwatch.com.

◆ What You Can Do with the Internet

Once you are connected to the Internet, you can

◆ View documents, browse, search for data, traverse other resources, see video and hear sound, explore interactive three-dimensional environments (via VRML), and publish your own material on the Internet via the *World Wide Web*.

◆ Send messages to friends and associates all over the world with *e-mail*.

◆ Experience broadcast-like content delivered to your computer via *push* technologies.

◆ Communicate with others in real-time written conversation via *chat* and in verbal conversations transmitted over the Net via *Internet telephone*. (Internet telephone usually does not involve long-distance charges to you or the recipient; all you're charged for is the call to your Internet service provider, and, if that's a local number, it's a local call.)

◆ Exchange ideas with other people in a public forum in Usenet *newsgroups* or private *discussion groups*. (Note that unlike e-mail, which is more or less private, newsgroups are quite public. Everyone in the newsgroup can read what you post there. Access to specific discussion groups may be limited to certain individuals, but within that group, the discussion is also out in the open.)

◆ Copy files from and to computers on the Internet with *FTP*. Many giant software archives, such as TUCOWS, hold literally gigabytes of files you can retrieve.

◆ Connect to other computers on the Internet and use programs on them via *Telnet*.

Many of these tools are used (either visibly or behind the scenes) in the course of using Communicator, so we'll talk about each one as it arises in later chapters. (We'll also cover some nifty things Communicator actually adds to the mix.)

What's Out There

TUCOWS, a huge archive of freeware and shareware for Windows, can be found at http://www.tucows.com.

And What, Exactly, Is an *Intranet*?

The corporate world is all abuzz about *intranets*. An intranet is an internal implementation of Internet technology. A company's intranet can look to its users and operate pretty much just like the public Internet, but it can be accessed only by those on the company's private network.

Communicator works quite nicely on intranets, thank you. In fact, many of the tools included in Communicator are designed specifically to enable and even enhance intranet use. To the user using Communicator in an intranet setting is little different from using it on the public Internet, so in this book, we focus on using Communicator on the Internet.

◆ The Internet As Medium

The Internet itself is just a medium, like television or print. There's plenty of room to develop services that make the most of the Internet, just as happened when the phone system was devised for simple communication, and then many products and services were developed that took advantage of its potential (ranging from voice mail, pagers, and automated banking, to the 911 system and, in fact, the Internet).

Today we see many big and small companies, organizations, and just plain people with good ideas racing toward the Internet to make the most of it. As this happens, it is important for all of us to remember that the Internet is not just a big billboard system, not a table onto which one can throw a brochure. Just as when one turns on the television, one expects to see more content than advertising (and even then the advertising must have some entertainment appeal if we're actually to watch it and not change the channel), the Internet must be content-driven, first and foremost.

The Internet's fundamental openness has been responsible for bringing forth a number of tools for use by the masses. A great example of this is, of course, Netscape Communicator.

The Internet via Communicator

Before we leap head first into using Netscape Communicator, an appreciation of the World Wide Web is in order. After all, Navigator, the highly popular Web browser, is a key component of Communicator. Let's take a quick look at the Web. Then we'll glance at what Navigator and the rest of Communicator can do.

If you know about the Web and how it works, skip ahead to Chapter 3 to start using Navigator. If you're looking for a brief introduction to the Web and Internet basics, read on.

◆ How the Web Came to Be

The World Wide Web (a.k.a. WWW, W3, or simply the Web) was originally developed to help physicists at Conseil Européen pour la Recherche Nucleaire (CERN), which in English is known as the European Particle Physics Laboratory in Geneva, Switzerland. CERN is one of the world's largest scientific labs, composed of two organizations straddling the Swiss-French border—the European Laboratory for High Energy Physics in Switzerland, and the Organisation Européen pour la Recherche Nucleaire in France. The physicists there needed a way to exchange data and research materials quickly with other scientists.

The Web technology developed at CERN by Tim Berners-Lee enabled collaboration among members of research teams scattered all over the globe. How? Through a system that allows for *hypertext* links between documents on different computers.

Unlike regular documents, with static information on every page, hypertext documents have links built in so that readers can jump to more information about a topic by (typically) simply clicking on the word or picture identifying the item. That's why they call it hypertext—it's not just text, it's *hyper*text. (The term hypertext was coined by computer iconoclast Ted Nelson.) Hypertext is what makes Navigator—and many multimedia tools—possible. The term hypermedia is sometimes used to refer to hypertext with the addition of other data formats. In addition to text, Navigator now supports graphics, video, sound, and a number of interactive formats, including VRML and Java.

In 1992, the Web grew beyond the confines of CERN, and now its use and growth increase exponentially. This was all part of the plan in a sense—the Web was meant to allow for open access—but it's hard to imagine that anyone could have expected the phenomenon that's occurred. The W3 Consortium, or W3C, was launched as the standard-setting organization behind the Web once CERN realized that the Web had grown beyond the bounds of CERN's responsibility.

What's Out There

CERN's own home page is at `http://www.cern.ch`. Meanwhile, the W3 Consortium, which sets the standards for the Web these days, can be found at `http://www.w3.org`.

Protocols, HTTP, and Hypertext: What It All Means

The Web's rapid expansion can be attributed in part to its extensive use of hypertext, held together by the Hypertext Transfer Protocol (HTTP). A protocol is an agreed-upon system for passing information back and forth that allows the transaction to be efficient (HTTP is a network protocol, which means it's a protocol for use with networks).

On "Mosaic" and Navigator

Netscape Navigator wouldn't be around today—at least not in the same form—had it not been for a piece of software called Mosaic.

The first version of Mosaic, which was developed by Marc Andreessen and a team of programmers at the National Center for Supercomputing Applications (NCSA), was X Mosaic for Unix workstations. Later, versions of NCSA Mosaic became available for Windows-based PCs and the Macintosh. NCSA Mosaic was, for a time, distributed freely via the Net itself. Anyone could download and use the software without charge.

In their wisdom, the folks at Netscape (Marc Andreessen again, along with some other very smart people) created and marketed a new Web browser—one that was faster and more reliable than Mosaic. They also made the new browser secure. (They wanted you to be able to conduct economic transactions, or in other words buy things, over the Internet without fear of someone stealing and using your credit card number.) The result of this venture, Netscape Navigator, took the World Wide Web by storm and was soon named by Wired magazine as one of its favorite products. Today it is estimated that over 70 percent of the people using the Web are using Netscape software to do their surfing.

Here's how this goes: If you (the client) go into a fast-food place, the counterperson (the server) says, "May I help you?" You answer something like, "I'll have a Big Burger with cheese, fries, and a cola." Then he or she verifies your order by repeating it, tells you the cost, and concludes the transaction by trading food for cash. Basically, when you walk into any fast-food place, you'll follow that same pattern and so will the person who takes your order. That's because you both know the *protocol*. The fast-food protocol is part of what makes it "fast food."

An Internet transaction is quite similar to a fast food transaction: One computer (the server or host) takes the requests of the other (the client), and delivers a product (usually data, not food). In just that way, HTTP, which is the protocol that was developed as part of the Web project, enables the kinds of network conversations that need to occur quickly between computers so that leaps can be made from one document to another. You can use other protocols to do the same things HTTP does

(Navigator is open-ended, meaning that it's designed to support other network protocols as well as HTTP), but HTTP is terrifically efficient at what it does.

◆ Information from Around the Globe

Web servers are located in many countries around the world, providing information on any topic you might imagine; a typical session using the Web might lead you through several continents. For example, your search for information in the field of psychology may start at Yale and end up at a research hospital in Brussels, all within a few mouse-clicks that lead you along a series of hypertext links from a file at one location to another somewhere else.

The caveat here is that links are forged by the people who publish the information, and they may not make the same kinds of connections you would. That's why it's important to keep an open mind as you adventure around in the Web—just as you would when browsing in a library. You never know what you'll stumble across while you're looking for something else; conversely, you might have to do a bit of looking around to find exactly what you're seeking. Fortunately, search tools such as those described in Chapter 8 have emerged to make finding your way easier, and other tools, built right into Navigator itself (see Chapter 4) make it a lot easier to track where you've been.

Who Makes This Information Available

Much of the information originally published on the Web existed thanks to the interest (and kindness) of the academic and research community; for a long time, almost all information about the Web (and the Internet) was available through the work of that community.

Increasingly, the Web has become a forum for commercial use. Given that the telephone system did not fully develop for personal use until it was seen by commerce as a tool for business, we see commercial use of the Web as a positive development. Commercial users of the Web must, however, adhere to the Internet philosophy in that they have to give to the Internet as well as use it. Along these lines, it's now not surprising to find useful information and entertaining content that have been created as a vehicle for a corporation's advertising (in a twist on the network TV model) or sponsored by some big company (in the PBS model). Not only will you find product information at a company's Web site, but you may find a full range of magazines and other online extravaganzas (as you do at Time Warner's Pathfinder site). These may be based on the corporate identity, but go way beyond selling the product (in Time-Warner's media empire, in this case).

What's Out There

Yahoo! Internet Life's Surf School feature is a great way to brush up on basics, no matter what your level of experience. Head for class at `http://www3 .zdnet.com/yil/filters/surfjump.html`.

Pathfinder, at `http://pathfinder.com`, is a mammoth site that includes not only online versions of Time-Warner's magazines, but "billions and billions" of pages of content.

Actually, anyone can become a Web publisher, as you'll see in Chapter 9. You, your neighbor, or an enterprising person almost anywhere on the globe might be compelled by an impulse to publish something you think interesting to others on the Web. Many Internet service providers offer to their users the opportunity to publish Web pages for free or for a very small fee. This makes the Web the ultimate vanity press as well as an extraordinary mass communications tool.

Web servers can be set up for strictly in-house purposes too. For example, a large organization with massive amounts of internal documentation or a smaller organization with shared documentation might publish that material on an in-house Web called an *intranet*. Intranets can also be made available through password-protection to outside contractors or telecommuting employees, making it possible to expand the idea of in-house to mean not just "in the building" but "company-wide." Just as members of a research team can use the Web to collaborate without having to be in the same location (fulfilling the original intentions of the Web's creators), so can members of a company's workgroup.

What's Out There

To investigate the nuts and bolts of intranets, read the Intranet FAQ at
`http://www.innergy.com/ifaq.html`.

What Types of Information Exist

Internet indexes like Yahoo!, which began as the project of two university
graduate students and is now a publicly traded company, cover specific
topics ranging from the entertaining to the academic (see Chapter 8).
Many, many traditionally print newspapers and magazines see publication
on the Web as opening new markets, and whole new types of Web-only
publications (Suck, Salon, and more) are sprouting up daily.

What's Out There

A growing number of high-tech companies are making information available
on the Web. Some familiar names—Microsoft, AT&T, and Sybex, for example—all maintain a presence on the Web. You can access these companies'
Web sites at:

`http://www.microsoft.com`

`http://www.att.com`

`http://www.sybex.com`

The magazines we mention here are easy to find: Suck makes fun at `http://www`
`.suck.com`, while Salon sips coffee at `http://www.salon1999.com`.

Consumer-oriented Web sites include Crayola (see Figure 2.1), which provides colorful background on the making of crayons and the removal of
crayon-based stains. You can tour Graceland via the Web, finding photos of
the "King" and listening to sound clips of Elvis music, and you can even
order a pizza using a Web order form. (This last is a pilot project so far; the
pizza will be delivered only if you live in Santa Cruz, California. Solamente
in California, eh?)

Figure 2.1:   Many companies see the Web as a way to put their messages in front of a wider audience.

What's Out There

We accessed Crayola with the URL http://www.crayola.com. Elvis Presley's Graceland, the Official World Wide Web Site, can be found at http://www.elvis-presley.com. If you live in Santa Cruz, click up a Pizza Hut delivery at http://www.pizzahut.com.

◆ The Role of the Browser

So far we've talked mainly about the structure and content of the Web, describing some of the links and information that make up the Web. So how does one jump into this Web thing and start cruising? You need a tool called a *browser*.

Now, at the risk of sounding like the nerds we've said you don't have to be, a browser, in technical terms, is a client process running on your computer that accesses a server process—in the case of the Web, the HTTP service—over the network. This is what's being discussed when people describe the Web as being based on client-server technology.

More simply put, the browser establishes contact with the server, reads the files—hypertext documents—made available on the HTTP server, and displays that stuff on your computer.

The document displayed by the browser is a hypertext document that contains references (or pointers) to other documents, which are very likely on other HTTP servers. These pointers are also called *links*. When you select a link from a hypertext page, the browser sends the request back to the new server, which then displays on your machine yet another page full of links.

In the same way you and a waiter at a restaurant have a "client-server" relationship when you ask for and receive water, a browser and the Web have a client-server relationship. The browser sends requests over the network to the Web server, which then provides a screenful of information back to your computer.

Before Web browsers like Navigator were developed, all of this had to be accomplished using text-based browsers—the basic difference between them and browsers such as Navigator is just like the difference between PC programs written for DOS and those written for Windows. (DOS was text-based, so using DOS required you to type in commands to see and use text-filled screens; Windows, like Navigator, is graphical, so all you have to do is point and click on menu items and icons to see and use more graphically presented screens.)

Let the Browser Beware

Remember that the Web is ever-changing by its very nature. In this book, we attempt to guide you toward a lot of sites that seem to have stable locations and an ongoing existence. Some others are just so interesting or unusual we can't pass them up, though. If you don't find a site we've described, it may be that it has gone the way of all things. Not to worry; something even more remarkable will probably crop up elsewhere. Another thing is that in the growing, ever-expanding Web, many of the servers you encounter may not be complete—their links may be "under construction." Sometimes you'll see a notice about this, but most of the time, you won't. Remember, the Web is by its very nature under construction; that's the beauty of the beast.

How HTML Fits In

In early 1993, the Software Development Group (SDG) of NCSA at the University of Illinois at Urbana-Champaign was researching an easy-to-use way to access the Internet. This led them to explore the World Wide Web and use of the Hypertext Markup Language (HTML). HTML was being used for marking up documents on the Web—it's HTML that is used to make the document; browsers such as Navigator simply allow you to look at it easily.

HTML, a mark-up language with which text can be made to look like a page, is the coding scheme used in hypertext documents that both handles the text formatting on screen and makes it possible to create links to other documents, graphics, sound, and movies. Figure 2.2 shows a Navigator document and the HTML coding that was used to create the document.

Remember, though, that Navigator is not just a way to look at visually appealing pages on the Internet. It also provides dynamic linking capabilities within a hypertext document and even search options. HTML, then, is the core building block of those capabilities. We'll get into this more and more as we go along...

```
Exploratorium Publications </A></P>
<P ALIGN=LEFT><A HREF="http://www.exploratorium.edu/general/membership/index.h
Membership</A></P>
<P ALIGN=LEFT><A HREF="http://netra.exploratorium.edu/jobs/index.html">
Job Opportunities</A></P>
<P ALIGN=LEFT><A HREF="http://www.exploratorium.edu/kudos/">
ExploraNet Kudos</A></P>
<P ALIGN=LEFT><IMG WIDTH=96 HEIGHT=12 SRC="images/home.gif" ALIGN="BOTTOM">
<BR><BR>
<A HREF="http://www.exploratorium.edu/Palace_History/Palace_History.html">
The Palace of Fine Arts</A></P>
<P ALIGN=LEFT><A HREF="http://www.exploratorium.edu/marina/index.html">
Filling in the Marina- An illustrated story</A></P>
<P ALIGN=LEFT><IMG WIDTH=74 HEIGHT=14 SRC="images/contact.gif" ALIGN="BOTTOM"
<BR><BR>
<FONT COLOR="#bcac58">Contact your webmaster<BR>
</FONT><A HREF="http://www.exploratorium.edu/ronh/index.html">Ron
Hipschman</A></TD>
<TD WIDTH="76%" VALIGN="TOP"><P><IMG SRC="images/explora_head.gif" ALIGN="BOTT
<P> <CENTER>
<TABLE WIDTH="98%" BORDER="0" CELLSPACING="2" CELLPADDING="2"
HEIGHT="23">
<TR>
<TD WIDTH="60%">
<P>
<CENTER>
<A HREF="http://www.exploratorium.edu/sports/index.html"><IMG WIDTH=200 HEIGHT
```

Figure 2.2: Here you can see the HTML coding (above) that makes this document (below) look the way it does.

Looking into HTML

If you want to see what HTML looks like, while viewing a Web page in Navigator, you can select View ➤ Page Source from Navigator's menu bar. A window will open showing the HTML for that page. You can't change the HTML you see, but you can copy pieces of it or even the whole thing to your Windows Clipboard (highlight what you want and press Ctrl+C) or you can save it as a text file to your local machine (see Chapter 3). Click on the Close button in the upper-right corner of your screen when you're done, and your view will once more be the document as it appears in Navigator.

◆ Using Navigator to Access World Wide Web Information

Using Navigator, you can skim material quickly, or you can stop and delve into topics as deeply as you wish. Let's take a quick look at a Navigator session in action.

A Typical Navigator Session

To start Navigator, we first start our Internet connection, then double-click on the Netscape Navigator icon on the Desktop. (We'll go over starting the software in detail in Chapter 3.) The Welcome to Netscape page (see Figure 2.3) appears on screen. From here we can traverse the Web by clicking on links, which appear on the home page as pictures and as underlined words in some special color (traditionally blue).

From Navigator's menu bar we select Edit ➤ Search Internet to open up Netscape's Net Search page—a convenient way to search the Internet for information.

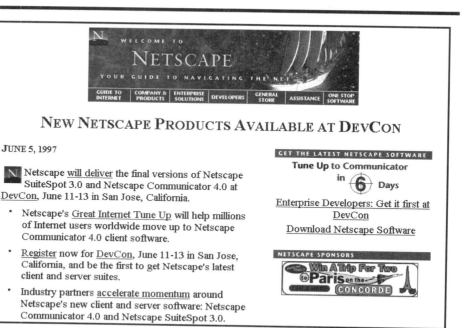

Figure 2.3:   The Welcome to Netscape page will be your first view of the Internet via Netscape Navigator.

Netscape's Net Search page allows you to search the Internet using a variety of high-profile indexes, directories, and search engines. See Chapter 8 for complete details about searching the Net. You can get to the Net Search page by clicking on the Search button on Navigator's navigation toolbar. There, you'll be offered a range of easy-to-use search options.

We type into the space next to the Search button a term to describe the topic of interest to us—in our case, the X-Files. Then we click on the Search button to start the search. Once the search is done, the results will appear on screen.

In the first entry we see, the phrase X-Files is in blue—it's a link to a site about the TV show. We click on the link to access the X-Files site, and the server there forks up the X-Files home page.

The X-Files home page is our entry point to a site with scads of information about the TV show. Here we can click on links to explore pictures, video clips, information about the sound score, a puzzle, and a contest.

We can, if we like, click on a link on this page to follow it to some other page about Mulder and Scully, or we can click on Navigator's Back button to return to the list of sites the search brought up and go from there to explore another aspect of Fox Mulder's doings. But our curiosity about the show is satisfied (the truth was in there), so we exit the program directly from where we happen to be by selecting File ➤ Exit from Navigator's menu bar.

What's Out There

The *truth* is out there, that's what. The Official X-Files site we just looked at lurks in cyberspace at http://www.thex-files.com.

◆ Navigator Is Fast

There can be an awful lot of data involved in transferring graphics, and your 14,400 or even 33,600bps modem acts as a bottleneck through which the data must squeeze. Many Web browsers halt all their other operations while they make you wait for images to appear. Navigator was designed specifically to get around this issue: Instead of waiting 'til the graphics appear, Navigator goes ahead and shows you the text on the page and allows you to start working with it. You can click on links in the text, for example, and move on to the next page of interest to you, before the graphics in the original page have appeared.

Further, you can decide whether you want the graphics to appear at all. Navigator, like other Web browsers, usually shows you both the text and the graphics in a given Web page. But if you find the graphics bogging you down, you can turn them off and see only the text.

To toggle off the graphics, making it so you'll see only text, you can turn off auto image loading using Communicator's Preferences dialog box. To open the Preferences dialog box, from Navigator's menu bar, select Edit ➤ Preferences. When the dialog box appears, click on the word Advanced in the category list. The dialog box will change to reflect your choice; find the Automatically Load Images option and deselect it. Click on the OK button to close the dialog box and return to Navigator's main window.

After you do this, the Web pages you view will include little markers where the graphics go, and the Smart Images button will appear on Navigator's toolbar. If you're viewing a page with graphics toggled off and you decide you want to see the graphics after all, just click on the Images button and the page will be reloaded, this time with its graphics.

To toggle graphics back on, so you'll see them loaded a moment after the text for each page appears, follow the procedure described above, and put that checkmark back where you found it.

Wanderers, Spiders, and Robots—Oh My!

In June of 1993, there were about 130 Web sites on the Internet. One year later, the number hit 2000. Now there are millions and millions. So how do you find what you need in this ever-expanding haystack? Wouldn't it be great to know what's out on the Web, and where?

You can find out by consulting World Wide Web indexes and search tools that use creatures known as *wanderers*, *spiders*, *crawlers*, or *robots*. An assortment of Web robots have been developed since the beginnings of the WWW; these programs travel through the Web and find HTTP files—the files that make up the content of the Web. Some robots were designed strictly to track growth on the Web.

The more interesting and useful Web crawlers are those that dump the information they gather into a place that's readable by the rest of us browsers. The information is then collected into a searchable database that's also sometimes indexed or otherwise catalogued—Yahoo!, Lycos, and AltaVista are all examples of this technology in action. Check out Chapter 8 for information about accessing indexes, guides, and search tools that use Web crawler technology.

◆ How Data Travels

Usually you can't install Communicator on your Windows computer and expect it simply to work. You have to go through a little rigmarole to get things going. The interface mechanism between the client—Communicator—and the Web server (the machine dishing up the information you want to view) depends on the Internet protocol known as TCP/IP (Transmission Control Protocol/Internet Protocol). TCP/IP creates packets (see Figure 1.3)—which are like electronic envelopes to carry data on a network—and then places the packets on the network. It also makes it possible, of course, to receive packets.

The Domain Name System and Packets

There is a system responsible for administering and keeping track of domains, and (believe it or not) it's called the Domain Name System (DNS for short). DNS is a distributed system that administers names by allowing different groups control over subsets of names. In this system, there can be many levels or domains, but the top-level domains are standardized.

In addition to the more familiar "English" names, all machines on the Internet have an Internet address in the form of four numbers separated by decimals; this is because, while a user might change the "English" address, an address is needed that will never change. This numeric address is organized in a system commonly called dotted decimal notation. An example of a host computer's address would be 130.19.252.21. These numeric addresses work fine for machines communicating with one another, but most people find them cumbersome to use and tricky to remember. To help people out, host computers were given names, such as *ruby* or *topaz*, making it easier to remember and to facilitate connecting.

However, other factors came into play, such as making sure that each machine on the Internet had a unique name, registering the names in a centrally managed file, and distributing the file to everyone on the Internet. This system worked adequately when the Internet was still small, but as it grew in size, so did the size of the file keeping track of all the host names.

The common standard American domains are as follows:

com	Commercial business, company, or organization
edu	Educational institution (university, etc.)
gov	Nonmilitary government site
mil	Military site
net	Any host associated with network administration, such as a gateway
org	Private organization (nonacademic, nongovernmental, and noncommercial)

These domains are referred to as descriptive domains. In addition, each country also has its own top-level domain, commonly called a geographical domain. Here in the United States, we are in the us domain. Other examples of countries represented with domains include:

au	Australia
ca	Canada
fr	France

Just as you need not know the internal workings of the U.S. Postal Service to use the system and get your mail, you don't need to know all about TCP/IP to use Communicator. But it does help to have some understanding.

TCP/IP is not part of the Communicator suite; it's part of your local network if you're on one. If you're not on a local network, though—if, for example, you're using your stand-alone machine at home or at work—you can still use Communicator. In that case, you have to have special network *drivers* loaded (not to worry, Windows 95 and NT includes them). These drivers make things go back and forth over your phone connection using the protocol Communicator understands. We'll talk more about this in Chapter 10.

If you're using a PC on a LAN that's already connected to the Internet, you're probably already set up with the TCP/IP software you need to run Communicator, and you can just use your company's connection. Your network administrator can clue you in to the details of running TCP/IP-based software such as Communicator.

◆ What Navigator Recognizes

Navigator has many big selling points, one of which is that it provides one-stop shopping for the Web by handling a variety of *data types*. Data types are just that—types of data. Having standard types of data makes it possible for one machine (indeed, a program) to recognize and use data that was created on another machine (and maybe even in another program). The data types recognized by Navigator include:

- ◆ HTML
- ◆ Text or Plain Text
- ◆ Graphics
- ◆ Sound
- ◆ Video
- ◆ Animation
- ◆ Virtual Reality (VRML)

The data type that the Web was designed around is HTML, the type the Hypertext Transfer Protocol we've talked so much about was designed to transfer.

HTTP servers, the servers that make up the World Wide Web, serve hypertext documents (coded with HTML, as we've discussed). These documents are not just what you view; these HTML documents actually guide you through the Web when you're cruising.

Navigator's Use of Plug-Ins and Helper Apps

For those data types that it can't handle directly, Navigator uses *plug-ins* and *helper applications*—these are two types of software that might specialize in displaying a graphic or playing a sound, a movie, or both. Plug-ins actually integrate into Navigator and allow new data types to appear right in the Navigator window. Helper applications (helper apps) are separate programs that launch themselves and appear in a distinct window when Navigator encounters a data type it needs help to run.

Communicator comes with a number of plug-ins and helper apps, for example a QuickTime movie viewer and the VRML viewer that lets you navigate 3D worlds. (See Chapter 7 for more on live content in general and plug-ins in particular.)

 Communicator also comes with very credible sound and video players integrated into Navigator so you can play most sound and video files you come across while surfing the Net. (Assuming you have a sound card....) Just click on the link to the sound or video clip, and (after a hefty download wait) the thing will play, either within the Navigator window or within a tiny player window.

How Plug-Ins and Helper Apps Work

Briefly, here's how plug-ins and helper apps work: Navigator looks at the first part (the header) of the file; the header tells Navigator what it needs to know to deal with the file appropriately. Text files are displayed on screen, in the very attractive way Navigator displays them. Compressed files, such as graphics, are uncompressed and then displayed. But when Navigator encounters a sound or video file, the program "knows" it needs help, and it launches the appropriate plug-in or helper app to "play" the file—if you have the plug-in or helper app on your machine, you won't see much evidence of this; you'll just hear the sound or see the movie on screen.

Many plug-ins and helper apps are available from many Internet sources (including anonymous FTP servers and the Web) and for all types of files. Netscape maintains pages at its Web site that describe plug-ins and helper apps.

E-Mail Addressing

Electronic mail, or e-mail, is the established form of communication on the Internet. In fact, typically this is where most of us encounter the Internet for the first time. A friend tells you his Internet e-mail address at work is `kmfez@schwartz.com` and asks for your e-mail address, and you begin exchanging messages that magically pop up in your on-screen e-mail in-basket. Users around the country—for that matter, around the world—readily grasp e-mail as a quick, convenient means for conducting business or just for staying in touch (and for doing so without the expense associated with a long-distance phone call). How does e-mail work? It's actually a lot like the postal service. E-mail uses addressing and a "store and forward" mechanism. This means that there is a standard way of addressing, and the mail is routed from one place to another until ultimately it appears at its destination. Along the way, if necessary, a machine can store the mail until it knows how to forward it.

Of course, there is a little more than that to sending e-mail on its way, but not much. The address in your e-mail header, much like the address on a postal letter, contains all the information necessary to deliver the message to the recipient. In the world of the Internet, a person's e-mail address is made up of two parts: a user name and a computer name, indicating where the user's ID is located.

In the example `kmfez@schwartz.com`, `kmfez` is the user portion of the address, and `schwartz.com` is the name of the domain (actually a host machine). The last part of the domain name, `.com`, is known as the high-level domain—in this case `.com` tells you that it is a commercial organization. If `.edu` appeared instead, you'd know it was an educational organization.

An address can actually contain many domains, which you see separated by periods, like this: `joke.on.you.com`.

If multiple domains appear in an address, they move in hierarchy from right to left. As you read to the left, the domains get smaller in scope.

Remember that plug-ins and helper apps are separate programs from Communicator (they are often produced by companies other than Netscape, and they are actually distinct programs from Navigator or any other component of Communicator) and that support in using them will come—if at all—only from their respective authors, not from the producers of sites where you got them. If you have questions about how to use any given plug-in or helper app, you must go to its author to get help.

With the help of plug-ins and helper apps, you can play video and sound clips with Navigator, but you should avoid doing so if you have a slow modem connection (as opposed to a LAN connection) to the Internet. Most sound and video files are multi-megabytes in size. As a rough estimate, each megabyte takes about 15 minutes to transfer with a 14,400bps modem (that is, on a good day with prevailing winds). It might take literally hours to access a single, relatively short video clip, although 33.6Kbps and 56Kbps modem users should have less problems.

These are just some of the ways you can extend Navigator to handle new data formats. Many, many new plug-ins and helper apps are being developed for use with Navigator all the time. Keep your eye on the Netscape site for announcements and links to help you stay in tune.

What's Out There

Netscape's guide to helper apps and plug-ins resides at `http://home .netscape.com/comprod/mirror/navcomponents_download.html`.

◆ Communicator As a Consistent Interface to Other Internet Resources

In addition to providing a nice graphical user interface to linked multimedia information, Communicator provides a consistent interface to other information types available on the Internet. Let's take a quick look at the kinds of resources that make up the Internet and that you can access using Communicator.

What's Out There

Zen and the Art of the Internet (`http://www.cs.indiana.edu/docproject/zen/zen-1.0_toc.html`) was written before anyone thought much of the Web. It's still a great way to learn about e-mail, FTP, newsgroups, Telnet, and those other text-type Internet tools.

E-Mail: For Fast Communications

As mentioned, most people's Internet experience starts with e-mail, the lightning-fast medium for communicating with other individuals or even (via *mailing lists*) with groups. In the past, some Web browsers allowed you to send e-mail, but they didn't let you receive it. Why was that? Well, basically, receiving requires a place for the mail to sit until you retrieve it (a mail box) and a way for you to read it (a mail reader) once you've got it. Netscape Communicator includes Messenger, a fully capable e-mail program that lets you both send and receive e-mail.

 Communicator's mail reader has lots of new power—it lets you view mail that includes graphics, fancy font effects, and color changes. See Chapter 5 for more on how to use Communicator's e-mail features.

We talked a lot about e-mail in earlier sections of this chapter; take a look at "How Data Travels" and "E-Mail Addressing" to find out how e-mail makes its way around the Internet world.

Discussion Groups: For "Public" Discussions

The first stop for new netizens (after e-mail and the Web) has often been Usenet news (also known as *newsgroups*). A newsgroup is like e-mail in that you are reading and possibly replying to messages, but unlike it in that you are able to partake of a broader scope of public conversations and discussions, with as little or as much participation as you want. You don't even have to take part—you can just stand back and watch if you'd prefer. (That's called *lurking*, and it's not looked upon as being as ominous as it sounds.) There are literally thousands of newsgroups available on nearly every subject imaginable; you can join in or just cruise through them as you like.

Communicator provides a nice interface for reading and writing to newsgroups. It also offers an option for creating and participating in more private discussion groups, which can be handy for situations where a group of people working together need to discuss aspects of their work, for example.

When you participate in newsgroups or discussion groups, it's very easy to work your way through the major headings and through the groups themselves. You can also subscribe (and unsubscribe) to your favorite groups as you like. We'll go over all this in detail in Chapter 5.

Behind the Usenet Scenes

The major (but not the only) source of network news is Usenet, which is a free service. Usenet was actually born before the Internet, and much confusion exists as to how the two interact.

Usenet is not a network like the Internet, there are no Usenet computers per se, and Usenet doesn't even need the Internet. Rather, what drives Usenet is akin to an agreement set up between those who want to distribute and those who want to read newsgroups. Network administrators arrange with other administrators to transfer newsgroups back and forth, which usually occurs via the Internet, but only because that's convenient.

The site that provides your site with news is called a *news feed*.

Some newsgroups end up being transferred by some computers, others by other computers, and so on.

Push: For Content Delivered Automatically

Push technology turns the World Wide Web inside out. Before *push*, content was generally *pulled*, in that getting the stuff required the use of a browser to contact a server, make a request, and accept the serving of the content. One had to pull the content from the server. Now the server will push it out to you automatically.

In using push technology, you subscribe to *channels*—which are similar to Web sites—and then the content on that channel is automatically delivered to your computer at regular intervals. The creator of the channel usually sets a frequency for delivery; for a news channel the frequency may be short—perhaps 15 minutes. For less time-sensitive stuff it may be longer. As a user, you can modify the frequency of delivery, overriding the channel producer's settings as you like.

Communicator includes a component called Netscape Netcaster that acts as a tuner for push channels. Netcaster allows you to get push transmissions and even subscribe to regular Web sites to have their content pushed your way. Netcaster also employs new extensions to HTML—called Dynamic HTML—allowing content developers to create truly compelling content with moving graphics as well as text, sound, video, and other forms of media.

 Netcaster is very, very new. (We talk about it more in Chapter 7.) Your copy of Communicator may not include Netcaster. To get it, or to find out about latest developments in push from Netscape, check the Netscape Web site at http://home.netscape.com. Also watch for updates to this book at the Sybex Web site, http://www.sybex.com.

Internet Phone: For Talking Online

Internet telephone software lets users tap into the Internet to conduct actual voice communications. The quality of transmission is not so hot, but Internet phone offers other features. For example, video conferencing and other collaborative tools become possible via Internet phone. Internet phone lets you use a microphone and speakers to actually speak over the Internet with other people (who, obviously, are also speaking over the Internet). Despite the currently poor quality of vocal transmission, this idea is just terrific and has been highly popular in the form of stand-alone programs.

Communicator includes an extra nifty program called Netscape Conference that offers Internet phone, chat (see the section that follows), whiteboarding, and collaborative Web browsing. These are highly dynamic and very innovative options for interactive communications. More on this stuff in Chapter 6.

Chat: For Real-Time Interaction

Chat, which has nothing much to do with actually speaking, is a means of real-time communication that takes place via typing messages that appear immediately on screen. As you type, your words are seen on screen by all the folks in this particular "chat room." As they respond, their messages are similarly seen by all. Some people just love chat. Chats are sometimes hosted by celebrities, sometimes centered on a specific topic, and sometimes just plain *chats*.

Communicator includes a good chat program, but chat can be accomplished on the Internet in any of a few ways, and Communicator does not handle all of them. The granddaddy of chat is Internet Relay Chat (IRC). IRC allows people all over the world to interact with each other in chat rooms. Communicator does not allow for using IRC, though you can use Communicator to download IRC software, which you'll generally get from a Web site hosting IRC chats.

Conference, Communicator's chat program, lets users conduct one-on-one chats with another user who has Conference. It can be handy for collaborative work, but to participate in IRC chats, you'll need IRC software. See Chapter 6 for more on Conference.

What's Out There

One site that incorporates chat into it's content is InterJazz, which has scheduled live chats with jazz artists at `http://interjazz.com`. To get IRC software, visit mIRC at `http://www.geocities.com/SiliconValley/Park/6000`.

FTP: For Transferring Files

For transferring a file or program from one machine (a server, for example) to another (yours, for example), FTP (File Transfer Protocol) is still the popular choice, although the mechanics of FTP are now often hidden behind a Web page link.

In its traditional modes, FTP only lets you see a list of the files on a computer and selectively transfer them to your machine, usually through anonymous FTP (see "Anonymous FTP Explained Here"). Still, FTP should not be overlooked for what it has accomplished and still does, namely, allowing users to bring home files, information, and software.

After retrieving a file, you may need to perform some additional steps if the file has been compressed to save space. This involves using a utility to uncompress, or *unzip*, the file to make it usable. There are many compression formats in use, so you may sometimes find yourself cursing rather than jumping for joy when you uncover just the file you are looking for but are unable to unzip it.

 More details on downloading and decompressing files are included in Chapter 8.

Navigator, the browser component of Communicator, presents FTP directories as a graphical menu using icons similar to those used by the Windows Explorer. Directories are represented by a folder icon; text files are displayed as the familiar sheet-of-paper-with-its-top-corner-folded-down. These items all appear as links—they are underlined so that you can click on them to move to the place in question.

Another advantage of Navigator, over say a regular FTP session, is that Navigator reads the file type, so it can display a text file on screen when you click on the link. A regular FTP session involves copying the file to your computer—similar to saving a document—and then opening it later using a text editor.

Likewise, Navigator will deal with sound, image, and video files that appear as links (in the FTP list) as it does in other contexts, displaying the text, picture, or movie, or playing the sound when you click on the link.

Anonymous FTP Explained Here

Anonymous FTP permits users to access remote systems without actually having user accounts on the systems. In effect, it allows for "guests" to visit a remote site, and it permits just enough computer privileges to access the resources provided. The process involves the user starting an FTP connection and logging in to the remote computer as the user "anonymous," with an arbitrary password that, for the purposes of Internet etiquette, should be your e-mail address. The beauty of using Navigator for anonymous FTP is that with Navigator you don't have to go through all the login steps, you don't have to use a text-based FTP program on your machine, and Navigator displays all the stuff on the FTP server in an easy-to-use graphical interface. You can tell when a Web document you are viewing in Navigator comes from an anonymous FTP site because the URL starts with `ftp:` instead of `http:`.

Navigator may have to be properly configured with the appropriate external player and viewer applications in order to play sounds or movies and display pictures, although it can automatically deal with popular sound formats such as WAV and AU and video formats such as AVI and MOV. Also, once Navigator plays the sound or movie, it's gone. You'll learn how to save the images, sounds, and videos in Chapter 3.

◆ The Human Side of Hypermedia

The Web offers a rich environment for exploring tangential or directly related information because the hypertext paradigm works the way people do when they're on the road to discovery. For example, if you were a kid in the '60s or '70s working on a book report about Native American cultures, your process might have looked like this: You began by reading the encyclopedia article on Indians (this, remember, is before Native Americans were referred to as such) when you came to a passage describing the dislocation of the Hopi people to a reservation near what is called today Apache Junction, Arizona.

Having never been near Arizona, you decided to find out about its climate, terrain, flora, and fauna. Putting the I volume aside on the floor, you grabbed the A volume and dipped into Arizona. Then you wondered, "What's it like today?" You called the Apache Junction Chamber of Commerce and asked for recent industrial and employment statistics. Later that day, curious about the status of any national reparations made to the Hopi in Arizona, you made a trip to your local library and had a chat with the reference librarian, who in turn brought you copies of various federal government policy statements.

Thus, the kind of discovery process supported by hypertext—and the Web—is really modeled after the way people tend to work when they're learning new things. It's easy to see why the hypertext paradigm and the Web have really taken off. If you want more information, you can just click on a Web page link and there you are: The linked item could be a Web page on a server 7500 miles away. If you were writing that book report today, you might travel all over the world, via the Web, without ever leaving your computer.

Moving Along

With all this backstory in place, you're ready now to hit the highway. Starting with the next chapter, we're going to dig into how you do what you do with Communicator. Let's take to the road.

Part Two:

Navigating, Communicating, and Publishing

Navigating via Navigator

Let's get working with Netscape Navigator. In this chapter, you'll learn how to start the program, how to open and save Web documents, and how to switch between documents and other hypermedia (sound and video, for example) via hot links. You'll also get a good look at navigating through *frames*, which are like window panes within a document.

 This chapter assumes you already have an Internet connection and have installed Netscape on your PC. For information on making your Internet connection work and on getting and installing Netscape, see Chapters 10 and 11.

◆ Launching Netscape Navigator

Launching Netscape Navigator is easy. If you follow the instructions for getting the software and setting it up in Chapters 10 and 11, you'll have a Netscape Communicator icon on your Desktop, and you'll have a new item in your Programs menu named Netscape Communicator. To start Navigator, follow these steps:

1. Start your Internet connection. How you do this depends on the sort of Internet service you have—see Chapter 10 for details about connecting to the Internet.

Netscape, Navigator, Communicator

When you hear people talk about *Netscape,* up until now, they were probably referring to the Web browser, which also included the ability to send mail and read newsgroups. Netscape also refers to Netscape Communications Corporation, the company that brings us all this lovely software (and a great Web site, too).

Netscape Navigator, the Web browser, is the central component of the suite of software called Netscape Communicator. Communicator includes not only the latest and greatest version of Navigator, but also Messenger and Collabra for using Internet e-mail and newsgroups (see Chapter 5); Composer, an HTML editor for creating your own Web pages (see Chapter 9); Conference, which allows two people to talk in real time over the Internet (see Chapter 6), and Netcaster, a nifty interface to the world of push technology and channels (see Chapter 7).

In this chapter, we're going to focus on using Netscape Navigator, the piece of software that lets you explore the World Wide Web (which is probably why you're reading this).

2. Now start up Navigator. You can do this in one of two ways:

◆ Double-click on the Desktop's Netscape Communicator icon, shown here. (Navigator will launch by default.)

or

◆ From the Windows 95 Start menu, select Programs ➤ Netscape Communicator ➤ Netscape Navigator. Either way, Netscape Navigator, the central component of Communicator, will open.

SLIP and PPP: The Communicator Connection

Before you can start using Communicator, you must start the connection software that you use to access the Internet. This may seem a bit more complicated than starting many other programs, but it's really no big deal.

Here's how it works: You start your connection software—it can be Windows 95 Dial-Up Networking, Netcom's Netcomplete, or whatever you choose—which then connects your computer to the Internet. This software "introduces" Communicator to the Internet—it is a vital link in your Internet connection. (At one time, this could be accomplished only through special SLIP/PPP software, but nowadays there are new and different technologies, included with Windows 95, for example, that accomplish the same purpose.) Your connection software and your provider will then do a little dance together, passing back and forth the TCP/IP packets that make it possible for you to run Communicator (which is on your machine). Voilà—your machine is accepted as a little network hooked into the bigger, more exciting network called the Internet, and you're on your way!

If all goes well (and it surely will), the Netscape Navigator window will open, and the Netscape icon in the window's upper-right corner will become animated: Comets will fly, the sun will rise, and the moon will fly on by. This tells you that Navigator is transferring data, which will appear in a few seconds in the form of a Web page. Whenever Navigator is "working" (downloading a document, searching, and so on), the Netscape icon is animated. It stops when the action has been completed.

Depending on your connection speed, the traffic level of the Internet, and how fast-acting the server that holds the Web page is, it may take more than a few seconds for the entire thing to load. In current Net parlance, that's known as *cometizing*—named for what the N icon does while you wait (and wait, and wait…).

What's Out There

You can find out all about Windows 95 Dial-Up Networking at `http://athos .rutgers.edu/LCSR-Computing/win95.html`.

When you first start Netscape Navigator, you'll see the Welcome to Netscape home page, with its sleek, colorful graphics. You can change this start-up home page to something else if you like; we'll tell you how to do that later, in Chapter 8.

The home page is where you begin, where Navigator first lands you on your Internet voyage. Think of it as one of many ports of entry into the Web. The Web, you'll recall, doesn't just go from here to there—it's a *web*. It doesn't really matter where you start, because everything's interconnected.

You can return to the start-up home page (the one you see when you start a Netscape Navigator session) at any time simply by clicking on the Home icon on the Navigator Navigation toolbar.

 You can always return to Netscape's own home page, no matter what else you've chosen as your start-up home page, just by clicking on the N icon in the upper-right corner of the Netscape Navigator window.

If you followed the steps earlier in this chapter and have Navigator running now, try clicking on the Search button in the Navigation toolbar. This brief exercise will test your Internet connection. The N icon should become animated, and in a few seconds Netscape's Search page should appear.

Now try clicking on the Back button. The N icon will again become animated, and Netscape's home page will reappear.

Home, Home on the Home Page

You are not limited to using the Welcome to Netscape home page as your start-up home page—you can make it so Navigator won't load a home page on start-up (see Chapter 8), or you can use the What's Out There page that comes with this book, or you can store and start up with one of any number of home pages that you find on the Internet. (Chapter 4 talks about storing and managing Web documents.) You can even create your own home page. (Refer to Chapter 9 for instructions on how to do this.) If you change the start-up home page and want to find the Welcome to Netscape home page again, you can use its URL, which is http://home.netscape.com/. Or you can just click on the N icon (the one that becomes animated when Web page files are arriving) in the upper-right corner of the Navigator window.

◆ What You See: The Navigator Interface

Let's look at the parts of the Navigator window. The interface shows the Document View window. Figure 3.1 shows you what's what.

Via the View menu, you can display or hide any of the toolbars, including the Navigation toolbar, the Location toolbar, and the Personal toolbar. Or, you can click on the blue arrow buttons at the left of any toolbar to collapse it (and expand it again later). You may want to hide this stuff if you want the page display area to be larger.

Title Bar   In the title bar, you can see the name of the page you are currently viewing.

Menu Bar   The menu bar in Navigator is similar to menu bars in other Windows applications: It provides you with drop-down menus. When you move the mouse to the menu and click on a selection, choices appear.

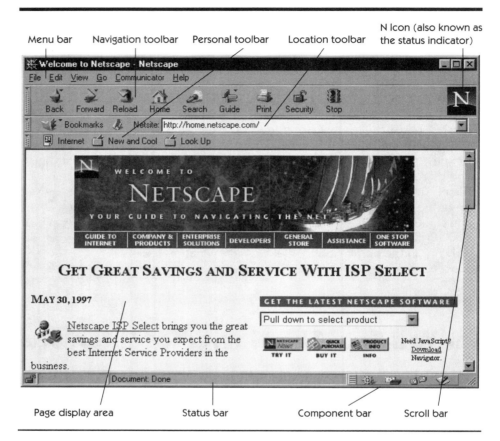

Figure 3.1: Here's the Navigator window with all its parts labeled so you can see what's what.

Navigation Toolbar   The Navigation toolbar performs some common actions. It's like other Windows toolbars in that all you have to do is click on the button for the specified action to occur. (If you point at a tool for a few seconds, a ToolTip will appear, telling you what the tool does. The ToolTip is simply a text box that displays the name of the tool to which you are pointing.) Let's quickly go over the Navigator toolbar buttons.

The Tool	Its Name	What You Do with It
Back	Back	Jump back to the previous page or document in your History list (that is, the page you were viewing just prior to the current page).
Forward	Forward	Jump forward to the next page or document in your History list. (If you're on the last item in the History list, this button is dimmed—it looks grayed out.)
Reload	Reload	Refreshes the document in the page display area.
Home	Home	Return to the start-up home page.
Search	Search	Visit Netscape's Net Search page.
Images	Images	This "smart" images button only appears when you have turned off image auto-loading.
Guide	Guide	Visit one of Netscape's Web pages.
Print	Print	Print the Web page you're currently viewing.
Security	Security	If this button is not grayed out, you can click on it to find out about the security of the current Web page.
Stop	Stop	When a page is loading, click on Stop to cancel the process of loading an incoming document.

Images load automatically unless you tell Navigator to do otherwise. If you have a slow Internet connection and prefer to decide whether or not you want to view pictures on a Web page, you can turn off Image auto-loading. To toggle image auto-loading from Navigator's menu bar, select Edit ➤ Preferences. In the Category column on the left of the Preferences dialog box, select Advanced. A checkmark will appear next to Automatically Load Images when auto-loading is turned on. When auto-loading is turned off, the Images button appears on Navigator's Navigation toolbar. You can click on this button to load images on a selected Web page.

Security is a topic of great concern to many users who want to protect their personal information—such as credit card numbers and bank records—from theft. Netscape Communicator has encryption and security features that make it the preferred Web client for accessing all types of commercial Web servers. Check out "A Few Quick Words on Security" in this chapter for more on Communicator's security features, and turn to Chapter 5 for a discussion of certificates. (A certificate provides a unique signature that can then be verified to protect an individual from being impersonated in Internet interactions.)

Location Toolbar   On the left is a blue folder icon you can click on to access bookmarks, which we discuss in Chapter 4. The rest of this toolbar is occupied by the Location text box, where you'll find the *URL* (the Uniform Resource Locator) of the current document. We'll get to a discussion of URLs a little later in this chapter.

Here's a sneaky trick: Click on the arrow on the far-right end of the Location text box, and any URLs you typed into the box recently will pop up. Select any one of them to visit that site again. Even neater than that: if you're in the habit of typing URLs directly into the Location text box, you'll be pleased to see a type-ahead feature there: type the first several characters of an oft-used URL, and Navigator will guess the rest for you.

Personal Toolbar   Below the Location toolbar is a toolbar that you can customize by dragging and dropping URLs into it using the page icon. You can find out more about the Personal toolbar in Chapter 4.

Page Display Area   This is the main portion of the screen—it's where you'll see what you came to the Web to see.

Status Bar   The status bar is at the bottom of the screen. As you move the cursor about the viewing area and come across links, the cursor changes into the shape of a hand with one finger pointing, and the status bar displays the URL for the link you're pointing to. When content is being transferred to your machine, you'll see numbers in the status bar indicating the progress of the transfer.

Scroll Bars   These are just like regular Windows scroll bars: They appear on the side of the viewing area, and possibly at the bottom, when the page is too big to fit in the window. Click on the scroll bars to bring into view whatever's off-screen.

Component Bar   Netscape Communicator includes a task bar with which you can open Navigator (the browser), Messenger's Inbox (the e-mail program), Collabra (the newsgroup reader), or Composer (the HTML editor). This component bar can be *docked,* meaning that it appears at the bottom of the Navigator window as part of the status bar; or it can *float,* meaning that it appears as a tiny window with buttons that launch the various Netscape components.

To make the component bar float (see Figure 3.2) when it's currently docked on the Navigator status bar, click on the gray bars at the left side of the component bar. Once it floats, you can drag it to wherever you'd like it to live for the time being. To dock the component bar, click on the little N icon on the floating component bar. Alternatively, you can use the Navigator menu bar and select Communicator ➤ Show Component Bar to float the component bar, or Communicator ➤ Dock Component Bar to anchor the component bar to the Navigator window's status bar.

Figure 3.2:   Communicator's floating component bar lets you open Communicator programs while you work.

◆ Opening Your First Document

You actually opened your first document when you started Navigator and the home page appeared. But let's dig around a little further and see what else we can do.

What's Out There

The Netscape Assistance area, online documentation for Netscape Communicator, is at http://home.netscape.com/assist/.

Following Hot Links

Moving around the World Wide Web is a snap, thanks to hyperlinks. It's as easy as a mouse-click on the link—each link points to some other piece of the Internet, just as Windows 95 shortcuts point to something on your hard drive.

As we've said before, hypertext is nonlinear. (That means you don't have to follow a straight path from point A to point Z, but rather you can skip around from one place to another to another, back to the first, round to a fourth, and so on.) Hypertext is hypertext because it has links—*hot links*, they're often called—to other sources of information. You follow these links through a document, or from document to document, document to image, or perhaps from server to server, in any way you like as you navigate the Web. (You can think of hypertext as both the text and the links—it's the navigational means by which you traverse the Web.) The great thing about the Web is that you don't have to know whether the information you're looking at is in Paris, France, or Paris, Texas—all you need to do is follow a link.

If you do want information about a link before you click on it, just check the status bar at the bottom of your screen. There you'll see a URL for anything from another site to a sound or video file, to an e-mail address. For example, if you drag your mouse over the linked word *Webmaster* on any given Web page, you might see the URL for the Webmaster's home page, an e-mail address provided by the Webmaster for feedback, or the URL for a Help page about the site you're viewing. Read on, and we'll tell you more about URLs later in this chapter.

How can you tell what is hypertext in a document? Words that are hyperlinks will usually be in a special color and underlined. On Netscape's home page, the special color is blue. A Webmaster (or producer) can choose any color at all to designate links, but in most cases the chosen color will be different from the color chosen for "ordinary" text. The words that stand out on a page are generally the links.

Images can also be links. Sometimes an image will have a border of color around it to designate its "linkness," but in any case, the cursor will almost always turn into a pointing hand when you drag it over part of a Web page that is linked to something else.

Just as both text and images on a Web page can be hyperlinks, these hyperlinks can lead you to many different kinds of information. A link could lead you through a single document, off to a different Web page, across the world to a page on a different server, or to an FTP server, Gopher site, newsgroup, or e-mail address.

Links can also lead you to images, sounds, movies, and multimedia files. We'll tell you more about how to experience the interactive Web in Chapter 6 and how to get tools to take advantage of the multimedia aspect of the Web in Chapter 7.

To Click or Not to Click?

When you click on a link on the Web, it may take a few seconds to access the information you requested. Don't click again; let Navigator do its job. Every time you click on a link, Navigator cancels the last order you gave it and starts a new one. So if you click on the same link four or five times, Navigator has to start all over again each time.

If we slowed this whole business down and showed you its underpinnings, you'd see that when you click on a hyperlink, Navigator contacts the machine (or machines) on the Internet that you told it to call. Then the dance between software and servers does one of these things:

◆ It gets and displays the document that the link specifies.

◆ It goes to another location in the current document.

◆ It gets a file, such as an image or a sound file, and through the use of a plug-in or an external viewer or player (another piece of software on your PC) displays the image or plays the sound.

◆ It gives you access to another Internet service, such as Gopher, FTP, Telnet, and so on.

If you still have the Welcome to Netscape home page open now, click on a few links. Don't be shy—just click on anything that looks interesting. You'll soon see why they call it the Web. Try jumping back and forth a couple of times, too, by clicking on those tools on the Navigation bar. When you've had enough, simply click on the Home button or the N icon to get back to the Welcome to Netscape home page.

When you look at a document that has a link to something you've already seen, the color of that link changes. These are called *visited links*, and this is Navigator's way of letting you know you've been to that place before.

What's Out There

Take a look at *On Internet Security,* Netscape's Web treatise on the subject, for the lowdown on Netscape Communicator's security features. The URL is `http://home.netscape.com/info/security-doc.html`.

Opening a Document Using Its URL

Sometimes you're going to want to go straight for the jugular—you know where the document is, and you just want to see it without starting on a home page and skipping through a lot of hot links. Maybe your pal just sent you the URL for the Exploratorium, a really wonderful interactive science museum in San Francisco.

To open a document using its URL, follow these steps:

1. From the Navigator menu bar, select File ➤ Open Page, or press Ctrl+O. The Open Page dialog box will appear.

2. In the Open Page dialog box (see Figure 3.3), type the URL of interest (in our example, `http://www.exploratorium.edu`).

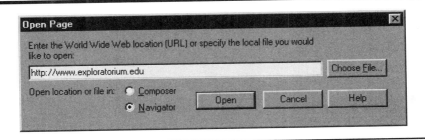

Figure 3.3: The Open Page dialog box

URLs Explained Here

Remember that talk about e-mail addresses back in Chapter 2? There's a standard addressing scheme with which Navigator and the Web work, too. It's called the Uniform Resource Locator (URL). The URL pinpoints the locations of documents and other information on the Web so Navigator and other browsers can find the stuff. The structure of a URL may seem complicated at first, but it's really straight-forward. These are the components of a URL:

◆ The type of resource

◆ The name of the machine containing the file (the document or information) to be transferred

◆ The full "path" that locates the file among the directories and sub-directories on the machine

For example, in the URL

```
http://home.netscape.com/home/welcome.html
```

the `http:` represents the resource type and transfer protocol (which, as you know, is Hypertext Transfer Protocol); the double slashes separate the protocol from the rest; the name of the computer is `home.netscape.com`; and the path and filename of the item on the computer is `/home/welcome.html`.

You will sometimes type into a text box the URLs of pages you want Navigator to find and deliver to you. One thing you should keep in mind in this situation is that, unlike e-mail addresses, URLs are case-sensitive—capitalization matters! This is because lots of Web servers are Unix machines; in Unix, filenames in upper-case letters are not considered the same as filenames in lowercase letters. All the punctuation marks you see in some URLs are significant too—one misplaced hyphen, period, or tilde (~) will trip up the whole works. So if you're typing in a complex URL, look at it closely as you type.

You can copy URLs from e-mail or other documents and paste them directly into either the Open Page dialog box or the Location text box.

3. Click on Open, and Navigator will find the document for this URL and display it on your screen. (See Figure 3.4.)

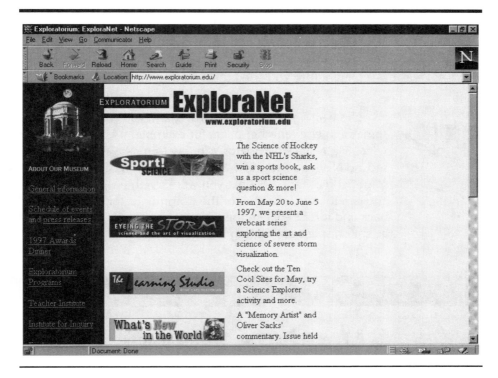

Figure 3.4: Here's the Exploratorium's home page. We found it using the URL a friend gave us.

You can also jump quickly to a document by typing or pasting its URL directly into Navigator's Location text box—that is, if you have the Location toolbar displayed. And you don't even have to type `http://` every time you want to type in a URL. You can start with the next bit of the URL instead. Navigator assumes that the URLs you ask for are HTTP URLs (Web pages) unless you tell it otherwise. In fact, you can often type just one word. For example, typing **Ford** and pressing ↵ will get you straight into that car maker's site.

The Web is very big. And it changes all the time. From time to time you might have difficulty locating or accessing content. The original may have been removed by its owner, the machine that holds the content may be unavailable or overworked when you try to access it, or the network path between your machine and the server might be down. If Navigator has been trying for a while to access a document without success, it will display a dialog box saying that it just plain cannot locate the document. (See "Error Messages Demystified" later in this chapter for the dish on error messages and what to do about them.) To go back to the document that was on-screen before you tried making the jump, just click on OK.

If you're waiting for a page to arrive, and you want to look at something else (another page, for example) while you're waiting, select File ➤ New Navigator Window from Navigator's menu bar. A second Navigator window will open, and you can use it to look at something other than what you were trying for in the first window. You can then use Alt+Tab or the Communicator menu to switch back and forth between the two open windows. Now who said attention spans are getting shorter?

A Few Quick Words on Security

Keeping the data that passes across the Internet safe and secure is an issue that bigwigs in both business and government are discussing now, and one that will soon become relevant even to the casual user.

You've probably noticed a lot of talk in newspapers and magazines and on TV about commercial ventures on the Web—merchants and malls all setting up shop and taking your credit card order, or banks offering home services through their sites. You can even use the Web to buy and sell stocks. If this data (your credit card number, your bank balance and access code, or your stock portfolio) is not safe, it can be read by some eavesdropper lurking in an electronic shadow. Well, you can surely see the concern!

Fortunately, the designers of Netscape Communicator had this issue in mind when they developed the software. Netscape Navigator was the first Web browser to allow secured transactions to take place (between your computer running Navigator and a Web server running Netscape's Netsite Commerce Server). In practical terms, this means that when you, running Navigator at home, connect to a home page on a special server that was purchased from Netscape Communications, the data sent back and forth can be secure from prying "eyes."

(continued on next page)

By now you may have noticed the little blue lock icon on Navigator's command toolbar. Usually, if you click on the security lock, a Netscape window will pop up and tell you that "There Is No Security Info for This Page."

If, however, you are connected to a secure page—one where such eavesdropping is not possible because the data is encrypted before it is transferred and decrypted upon arrival—clicking on the lock will open a similar window, but one that's filled with tasty, reassuring data that offers copious detail about the relative security of the Web page.

Netscape Communicator (and therefore Navigator 4) offers even more sophisticated security with the addition of *certificates* to its features. Certificates are meant to prove your identity to Web servers through a system of verification. Look for this technology to become an increasingly important security feature as Web producers upgrade their sites to take advantage of new versions of Netscape's server software using certificates.

You can find out more about security by selecting Help ➤ Security from the Navigator menu bar. To get a directory of sites using Netsite Commerce Servers and other Netscape software, visit Netscape's Customer Showcase at http://home.netscape.com/home/netscape-galleria.html. To find out more about the current document on screen, select View ➤ Page Info from Navigator's menu bar.

◆ Changing the Size and Color of Displayed Text

If you've been working along with this chapter, you'll notice that text appears on your screen in different sizes. Usually, the text that makes up the substance of the page—the *body text*—is about the size you'd expect, while the title of the page is larger. (For a more complete discussion of the composition and elements of Web pages, see Chapter 9.)

Changing Fonts and Type Sizes

Some folks are annoyed by gigantic titles all over the page that necessitate scrolling around a lot, while others can deal with big headlines in order to make the main text of the page larger and easier to read. Whichever you prefer, you can change the font and size of displayed text in Navigator.

Here's how you do it:

1. From Navigator's menu bar, select Edit ➤ Preferences. The Preferences dialog box will appear.

2. In the Category column along the left of the Preferences dialog box, double-click on Appearance (or click on the plus sign next to that word). The Preferences dialog box will be updated to reflect your choice.

3. Indented below the word *Appearance*, you'll see the word *Fonts*. Click on that word, and once again, the Preferences dialog box will change to reflect your last click.

4. Now, in the Fonts and Encodings area, you can set either a variable width or a fixed font. Just click on the menu boxes for either the font face or the font size to choose any font and size available on your machine.

5. When you're finished making your selections, click on OK to return to the Navigator window.

The variable width or proportional font is the one used for most of the text—body, head, and lists. The fixed font is the one used for preformatted text, which is a rarely used HTML element, but it also happens to be the font that appears when you type stuff in to the forms that some pages offer; for example, when responding to surveys.

Leave the Preferences dialog box's "encoding" set to Western. Western is the proper setting for English and most European languages. Note too that while other choices are apparent in this dialog box, they aren't really available to you unless you have a version of Windows that's been localized to a specific language or country. Leave this stuff alone unless you know what to do with it.

As a shortcut, you can change font sizes without opening the Preferences dialog box at all. From Navigator's menu bar, select View ➤ Increase Font or View ➤ Decrease Font, depending on what you want to accomplish.

You might wonder as you go along, How does changing one font size change the style of more than one kind of text on a single page? Good question. Basically, Navigator displays different sizes of text (the title, headings, body text, and so on) in comparison to one "measure"—the basic font size. Navigator will display the title so-and-so many times larger than this base measure, and so forth. It is the base measure that you are changing in the procedure we just described.

A good rule of thumb is to select the font you find the most readable as your Proportional Font. A font such as Times New Roman or Bookman Old Style would be a sensible choice. For the Fixed Font, which is generally supposed to resemble a computer code look, Courier New or some other typewriter type of font will work well. A size of 12 or 14 for both fonts will make text readable on almost any screen.

Changing Colors

In Navigator, you have the option of changing the color of text. Imagine that! To do so, follow these steps:

1. From Navigator's menu bar, select Edit ➤ Preferences. The Preferences dialog box will appear.

2. If the word *Colors* is not already visible in the Category column along the left of the Preferences dialog box, double-click on Appearance (or click on the plus sign next to that word). The Preferences dialog box will be updated to reflect your choice.

3. Indented below the word *Appearance,* you'll see the word *Colors.* Click on that word, and the Preferences dialog box will show Navigator's true colors (see Figure 3.5).

You can choose whether you want the selections you are about to make to override any existing settings in the documents you'll be viewing. For example, you might want all the text other than links in all the documents you view to be purple, even if the document's designer made the text black. Or you might want the document designer's wishes to outweigh your own.

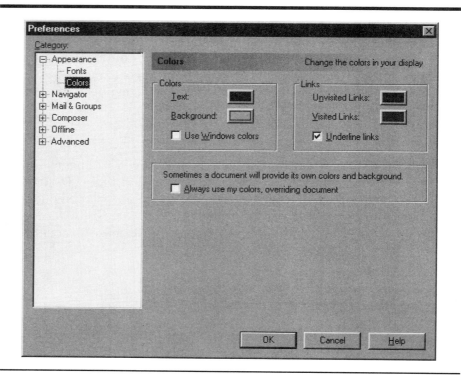

Figure 3.5: The Preferences dialog box displaying color information

4. To make your upcoming color choices override any other settings, select the checkbox Always Use My Colors, Overriding Document.

or

To allow the settings that exist in a given document to override the color choices you are about to make, deselect the checkbox Always Use My Colors, Overriding Document.

5. As you can see in Figure 3.5, you have four color choices available to you. These include:

◆ Text

◆ Background

◆ Unvisited Links (the ones you haven't been to yet)

◆ Visited Links (the ones you've seen already)

Click on any of these buttons to adjust the color choice for that option. The Color dialog box will appear.

6. In this dialog box, you can select any of a number of predefined colors by clicking on one in the Basic Colors area.

   or

   You can define a custom color by clicking on the Define Custom Colors button. In that case, the window will expand to include a wide range of colors. Click in the box wherever a color you like appears, and then click on the narrow panel to the right of the main color box to specify the shade (lightness and darkness) of that color. Click on the Add to Custom Colors button. The color you have specified will appear in the Custom Colors part of the Color dialog box. Click on it to make it your selected color.

7. Click on OK to close the Color dialog box. The Preferences dialog box will reappear, with the color(s) you've chosen appearing in place of the default Netscape colors that were there before.

8. You can repeat steps 4–6 for all four elements (text, background, unvisited links, and visited links), if you like.

9. When you are done specifying Navigator's colors, click on OK. The Preferences dialog box will close, and you will once again see the Netscape window.

The changes you've made will take place immediately. If you don't like the results, you can always go back and repeat the whole color-changing process, selecting something new and different.

Guestbooks, Surveys, and Forms—Gee Whiz!

When you see a box on a Web page that lets you type stuff in it, that's often what's called a *form*. Forms are used by Web site producers to let users like you participate in Internet surveys, order merchandise, "sign" guestbooks, and give feedback, among other fun things. The purpose of a form is usually obvious, as is the way you use it. You'll type some words in a text box, then perhaps click on a few radio buttons and checkboxes, and finally press a button at the bottom of the

(continued on next page)

page that whisks that information on its way. You may be invited at some sites to fill in a guestbook with your name, e-mail address, and a message to tell the Webmaster and other Web users what you think about the Web page you just visited. Or you may be asked to fill out a survey or registration form as a prerequisite to seeing the rest of a site. Sites like HotWired (`http://www.hotwired.com/`) want to know who's using their services, and so they offer a free registration process in which you tell them who you are, and in exchange they let you visit all of HotWired's chat rooms and live broadcasts.

Sites like Time Warner's Pathfinder (`http://pathfinder.com/`) and the CNET site (`http://www.cnet.com/`) offer entertaining e-mail newsletters in exchange for your registration. Other sites may offer you contests or giveaways in exchange for your completed questionnaire.

This process is usually quick, simple, and free. However, if you're not sure exactly who might be receiving personal information, and if you don't want your e-mail box cluttered with junk from strangers, you may want to think twice about filling out every survey or questionnaire you run across. Watch for sites that do not sell their mailing lists—they usually tell you as much, and they usually stick to their word.

If choices like laundry detergent, breakfast cereal, and link color stymie you, you can choose the default Windows color scheme as your very own. In the Colors area of the Preferences dialog box, simply place a checkmark next to Use Windows Colors.

◆ Saving Stuff to Your Local Machine

Let's say you've been skipping around the Internet and looking at a lot of stuff, and you've found something really nifty you want to hold on to.

Saving takes up valuable disk space. This means you don't want to save *everything*. You do want to save things you want to keep for reference or access quickly in the future. For alternatives to saving, see Chapter 4's discussions of Bookmarks and Internet shortcuts.

So What If You Have a Different Browser?

One line of thinking goes that Web documents should be viewable by any person with any Web browser, so pages should be thoughtfully designed to take into account the failings of browsers other than Navigator. Another line goes that one should exploit all the wonderful features Navigator has to offer, including fancy things such as special colors and the use of columns, frames, and tables, even though people using Web browsers other than Navigator might not be able to view that stuff as it was intended to appear. You can sometimes see the evidence of this debate on the Web in the form of messages that say something like "Use Netscape for best viewing" or "Netscape not required." Let's take a look at what all this talk is about.

Netscape Navigator, since its nascent moment, has always pushed the envelope of what a Web browser can do. Netscape Navigator 1 supported HTML version 1 and some of the proposed HTML+ extensions; at the time, all other Web browsers were offering only HTML version 0.9. Netscape Navigator 1.1 supported the newly proposed HTML 3 standard. Netscape Navigator 2 was the first commercial browser to support Java, which allows designers to add more interactive and animated functionality to Web pages. Other enhancements that became available included frames, JavaScript, helper applications, and plug-ins.

Netscape Navigator 3 added new capabilities, allowing Web designers to create more attractive pages with new tabling techniques, providing more secure communication over the Internet via certificates, and opening up access to interactive three-dimensional experiences through VRML.

And Netscape Communicator, including Navigator 4, includes even more versatility in page design, including support for style sheets, Web fonts, absolute positioning of items on a page, and layering of text and images. (And that's not even counting the huge enhancements to Navigator itself, as well as to the other programs in the Communicator suite).

What does all this advanced thinking mean to you? Well, by using all the advanced HTML and Java features that Netscape Communicator supports, Web page authors can create state-of-the-art Web sites.

The only drawback in using these amazing features is that many Web browsers other than Navigator cannot (yet) display them on-screen correctly. Netscape is usually a step or two ahead of the pack in this regard, and a document designed to take full advantage of Netscape Communicator's advanced features can look disappointingly different when viewed with some other Web browser. But you have Netscape Communicator, so you'll be just fine, right?

You can save a document to your local hard drive in three ways. We'll get to those in a second; first, a word or two on naming files in general and hypertext files in particular.

Saving Stuff You Can See

Saving documents and images to your hard drive can be a good idea if you want to look at them later without paying for connect time. You can also use your store of saved documents as a library to jog ideas in constructing your own home page—this may be an easier process if the page is on your hard drive. See Chapter 9 for more on creating your own Web pages.

Saving Web Pages

Here's how to save the page you are viewing at the moment to your hard disk:

1. From the Navigator menu bar, select File ➤ Save As. The Save As dialog box will appear (see Figure 3.6). This is much like a Save As dialog box you'd see in any other Windows application.

2. In the File Name text box, type a filename. Navigator will usually assign either .htm or .html as the extension automatically—these are the extensions for hypertext files. (If you want to be sure the program is assigning one of those extensions, just take a look at the bottom of the dialog box, where the Save As Type drop-down list appears.)

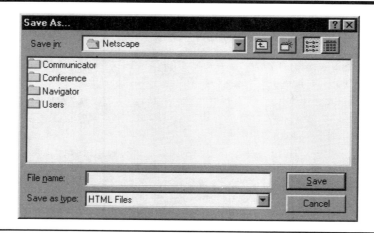

Figure 3.6:   The Save As dialog box

Some files on the Web don't end in .html or .htm—they end in trailing slashes, as in http://www.webpage.com/ (rather than http://www.webpage.com/home.htm), or they end in some sort of goop given them by a CGI or other interactive script. Generally, Navigator rolls with the punches and gives the file an attractive name ending in .html, but you may want to double-check your filenames before you save them anyway.

 If you want to save just the page's text, and not the HTML format, you can select Plain Text as the file type. This might be useful if you want to save, say, one of Shakespeare's plays or a lengthy magazine article—in those cases the links may be less important to you than the text alone.

3. Pull down the Save In list by clicking on its down arrow. From the list, select the drive to which you want to save the file. Below the Save In drop-down list, the contents of the drive you selected will appear as a list of folders and icons.

4. In that list, double-click on the directory into which you want to save the file.

 If you want to place the file in a subdirectory (within a directory), first double-click on the directory that contains that subdirectory so you can see it. For sub-subdirectories, repeat this process as needed until you find the target subdirectory.

5. Click on the Save As dialog box's Save button.

Perhaps this is obvious, but you won't see the document you've saved on-screen when you save it. You'll know it's been saved when you check the Directory list and see the filename there.

Saving Images

You might want to save one special image to your hard drive instead of a whole Web page. What for? Well, you can use that image as desktop wallpaper for your computer, send it as a map to a friend who's coming to town, or print it to hang over your desk at work. If the image is clip art (or otherwise in the public domain), you can also use it on your own home page. (See Chapter 9 for more on creating Web documents.)

Saving an image to your hard drive is easy. Just do this:

1. Using your right mouse button, click on the image of interest. A pop-up menu will appear asking you what you want to do.

 Your other choices from this menu include viewing the image on a separate page, or if the image is a link, creating a Bookmark or Internet Shortcut to the page it's pointing to. See "Pop-Up Menus and You," later in this chapter, for more on how to use your handy right-mouse-button tool.

2. From the pop-up menu, select Save Image As. The Save As dialog box will appear.

3. Now follow steps 2 through 5 in the section titled "Saving Web Pages," earlier in this chapter. Navigator will automatically detect and choose the correct file format (usually either GIF or JPEG) for the image.

4. To verify that the save was successful, you can use Windows Explorer to look in the directory to which you just saved the file. You should see the file listed.

Saving Stuff That's Not in View

Let's say the page you are viewing at the moment includes a link to something (maybe to a sound or to an image) that you want to save to disk to check out later. You can save the stuff at the other end of the link without first having to travel that link. Just follow these steps:

1. Pointing to the link that goes to the stuff you want to save, click the right mouse button. A pop-up menu will appear.

2. From the menu, select Save Link As. The Save As dialog box will appear.

3. Now follow steps 2 through 5 in the section titled "Saving Web Pages," earlier in this chapter.

To verify that the save was successful, you can use Windows Explorer to look in the directory to which you just saved the file. You should see the file listed.

 When you save an HTML document to your hard drive, what you get is the HTML code and the text—not the images. When you load the page later into Navigator, the images won't be there. This is because HTML documents tell Navigator where to find images, but they don't actually contain any pictures. An image in a Web page is really a link to a picture located on the Internet—but Navigator loads the pictures onto the page instead of just linking to them.

◆ Viewing Documents You've Saved

You can view a document you've saved to your local hard drive by selecting File ➤ Open Page from Navigator's menu bar.

 You don't have to be running your Internet connection to use Navigator to look at files on your computer.

The Open Page dialog box will appear; to open a file on your local drive, click on Choose File, and the standard Open dialog box will appear. Again this is a standard Windows dialog box. Select and open the HTML file of interest by double-clicking on it. Once you're back at the Open Page dialog box, click on the Open button to display the file in the Navigator window.

By the way, saving a file and then viewing it this way is a lot faster than accessing and viewing it when it's somewhere else in the world; the drawback is that if the owner of the document has made changes to it, you won't know about them. A really cool aspect of this, though, is that when you view a document that's been saved to your local machine, the links have been saved with it, and you can simply click on those links and start up your Web travels again—assuming you're dialed in for the clicking part.

Pop-up Menus and You

Netscape Navigator offers a lot of handy shortcuts that are no further away than your right mouse button. The available shortcuts change depending on where you point your cursor when you click. Try these:

◆ Point at some white space or nonlinked text, click the right mouse button, and a pop-up menu will appear offering options for going back or forward and for adding a bookmark or Internet shortcut for the page you're currently viewing, among other things.

◆ Point your mouse at a link, click with your right mouse button, and a pop-up menu will appear offering options to copy the link's URL to the Clipboard, to add a bookmark or an Internet shortcut, to save the document behind the link to your hard drive, to open the link in Netscape Communicator's HTML Editor, or to open the link in a new window instead of the one the link is in.

◆ Point at an image, click with the right mouse button, and a pop-up menu will appear offering options for saving the image to your hard drive, copying the image's URL, or viewing the image in a separate window.

◆ Jumping Back and Forth While Viewing a Document

The Back and Forward buttons on the toolbar provide a convenient way to jump back and forth among the hot links you've followed.

This is because Navigator tracks the documents you visit in a History list. The Back and Forward buttons actually let you travel through the History list. If you have Navigator running, try clicking on the Back button to jump backward along the links you just followed, and then try clicking on Forward to jump forward.

In addition to going back and forward one page at a time, try clicking on the Back button and holding down the left mouse button for a second or two. A small pop-up menu will appear, listing the last five pages you've visited. You can do the same thing with the Forward button; the menu will list the next five pages in your History list. (You can find out more about using the History list in Chapter 4).

There is an end to this—if you jump back to the first document you viewed in a session, or forward to the last one, you reach the end of the History list. The Back or Forward button, depending on which end of the history you reach, will be grayed out. (You can, as always, create more history— click on another hypertext link to explore further.)

Nothing's Showing Up! What to Do?

Sometimes the N icon will be animated, its comets flying along, and either nothing shows up, or the text arrives sans any images. What's going on?

When a Web server is busy, overloaded, or just plain slow, you'll get the text and basic HTML from it first and the images last. Images are a lot bigger (file-size-wise) than text, so they take longer to load. You can try any of these ways to address this:

◆ **Stop:** Click on the Stop button. Often, the images that were trying to load are mostly there, and hitting Stop will say, "Hey images! Hurry up and load!" Many times, they will.

◆ **Reload:** If that doesn't work, click on the Reload button. In fact, if a Web page ever looks funny or incomplete in some way, try reloading it.

◆ **View Image:** If a single image hasn't shown up, but the rest of them have, click the right mouse button over the placeholder (that funny-looking picture that represents an image that should be there, but isn't). When the pop-up menu appears, select View Image. Navigator will then try to retrieve that single image and load it onto the page you're viewing.

◆ **Give up:** Sometimes Webmasters goof up, and sometimes, particularly if the Web server you're trying to access is halfway around the world, the connection is just too danged slow. Oh, well. If you really want to see that picture of Joe Namath as a baby, try your luck again some other time.

At the bottom of many documents, you'll find a hot link that says something like Go Back. If you click on this link, you won't necessarily go back to where you came from; instead, you'll visit the page that the Webmaster assumed you just came from (usually another page at the same site). If you want to go back to where you were before, click on the Back button on the Navigator toolbar.

◆ Getting Around in Frames

Frames are popping up all over, ever since they became a design option in version 2 of Netscape Navigator. Frames appear on a Web page looking like a bunch of panes within the larger viewing area window; these "panes in the window" each hold some piece of the larger whole. Like everything else in life, frames are good when used purposefully, and not so good when they're used gratuitously. In Figure 3.7, you can see News of the Day, a Web page that uses frames to enhance the organization of the page by offering a navigation frame on the left and a larger frame in which various news sources appear on the right.

Having too many frames in a Web site is like putting too many bows on a dress—too much. Frames are best used when no other option will do. To be fair, many sites use frames quite well—one of the most practical applications of frames are pages that offer a table of contents in one of the frames. That index stays put (in some form or other) the whole time you're navigating the rest of the site.

Many frames-based sites are quite apparent—there are solid lines of one sort or another, and maybe even scroll bars, that make it clear that the Navigator viewing area is being divided into little window panes. Recently, however, it's become possible to create a site that uses *borderless frames*—the usual, obvious gray lines and bars that divide the window are invisible. You may not even notice that some sites use frames until you start navigating through them and notice that only part of the page is changing while you click.

Whatever their purpose in a Web site, each individual frame has its own URL. They also can have their own scroll bars, various background colors, images, text, Java or JavaScript elements—anything, in short, that a nonframe Web page can have.

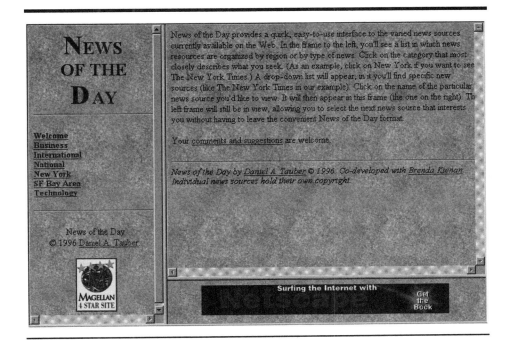

Figure 3.7: The News of the Day page uses frames to enhance navigation of its contents.

When you click on a link in one frame, often another frame on the page will change to reflect that click. That means you can easily get lost trying to find some information that was in a frame you saw five clicks ago.

What's Out There

Two of HotWired's sites use frames really well: Cocktail is located at http://www .hotwired.com/cocktail/, and Net Surf is at http://www.hotwired.com/ surf/. News of the Day is at http://www.dnai.com/~vox/news/. For a lesson in creating frames in your Web pages, check out Netscape's Frames Tutorial at http://home.netscape.com/assist/net_sites/frames.html.

Still, using frames, you can easily get back to where you once belonged. The easiest is to use the Back button—in Navigator 4, the Back button sends you back one frame at a time until you reach the beginning of a framed-up site. You can also use the right mouse button to navigate backward—click, and when the handy pop-up menu appears, select Back. You'll navigate backward one frame at a time.

 You can bookmark a document or a frame; this is much like putting a bookmark in a book in the sense that it helps you find where you've been without having to retrace your steps. See Chapter 4.

◆ Caching and Reloading

Navigator stores the pages you visit in what's called the *cache* (pronounced "cash"). A cache (noun) is just a chunk of storage—it can be RAM or the disk drive—on your computer that's been set aside as a temporary storage place. Your PC caches (verb) parts of the programs that you're running in its cache to make them run faster. Similarly, Navigator caches the Web pages you look at, so when you go back and forth between pages, you don't have to access the Internet anew every single time you look at the same page. Instead, your machine accesses the copy of the page that's in the cache.

 Navigator actually maintains two caches of documents—one in your computer's memory that goes away when you end your Netscape session, and another on disk that it uses between sessions. When you access a Web page, Navigator first checks to see if you have a current copy of the page either in the memory cache or in the disk cache. If a copy of the current page is located in either of these places, that copy is displayed instead of a fresh copy, relieving Navigator of the slow process of downloading the page from the Internet anew. (This is also true of images, sounds, video—in short, anything on the Net you access via Navigator.)

As you continue to visit new sites on the Web, old stuff in the cache is flushed out, and the newer stuff you visit in your travels is added. Sounds reasonable, eh?

There is a big drawback to this scheme: When you click around from page to page, you may not be seeing the most current version of a Web page; you may instead be seeing the cached version. This can be a drag if the page changes a lot and you want the fresher version. Certain pages, like weather maps, newsfeeds, and live camera links, for example, change minute by minute, and you want the freshest view of them.

 If you ever doubt that you're seeing the most current version of a page, just click on the Reload button and the page will appear from scratch, rather than from the cache.

Specifying How Often to Check the Cache

You can specify how you want Navigator to approach this matter by checking the cache Every Time, Once per Session, or Never settings in the Network Preferences dialog box.

The default is Once per Session. It's best not to mess with this unless you have some compelling reason and know what you're up to, because it'll slow down other operations. But here are the details:

1. From Navigator's menu bar, select Edit ➤ Preferences. The Preferences dialog box will appear.

2. In the Category area of the Preferences dialog box, double-click on the word *Advanced*. The Preferences dialog box will change to reflect this choice, and some other options should become visible, indented beneath the word *Advanced*.

3. Click on the word *Cache,* and the Preferences dialog box will be updated once again (see Figure 3.8.).

4. Locate the label marked "Document in cache is compared to document on network." Below the label you'll see three radio buttons, one for each option:

Option	What It Means	When It's Good
Once per Session	Navigator will go looking for each page once (the first time you access this particular Web page in this particular session).	During your usual activities; this is the default, and it's best to call this a keeper.

Option	What It Means	When It's Good
Every Time	Navigator will not look at your disk cache and will always retrieve from the Internet instead of locally.	When you're viewing lots of pages that change frequently, and especially if you're on a high-speed line.
Never	Navigator will always go for the copy in your disk cache unless it becomes unavailable (or unless you click on the Reload button).	When you're not dialed in to the Net, and you want to look at pages in the cache.

Click on the button of choice. Then click on OK to close the dialog box. Navigator will hereafter comply with your choice.

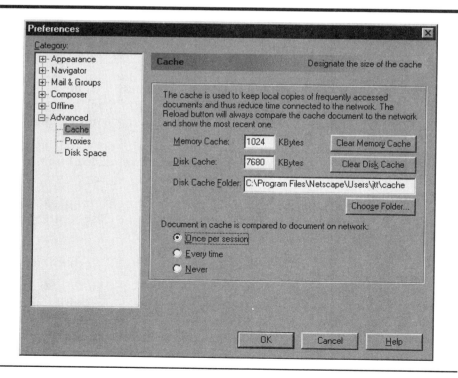

Figure 3.8:   The Preferences dialog box displaying information about the cache

Increasing the Size of Your Disk Cache

As a default, Communicator sets the disk cache at 7680K unless it picked up your Preferences from a previous version of Navigator. This is a good minimum, but you may want to increase it, depending on how much disk space you want to dedicate to Net surfing. The more disk space you allocate to Navigator's cache, the more stuff it will hold.

 It makes a lot less sense to increase the size of the memory cache than to increase the size of the disk cache. The other programs you're running, including Windows 95, need all the memory they can get. Don't shortchange Windows for the sake of Navigator or other applications that rely on Windows.

To increase your disk cache, follow this simple procedure:

1. Follow steps 1–3 in the "Specifying How Often to Check the Cache" section to display the Cache area of the Preferences dialog box, as seen in Figure 3.8.

2. In the Disk Cache text box, type the number of kilobytes (K) you want to reserve for Navigator's disk cache. The default is 7680K (or 7.7MB); 20000K (20MB) is a better choice if you have that much disk space to spare.

3. Click on OK. The dialog box will close, and you'll find yourself in the familiar Navigator window.

From this moment forward, you should find accessing the pages you visit most often a lot faster than it was before.

◆ Error Messages Demystified

The Internet works really well most of the time, but both computers and humans are fallible, and sometimes you'll click on a link or enter a URL and get an unhappy message from Netscape instead of the Web page you wanted. See Table 3.1 for a listing of error messages and what they mean.

A few general tips:

◆ Most errors aren't permanent. If you get an error, try a few minutes, hours, or even days later, and the page you want will usually come back.

◆ You're more likely to get Busy or Connection Refused messages during peak hours, like lunchtime and right after the workday ends. Try accessing busy pages during off-peak hours.

◆ Good Webmasters do routine maintenance on Web pages fairly often, and this can increase the chances of certain parts of a server being off-limits. If you try accessing the site a day or two later, you'll usually be able to access the page you want, or you'll be given a pointer that says the site has moved.

◆ If a page disappears inexplicably or permanently, check your favorite search engine to see if it can locate an alternate address for the page.

◆ There are probably lots of other error messages you could get, and a good rule of thumb is to try the page again later, especially if you know you've been there before, or to check the spelling and format of the URL.

 As always, when in doubt, click on Reload and see what happens.

Table 3.1:   Navigator Error Messages We Know and Love

Error Message	What It Means	What To Do
Too Many Users	This Web site may restrict the number of accesses allowed per day or per hour.	Try again later.
A Network Error Occurred. Unable to Connect to Server	Either the host is busy, the URL is spelled wrong, or something else is funny.	Make sure you actually put the forward slashes in after `http:`. If so, just try again later.
Broken Pipe	Something went wrong en route and some data got lost.	Click on the Reload button, or try again later.
Connection Refused	The line is "busy," and this is the Web's busy signal.	Try again later.
Document Contains No Data	The Web page you tried to link to is there, but there's nothing on it.	Forget about it. Whoever pointed you there made a mistake.

Table 3.1:   Navigator Error Messages We Know and Love (continued)

Error Message	What It Means	What To Do
The Location (URL) Is Not Recognized.	You asked for a type of URL that doesn't exist.	Look for typos in the URL you entered, especially the http:// part.
The Server Does Not Have a DNS entry.	This server doesn't exist right now, at least not the way you spelled it.	Check your spelling of the domain name. If it's spelled correctly, try again later.
Netscape Is Out of Memory	Boy, you've been looking at a lot of huge Web pages today!	Quit Navigator, and then launch it again.
403 Forbidden	The part of the Web server you're trying to access is off limits right now.	Try it again tomorrow or next week. If that doesn't work, forget about it. Someone doesn't want any visitors.
Please Enter Username and Password	If you don't have an account on this server, it won't let you in.	Try visiting the site's home page to see if they require you to complete a registration process.
404 Not Found	The page you tried to link to may be gone forever, or there may be a typo in the URL you entered.	Try it again tomorrow or next week. If that doesn't work, the thing's probably gone.
409 Fire, Flood, and Pestilence	This is a joke.	Ignore this geek humor and go on with your life.

◆ Printing a Document or a Single Frame

To print a Web document, you must first have it open. Then, follow the usual printing procedure:

1. From the Navigator menu bar, select File ➤ Print. The Print dialog box will appear.

2. Fiddle with the dialog box to specify what you want exactly, and click on OK.

The whole document will pop out of your printer. Note, however, that the document probably will not be a single page long (unless it's a very brief home page, for example). This, of course, is because Web pages do not have the same physical boundaries as paper pages. So a single Web page may be several paper pages long.

It may be helpful to print out a page at less than 100 percent scale. If your printer dialog box has options for printing a page at 75 percent of its normal size (or some other likely ratio), give that a try.

Also, perhaps obviously, if you want to print other pages linked within a single site, you'll have to go to those pages and print them separately. (Of course, you can't click on a printed-out Web page. But you already knew that, right?)

With frames, the matter gets a little stickier. You can't print out an entire Web page full of frames, because each pane in the window is technically a distinct document. To select the frame you want to print, again with the page (with frames) open,

1. Click on some blank space within the frame, and that frame will appear highlighted.

 To see how this works, try clicking from frame to frame in a site that uses frames. Try News of the Day, which is located at http://www.dnai.com/~vox/news. You can see how each individual frame gets highlighted as you go from frame to frame. Keep in mind, though, that the highlight may not be apparent in sites that use borderless frames.

2. From Navigator's menu bar, select File ➤ Print Frame. The Print dialog box will appear.

3. Fiddle with the dialog box to specify what you want, and click on OK.

 To make sure you're printing the frame you want, you can select File ➤ Print Preview from Navigator's menu bar before you print. A window will appear showing you what you're printing, how many pages long it is, and other nifty things about the page. To exit Print Preview and return to the Navigator window, click on Close from Print Preview's toolbar. To go ahead and print, click on the Print Frame button.

The frame you selected will pop out of your printer. Now, the thing to remember is that it's one frame that you've printed, and a whole Web page can be made up of several frames. If you want to print an entire Web page with all its frames, you'll unfortunately have to print each frame individually.

◆ Quitting Netscape Navigator

You can quit Navigator any ol' time—even when the N icon is animated. To leave Navigator, simply do the following:

1. If the N icon is animated, click on the Stop button on the toolbar. This will cancel whatever Navigator is trying to do at the moment. (If the N icon is not animated, skip this step.)

2. To actually quit the program, click on the Control button in the upper-left corner of the screen, or select File ➤ Exit from the menu bar. The Windows Desktop will reappear.

3. Remember, even if you aren't running Navigator, you are still connected to your Internet service provider, and you must break this connection, using whatever techniques are appropriate. (Check with your Internet service provider to find out about that.)

If you have more than one Navigator window open, or another Communicator component, such as Messenger, running, you can exit all Netscape windows at once by selecting File ➤ Exit from any Communicator menu bar. A dialog box will appear asking if you wish to close all windows and exit Netscape Communicator. Click on Yes to close all the windows. Click on No to continue Communicator.

Keeping Track

Now, with your basic skills in place for navigating the Web via Netscape Navigator, let's take a look at how you can more closely track where you've been by using Internet shortcuts and bookmarks, and how you can manage your bookmark list as it grows and grows.

What's Out There

Want to be hip to what's happening on the Net? The latest Net Happenings are the topic at http://www.gi.net/NET/. And you can get advance information about new versions of Netscape and other Web browsers via the Browser Watch site at http://browserwatch.iworld.com/.

Been There, Going Back

In your Web travels, you're bound to come across some sites you think are worth visiting again. It's highly unlikely you'll be able to remember where this stuff is or follow a trail of bread crumbs back to it—you need to mark your favorite places on the Web, so you can go back easily. You can mark these spots easily with bookmarks or Netscape Navigator's Personal toolbar. Alternatively, you can use the History window, the Go menu, or even an Internet shortcut to track the sites you've seen.

◆ You Can Get There from Here in a Snap: Bookmarks

A big part of managing your Navigator tour of the Web is tracking what you found and liked. One way you can revisit what's worthy is to save files to disk, a process we described in the preceding chapter. But you don't always want the stuff on your disk—it takes up valuable space. When you stumble across something on the Web that you want easy access to in the future, you should mark it with a bookmark. In the menu bar (and on the Location toolbar), you'll find a drop-down menu devoted entirely to bookmarks. Let's take a look at it.

When you install Communicator for the first time (or create a new user profile), your Bookmark list will include some preselected bookmarks and folders from those helpful folks at Netscape. You can rearrange or delete these bookmarks, if you so desire. Read on to find out how to do whatever you like to your Bookmark list.

What's Out There

To find sites worth bookmarking, try the Cool Site of the Day at `http://cool .infi.net/`, or NetGuide Live at `http://www.netguide.com/`.

Bookmarking Documents

When you're viewing a page or a document that you like so much you want to view it again later, bookmark it. There are four very easy ways to add a site to your Bookmark list:

◆ From Navigator's Location toolbar, click on the blue QuickFile folder icon and select Bookmarks ➤ Add Bookmarks. Poof! The site is bookmarked.

◆ Press Ctrl+D. Poof!

◆ Press the right mouse button, and a pop-up menu will appear. Select Add Bookmark. Poof (again)!

◆ Using the Bookmarks QuickFile menu, you can drag a bookmark directly into a folder (see "Using the Bookmarks QuickFile Menu" later in this chapter). Super-poof!

When you're using the right-mouse-button trick, you have two options. If your mouse is pointing at a link, you can bookmark that link whether you've visited it or not. If your mouse is pointing at white space, you can bookmark the page you're looking at right now.

The name for whatever page you're so taken with will appear immediately on your Bookmark list, which you can access by clicking on the blue

QuickFile icon in Navigator's Location toolbar. A drop-down menu will appear, with all your bookmarks listed. Any bookmarks or folders you add later will also appear there, directly below the Edit Bookmarks option.

Keep in mind that you're not saving the page itself when you create a bookmark—you're saving the page's URL. This means that when you revisit the page you found so interesting, it may have changed. This can be both an advantage, in that you may find even more interesting stuff there next time, and a disadvantage, in that whatever you liked so much the first time might be gone on your next visit.

Using The Bookmarks QuickFile Menu

Navigator's Location toolbar (see Figure 4.1) also holds the Bookmarks QuickFile menu. The big blue icon there is the button for that menu; the icon depicts a little bookmark in a folder. You may have noticed that when you move the mouse pointer over the other icon on this toolbar, the page icon, the mouse pointer turns into a hand, and the bookmark part of the page icon does a little dance. When the little hand appears, you can click on the page icon and drag it into the QuickFile menu. Not only can you drag it there; you can drag it to any place in the QuickFile menu, including folders (and folders within folders). We'll tell you how to make those folders in "Managing Your Bookmarks," later in this chapter. For now, you can follow this simple process to drag and drop bookmarks directly to the QuickFile menu:

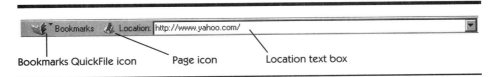

Figure 4.1: Navigator's Location toolbar allows you to see where you're going and mark where you've been.

1. With Navigator up and running and the page you want to bookmark in the Navigator viewing window, move the mouse pointer over the page icon until the mouse pointer turns into a little hand.

2. Click on the page icon, and drag it to the blue folder icon. That folder icon accesses the Bookmarks QuickFile menu. The mouse pointer turns into a little chain link (a link, get it?). You can position

this link anywhere in the Bookmarks QuickFile menu, including within a folder (or within a folder within a folder). See Figure 4.2 to see what we mean.

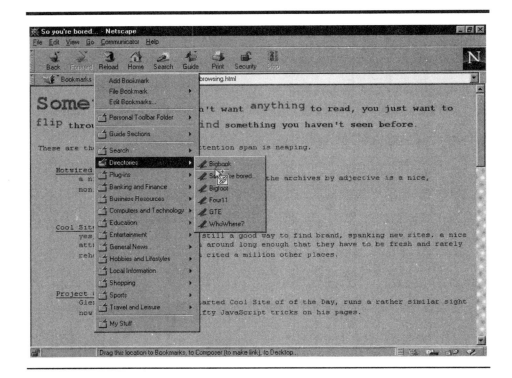

Figure 4.2:   Here we are, dropping a new bookmark into the Bookmarks Quick-File menu.

3. When the bookmark is where you want to leave it, let go of the mouse button, and the bookmark will stay where you put it. That's all there is to it. You'll be surfing as usual in Navigator, and the next time you access the Bookmarks menu, you'll have your new bookmark.

Quickly Jumping to Documents on the Bookmark List

Any time you are using Navigator, regardless of where you are or what you're viewing, you can jump to any page you've bookmarked. To do this, with your connection going and Navigator running, simply click on the Bookmarks QuickFile icon, and in your Bookmark list, highlight the name of the page that interests you and click on it. The N icon will become animated, and presumably the page will appear.

What's Out There

Bookmark this: The Discovery Channel Online (http://www.discovery.com/).
And: Yahoo! Internet Life (http://www.zdnet.com/yil/).

Managing Your Bookmarks

After a while, when you've bookmarked a lot of pages, you may find the list growing to unwieldy proportions. You can drag a bookmark to wherever you want using the Bookmarks QuickFile menu, but if you use Ctrl+D or the right mouse button to add bookmarks, they'll show up in the order you added them—or you might not remember to organize as you drag and drop. Either way, unless you're very tidy, your bookmarks might seem to be in no particular order.

Fortunately, Navigator allows you to impose some order on all this seeming chaos. You can toss out the old and unused stuff if you want, but you can also shift things around so that they make more sense to you. You can put related pages next to one another on the Bookmark list; and you can even group related pages under folders, which then appear as submenus of the Bookmarks QuickFile menu.

Rearranging Bookmarks

You can easily rearrange items in your Bookmark list. Communicator comes loaded with bunches of folders and bookmarks, and you can rearrange them as you see fit. Here's how to arrange items on the Bookmark list:

1. From Navigator's menu bar, select Communicator ➤ Bookmarks ➤ Edit Bookmarks. The Bookmarks window will appear, as shown in Figure 4.3 (where Communicator's preselected bookmarks are displayed).

Bookmarks have their own separate window in Navigator. From Navigator's menu bar, select Communicator ➤ Bookmarks ➤ Edit Bookmarks, and a separate window will appear that lets you do whatever you want with your bookmarks. You can also press Ctrl+B to the same end. To visit a bookmark from this window, just double-click on its icon.

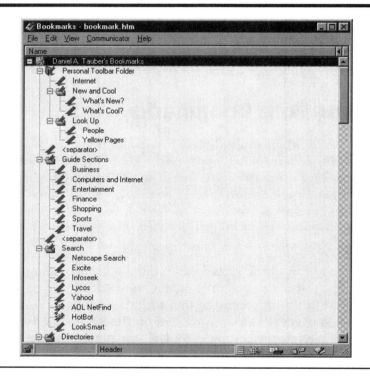

Figure 4.3: The Bookmarks window, where you can tinker with your Bookmark list

2. Highlight the bookmark you want to move by clicking on it, (by holding down the mouse button as you move the mouse) and then drag it up or down to its final resting place. Once you have moved the mouse pointer to the bookmark's final location, release the mouse button. You'll now see the bookmark in the new location.

That's all there is to it.

You can cut a bookmark by highlighting it with a mouse click and pressing Ctrl+X. Then you can paste it into a new location by positioning your mouse where you want the bookmark and pressing Ctrl+V.

Creating Folders

When you've created a long, long list of bookmarks, rearranging them may seem tedious. In the end, it's also a poor solution to your organizational woes—you'll still find yourself searching line by line through the list. Worse yet, you'll end up with a Bookmark list too tall for Navigator to display all at once. A better way to deal with the problem is to group bookmarks in folders, which will appear on the Bookmark list as submenus. (Bookmarks grouped under a folder will appear as options on these submenus.)

Here's how to create folders:

1. If it's not already open on your screen, open the Bookmarks window by selecting Communicator ➤ Bookmarks. Click on Edit Bookmarks.

 Navigator conveniently provides useful information about any high-lighted bookmark in the Bookmark Properties dialog box. To view the Bookmark Properties dialog box for the highlighted bookmark, select Edit ➤ Properties from the Bookmarks menu bar. You'll find the name of the highlighted page, its URL, and the dates when you created the bookmark and when you last visited the page. There's even a text box into which you can type your own description of the bookmarked page.

2. From the Bookmarks window's menu bar, select File ➤ New Folder. The Bookmark Properties dialog box will appear (Figure 4.4).

3. In the dialog box's Name text box, give the new folder a descriptive name—one that will help you find this stuff when it appears on the Bookmark list. Once you have entered a name, click on OK. The dialog box will close, and the Bookmarks window will reappear with your new folder listed.

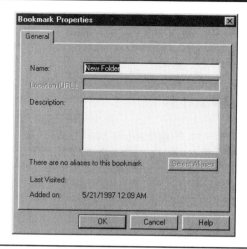

Figure 4.4:   You can edit a particular bookmark or folder using the Bookmark Properties dialog box.

4. Highlight and drag the folder to a position above the bookmarks you want to appear in the folder.

5. Now that you've created and named a new folder, you'll have to group bookmarks under it. Highlight and drag a bookmark to the folder. As you move the bookmark over the folder, a highlight will appear over the folder. When this highlight appears, release the mouse button. The bookmark will appear as an item in the folder— the bookmark's title will be indented under the folder's title.

6. Repeat step 5 for each bookmark you want to place in a folder. When you've finished, close the Bookmarks window by selecting File ➤ Close from the menu bar.

Now, if you pull down the Bookmarks QuickFile menu, the folder you created will appear as a submenu (marked on its right side by an arrow), but the bookmarks you placed in it won't be listed there. Not to worry— move the cursor to the new folder, and the bookmarks grouped in it will appear.

After all that filing of bookmarks, did you forget where you put that valuable hot link to the Donnie and Marie Fan Club? Not to worry. From the Bookmarks menu bar, select Edit ➤ Find in Bookmarks, and up will pop a Find Bookmark dialog box. Type in a word or two and click on OK, and the search function will highlight the first bookmark it finds that matches your search words. This feature will search titles, URLs, and even text you've typed in the Description field of the Properties dialog box. To keep searching for the same words, select Edit ➤ Find Again from the Bookmarks menu bar.

Choices, Choices: Displaying the Bookmark List

Suppose you're doing research on Mad Cow Disease or the geological origins of the Grand Canyon. While you're doing research, you may want to place all your bookmarks directly into a specific folder instead of sorting them later on. Or say you have a lot of bookmarks already, and you're surfing for information on your favorite bands—you might want to make it so your Music folder appears temporarily in place of Bookmarks on the menu bar. Here's how you can customize the delivery and appearance of the Bookmarks feature on the menu bar:

New Bookmarks Folder   Once you've created a folder, you can tell Navigator to put any new bookmarks directly into it. By default, you see, Navigator will put a new bookmark at the top level of the Bookmark list, which means directly on the main Bookmark list and not in any folder you've created. To change this and to put any new bookmarks automatically and directly into a folder, first open the Bookmarks window. Then, highlight the folder you want to use, and from the menu bar, select View ➤ Set as New Bookmarks Folder. It's that simple.

When you're displaying the Bookmarks window, the new bookmarks folder will have a little icon on it that looks like a piece of newsprint (code for new, hmm?).

Bookmark Menu   Navigator also allows you to "shrink" the Bookmark list so that when you pull down the Bookmarks QuickFile menu, only the bookmarks contained in one folder are displayed. This may be useful if you've got a lot of folders but are only going to be using one group of bookmarks in a given Web session. To do this, open the Bookmarks window (you can press Ctrl+B to do this) and highlight the folder you want to become the Bookmarks QuickFile menu. Now, from the menu bar, select View ➤ Set as Bookmark Menu. To change the list back and display all bookmarks (and folders) again, highlight the topmost folder in the Bookmarks window (usually the one bearing your name), and from the menu bar, select View ➤ Set as Bookmark Menu.

Whichever folder you choose to be the Bookmark Menu, you'll see that the little bookmark icon displayed on each bookmarks folder has changed from dark green to the light green that signifies the menu folder. And the next time you look at the Bookmarks QuickFile menu, you'll see only what's in that folder.

Renaming Items in Your Bookmark List

When you bookmark a Web page, the title of that page appears in your Bookmark list, the Bookmarks QuickFile menu, and the Bookmarks window. (They're all the same list, of course.) This is usually just fine, but sometimes you'll want to rename the item—to clarify what the page is about, for example, or perhaps because the page's creator gave it no title in the first place. You can easily change the name of any item that appears on your Bookmark list (including folders). Just do this:

1. From the Navigator menu bar, select Communicator ➤ Bookmarks ➤ Edit Bookmarks to open the Bookmarks window.

2. In the Bookmarks window, highlight the bookmark or folder you want to rename.

3. From the Bookmarks menu bar, select Edit ➤ Bookmark Properties. The Bookmark Properties window will appear.

4. In the Name text box, you'll see the name of the bookmark or folder you highlighted. Type the new name you want to assign to this item in the text box.

5. Click the OK button. The Bookmark Properties window will close (and your change will take effect).

6. If you want to rename another item, repeat steps 2–5.

7. When you've finished renaming bookmarks and folders, select File ➤ Close from the Bookmarks window's menu bar to return to the Navigator window.

The Ol' Bookmark-List-Becomes-a-Web-Page Trick

Here's a nifty trick. You can make your Bookmark list into a Web page that links you to all your favorite places. This is possible because Navigator stores your bookmarks in an HTML file that can be viewed and navigated like any other Web page. With Navigator running, follow these steps:

1. Press Ctrl+B. The Bookmarks window will appear.
2. From the Bookmarks menu bar, select File ➤ Save As. The Save As dialog box will appear.
3. In the dialog box, type a filename—something like faves.htm or whatever you like that will remind you that this is your own personal Bookmark List page. Click on the Save button. The Bookmarks window will reappear. From here, you can close the Bookmarks window, or you can click on the Navigator window to leave the Bookmarks window open in the background.

Now you can open up faves.htm (or whatever you called it) just as you would any other HTML file you've saved to your local machine (by selecting File ➤ Open Page from the menu bar, for example). The first cool thing is that you'll find you have created a Web page version of your Bookmark list, which you can use as your own home page or pass on to friends and colleagues for their use. The second cool thing you'll find is that all the headings and organization you've done in your Bookmark list will be included in the page (Figure 4.5). The third cool thing is that any descriptions you've provided for individual items (in the Bookmarks window's Description box) will appear as text describing those links. Yes, we said links. Because, of course, all the items you've bookmarked appear in this page as clickable links to those resources you found so appealing or useful that you just had to bookmark them.

Be careful, though: this page is not the same exact file as your regular bookmarks file—when you add new bookmarks during your regular Navigator use, they won't automatically get added to faves.htm. You can throw out the old faves.htm and replace it with a new one monthly, weekly, or however often you'd like—this is also a pretty smart way to make a backup of your bookmarks.

To rename the Web page you created from your Bookmark list (as described in "The Ol' Bookmark-List-Becomes-a-Web-Page Trick"), just rename the topmost folder of your Bookmark list—usually you'll find your actual name there; you can rename the folder anything you like, then open the list as a Web page and it'll have the new name you gave it.

Removing Items from Your Bookmark List

Out with the old and in with the new! You can remove any bookmark or folder from your Bookmark list, making room for fresher material.

To delete items from your Bookmark list, follow these steps:

1. From the Navigator menu bar, select Communicator ➤ Bookmarks ➤ Edit Bookmarks to open the Bookmarks window.

2. In the window, highlight the bookmark or folder you want to remove.

3. Press Delete.

or

From the Bookmarks window's menu bar, select Edit ➤ Delete.

 If you delete a folder from your Bookmark list, any bookmarks under that folder will also vanish.

4. When you've finished removing bookmarks and folders, select File ➤ Close from the Bookmarks window's menu bar to return to the Navigator window.

The items you deleted will no longer appear in the Bookmark list (that is, on the Bookmarks QuickFile menu).

Updating Bookmarks

Navigator includes a great feature that allows you to see which of your book-marked Web pages have changed since the last time you visited them. To get the latest, highlight the page(s) of interest in the Bookmarks window (or high-light nothing if you want to check all the bookmarked pages), and from the menu bar, select View ➤ Update Bookmarks. The What's New dialog box will appear. Click on All Bookmarks to check all the sites you've collected, or Selected Bookmarks to limit your search to those bookmarks you've highlighted. Then click on Start Checking.

Navigator will venture forth to check the Web pages and report which of them have been modified since your last visit. The title of any page that has changed will appear as usual in the Bookmarks window, but its icon will have little blue "Hey! Lookee!" lines beaming from it. Pages that Navigator can't verify will bear little question marks—for example, some pages that use interactive scripts may be impossible to verify and will appear with question marks. (You'll have to check into them manually, by clicking on their icons to visit them separately.)

Bookmarking a Single Frame

You may have noticed that no matter where you go in a site that uses frames, the URL that appears in the Location text box changes not a bit—until you move on to a different Web site, that is. This is because, while each frame technically has a different URL, the entire page has just one URL—the one that appears in the Location text box.

Suppose you like one part of this framed Web page, and you want to bookmark the contents of just that specific frame. There are two ways to do this:

◆ Right-click in the frame containing the material of interest, and from the Navigator menu bar that appears, select Add Bookmark. Then you can open and check the Bookmarks window to make sure that you bookmarked the contents of the frame you wanted instead of the whole page.

◆ Go back to where you saw the link to what you like. Point and click the right mouse button on this link, and a pop-up menu will appear. Select Add Bookmark from the menu. The bookmark will then appear on your Bookmark list.

When you visit your new bookmark, you should find that it takes you to a frames-free page that contains just the stuff you bookmarked—that's because you bookmarked only part of the site.

Importing Bookmarks You Already Have

If you've been using an older version of Navigator or a copy of Navigator on another machine, or if you've been surfing in another browser, you may wonder how you can get your bookmarks from those browsers into this copy of Navigator. Importing bookmarks, as this process is called, is very simple.

 If you want to get a bookmark file that's on another machine to where your current copy of Navigator is, see "The Ol' Bookmark-List-Becomes-a-Web-Page Trick," earlier in this chapter. Instead of saving the file elsewhere on your hard drive, save it on your A drive or other floppy drive, or e-mail it to yourself.

Okay, before we start, you need to know where that other bookmark file is located and what it's called. Once you're all set, it's an easy process:

1. You don't need to be dialed in to the Internet to import bookmarks, but you do need to have Navigator open. From the Navigator menu bar, select Communicator ➤ Bookmarks ➤ Edit Bookmarks. The Bookmarks window will appear.

2. From the Bookmarks window menu bar, select File ➤ Import. The Import Bookmarks File dialog box will appear, as seen in Figure 4.5.

3. Locate the bookmarks file you wish to import by browsing through your computer directories, just as you would to open any other file. When you've located the file you want, highlight it with a click and then click on the Open button. The Import Bookmarks File dialog box will close, and you'll be returned to the Bookmarks window.

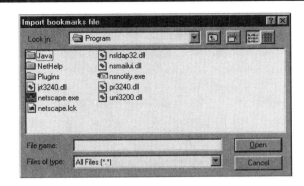

Figure 4.5: The Import Bookmarks File dialog box looks just like any old Open File dialog box.

Navigator will have imported all the bookmarks in the file you just opened into the contents of a single bookmarks folder. You can rename this folder and move all the bookmarks to wherever you like. When you're done moving around the bookmarks you imported, you can close the Bookmarks window and go back to surfing.

◆ Make Your Own Buttons with the Personal Toolbar

You may find that there are a few sites that you visit quite often—so often that you wish you could get to them even faster than you can with bookmarks. Now you can, with Netscape Navigator's Personal toolbar feature:

This Personal toolbar allows you to create new buttons, as we've done above by adding Hotwired, CNET, and HoTMaiL. You can get to these sites with one single click of the mouse. Navigator comes loaded with two buttons you can use right now: What's New and What's Cool. These buttons take you to some Web pages made by Netscape that describe, well, what's new on the Web and what sites Netscape calls cool. To get to these pages, just click on their buttons. Now let's look at how to add (and remove) buttons to this toolbar.

Before you can use the Personal toolbar, it has to be visible. If you don't see the Personal toolbar, it is either turned off or closed. To turn the Personal toolbar on when it is turned off, from Navigator's menu bar, select View ➤ Show Personal Toolbar. If the menu lists Hide Personal Toolbar instead, the toolbar is already turned on, but it's closed. To open the toolbar, click on the third blue toolbar arrow, and it should be displayed. When the toolbar is open, you should see buttons that say "What's New" and "What's Cool."

What's Out There

To get to What's New and What's Cool by their URLs, go to `http://home.netscape.com/home/whats-new.html` and `http://home.netscape.com/home/whats-cool.html`, respectively. To try out HoTMaiL, the free e-mail service, visit `http://www.hotmail.com/`.

Creating New Buttons by Dragging and Dropping

Once you've decided which sites you want to add to your Personal tool-bar, getting them there is a piece of cake. There are two easy ways to add buttons to the Personal toolbar. We told you earlier in "Using the Bookmarks Quick-File Menu" how to drag a bookmark to the QuickFile menu by dragging the page icon into the QuickFile menu and dropping it where you want it to go. Adding buttons is similar; just follow this simple process:

1. With your Internet connection active and Navigator open, go to the page you'd like to make into a button. You can do this by typing the URL into the Location text box or accessing a bookmark you already have.

2. When the page appears, click on the page icon and drag it to the Personal toolbar. When you let go, the name of the page will appear as a new button with a little Web page icon next to it. The next time you click on that button, you'll go right to the page you just made into a button.

Adding a Button with the Bookmarks Toolbar Folder

If you want to place a new button between a couple of other buttons, you can add the button to the Personal toolbar folder. We do this by following the same procedure we described in "Using the Bookmarks QuickFile Menu."

1. With Navigator up and running and the page you'd like to make into a button in view, click on the page icon and drag it to the Bookmarks QuickFile icon until the Bookmarks QuickFile menu appears.

2. When the Bookmarks QuickFile menu appears, drag the page to the Personal Toolbar folder. Position the bookmark where you want it and let go. The Bookmarks QuickFile menu will disappear, and in a few seconds, your new button will appear on the Personal toolbar.

Pretty neat!

Editing and Deleting Buttons from the Personal Toolbar

So what happens when you want to rename or delete a button from the Personal toolbar? Maybe you changed your mind about wanting that button, or maybe a new Web site about polka dancing has become your favorite site and the John Travolta home page has fallen by the wayside. You can edit the Personal toolbar in the same way you edit any other part of the Bookmark list: move stuff around in it, rename it, delete it, and add to it from other parts of the Bookmark list. Doing any of these things is easy, but first we need to open the Bookmarks window to edit the Personal Toolbar folder.

1. From the Navigator menu bar, select Communicator ➤ Bookmarks ➤ Edit Bookmarks. The Bookmarks window will appear.

2. Open the Personal Toolbar folder by double-clicking its icon. When it opens, you'll see all the buttons in the Personal toolbar represented as bookmarks indented beneath the Personal Toolbar folder.

Now we're ready to delete, edit, and add buttons.

Editing Button Names

You may want to edit the name of a button, especially since only a part of the page name will appear on the button itself. (For example, instead of "Welcome to CNET," we want our button just to read "CNET.") Changing the name of a button is a simple process:

1. With the Bookmarks window open and the Personal Toolbar folder open, highlight the name of the button (bookmark) you wish to modify by clicking on its name.

2. From the Bookmarks window's menu bar, select Edit ➤ Properties. The Bookmark Properties dialog box will appear.

3. In the Name text field, type the new name for your bookmark. When you're finished, click on the OK button. The Bookmark Properties dialog box will close and return you to the Bookmarks window, where you can see that your bookmark has been renamed.

4. Close the Bookmarks window to return to Navigator. When you look at the Personal toolbar, you will see that the button you just edited has been renamed.

 You can also edit the URL and description if you'd like, just the same as for any other bookmark.

Moving Bookmarks in and out of the Toolbar Folder

You may decide to remove a button from the Personal toolbar, but you want to keep it as a bookmark. Or you may decide that you want a bookmark you already use to turn into a button. Either way, moving bookmarks in and out of the Personal Toolbar folder is easy:

1. From the Location toolbar, click on the blue Bookmarks QuickFile icon. When the QuickFile menu appears, select Edit Bookmarks. The Bookmarks window will appear.

2. If it's not already open, open the Personal Toolbar folder by double-clicking on its icon. Click on the name of the bookmark you wish to move and then drag it into another folder of your choice. Or click on the name of a bookmark that's in another folder and drag it to the Personal Toolbar folder.

You can repeat this process as often as you like to add and remove bookmarks to and from the Personal Toolbar folder—that's to say, the Personal toolbar.

You can also rearrange the order in which the buttons appear on the Personal toolbar by moving them about in the same way. In this case, however, you leave them in the Personal Toolbar folder and simply rearrange their order by clicking and dragging them.

Deleting Buttons from the Personal Toolbar Folder

If you decide you no longer want a Personal toolbar button, and you don't want it sticking around as a regular bookmark, it's easy to get rid of it entirely:

1. With the Bookmarks window open and the Personal Toolbar folder open, highlight the name of the button (bookmark) you wish to delete by clicking on its name.

2. Press the Delete button. Your button is gone.

You can delete any location buttons, including the What's New and What's Cool buttons, if you like. If you end up deleting these built-in buttons, you can still get to them by opening Navigator, clicking on the Guide button in the Navigation toolbar, and selecting What's New or What's Cool from the menu that appears. If you want to add the What's New and What's Cool buttons to the Personal toolbar again, you can do so by completing the process for adding buttons described earlier.

Get Your Own Bookmark List with the Profiles Wizard

If you're sharing a machine with other folks in your home or office, you can take advantage of the Netscape Profiles feature for each user who has access to the machine. This feature allows users to keep their own sets of bookmarks, as well as separate e-mail boxes.

When you started Communicator for the first time, the first thing that launched was the Profiles Wizard. To create a new user profile, exit Communicator and, from the Windows 95 Start Menu, select Programs ➤ Netscape Communicator ➤ Setup New User Profile and follow the instructions (see Chapter 5 for more on the Profiles Wizard).

In this way, you can assign yourself a new username. The Users folder contains a folder for each person who creates a Profile with the Profile Wizard, and each person's folder contains their personal bookmarks and mail files. For more on Netscape Messenger and using e-mail with Netscape Communicator, see Chapter 5.

◆ The History Window As Bookmark List

You might think of the History window as a pseudo-Bookmark list. The History window, which appears in the Navigator menu bar under the Window option, is a log of every move you make in your Navigator session. The first time you launch Navigator, the History window starts empty; then it fills up with a list of your moves as you go along. To see the History window, select Communicator ➤ History from the menu bar (a highlight appears over the name of the current page, as seen in Figure 4.6). You can then double-click on any page listed there and jump to that item, or choose File ➤ Open Page. Thus, you can use the History window as a kind of short-term Bookmark list.

Here's a nifty History trick: The column headings that describe the information the History window contains are actually buttons. These buttons include Title, Location, First Visited, Last Visited, Expiration, and Visit Count. Click on any of them, and the History window's contents will be sorted by the category you clicked on.

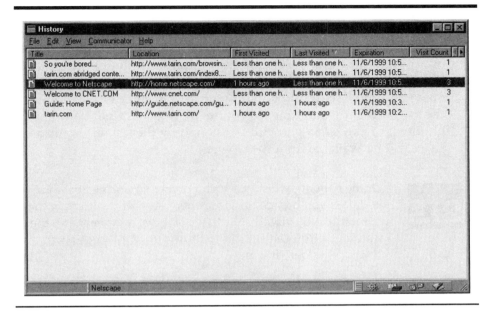

Figure 4.6:   The History window shows you where you've just been.

Note that short-term means *really* short term. The contents of the History window turn themselves over every few days; nine days is the default. You can change the amount of time that Web site addresses stay in your History list by selecting Edit ➤ Preferences from any Communicator window. The Preferences dialog box will appear. In the Category column, click on Navigator, and the Preferences dialog box will change to reflect your choice. In the text box under History, you'll see a number (probably nine, the default). You can choose any number from one on up. This number also determines how long your visited links stay marked as such.

 To add items from the History window to your Bookmark list, highlight the item of interest in the History window, and from the History window's menu bar, select File ➤ Add to Bookmarks. The next time you check into your Bookmark list, you'll find a new bookmark there.

◆ Go Gets You There, Too

The Go feature on the menu bar is one of the most useful—and most overlooked—features of Netscape Navigator. After you've gone a lot of places during a Navigator session, select the Go menu from Navigator's menu bar. You'll see a list of places you've been since you started surfing the Web this particular time. Of course, there is a limit. If you've visited hundreds of pages in a particular session, only the last dozen or so of those pages will be available from the Go menu.

 Oddly enough, when you visit a page that you've already visited, and then you branch off somewhere else, all the items in the Go menu that you visited after that point will disappear and the list will start anew. You can still get to those "missing" pages with the History window, though.

To take advantage of the Go feature, from the Navigator menu bar, just select Go. From the menu that appears, you can go Back, Forward, or Home, or (here's the true value) you can select any of the pages listed—the pages you've visited most recently. Between this and the History window, you're pretty much covered.

◆ Using Internet Shortcuts to Web Documents

As an alternative to bookmarking Web pages or saving them to your local machine, you can create Internet shortcuts. These shortcuts are a Windows feature; they look just like files on your local machine—appearing as icons on your Desktop, files in folders, or the like, but instead of being a document (like a word-processed document, for example) they point to documents on the Web. Internet shortcuts offer you the advantage of having direct access to Web documents regardless of whatever else you happen to be doing on your com-puter. You can embed an Internet shortcut in any application that takes advantage of current OLE technology (that means most Windows 95 applica-tions) or on your Desktop; it'll be there for your convenience when you want it.

The difference (to the user) between an Internet shortcut and a bookmark is that the shortcut can appear on your Desktop or in another Windows application document, whereas a bookmark appears only on the Bookmark list in Navigator. Assuming your Internet connection is going, when you click on an Internet shortcut, the shortcut will launch Navigator and load the page of interest in one fell swoop.

The big advantage to having and using an Internet shortcut as opposed to saving the actual Web document on your machine is that the shortcut takes you to the Web document of interest as it exists "live" on the Net. When you save and view a document, on the other hand, you'll be viewing the document as it existed when you saved it—you may not be seeing the most current version, and you won't have the images unless you saved each one.

 Shortcuts conserve disk space—a shortcut takes up only a few bytes of disk space, regardless of the size of the original document, while saving a whole document may take up tens of thousands of bytes.

The drawback to shortcuts (it isn't much of a drawback) is that you must be connected to the Internet to view documents with them. (They're shortcuts to documents as they exist on the Web, not the documents themselves, remember.) This means that the best use of shortcuts is for getting to Web documents you need to see "live." If you want to save a document you don't expect to last long on the Web, or if you don't want to pay for connect time to view a document, you may want to save the document instead of using a shortcut to get to it.

Creating an Internet Shortcut

You can create an Internet shortcut to the document you are currently viewing in Navigator by following a few simple steps.

Creating an Internet Shortcut on Your Desktop

Creating an Internet shortcut on your Desktop is an end in and of itself and is the means to creating one in a Windows application. Here's how to do it.

1. With Navigator running and the Web page of interest in view, point your mouse any place on the Web document that is not a graphic or a link. (White space is a good choice.)

2. Click the right mouse button. A pop-up menu will appear.

3. From the menu, select Create Shortcut. The Create Internet Shortcut dialog box will appear (Figure 4.7).

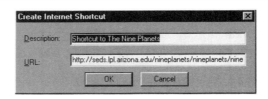

Figure 4.7: The Create Internet Shortcut dialog box allows you to confirm the URL and title of the Internet shortcut you are creating.

 You can check the location of the Internet Shortcut you just created by double-clicking on it and seeing where Navigator goes.

4. You may want to type a shorter title than the one the page already has. For example, if the page is called something like "Welcome to John Jacob Jingleheimer Schmidt's Home Page on the Web," you may want to shorten it to just "John Schmidt's Home Page."

5. Click on the OK button.

You won't see any immediate difference on screen, but the next time you minimize or close Navigator, you'll see your new Internet shortcut appearing as an icon on your Desktop. It'll look like a little globe with a document attached, with the name of the Web document under the icon.

 Just as you can bookmark a link you haven't yet visited by right-clicking on the link, you can create an Internet shortcut the same way by right-clicking a link and, from the pop-up menu, selecting Create Shortcut. You can also create an Internet shortcut by clicking on a hypertext word or phrase (or any other link) in a Web document and then dragging that link from Navigator's window to the Desktop. When you release the mouse button after this clicking and dragging procedure, an Internet shortcut will appear where you placed it.

Placing a Shortcut in a Windows Program

Having created an Internet shortcut for the Web document of interest on the Desktop as described in the previous section, you can now pick up the shortcut from there and place it in a Windows application. It's easy.

1. Follow the procedure for placing an Internet shortcut on your Desktop, as described in "Creating an Internet Shortcut on Your Desktop."

2. Open the Windows application and the document (or spreadsheet, or whatever) where you want the shortcut to conveniently be at your disposal.

 In Microsoft Office programs such as Microsoft Word, the Navigator Internet shortcut will be treated as an *object* and can be manipulated in the same way as imported graphics and charts. In these and other programs, the name may be truncated if it's too long, so renaming the shortcut at the Desktop level may be the best way to avoid odd treatment of the name of the Web page.

3. Resize or otherwise position the application's window (containing the document into which you want to place the shortcut) so that you can see both it and the shortcut that appears on your Desktop.

4. Click on the Internet shortcut of interest and drag it to the document in the application's window, dropping it where you want it to appear. The name of the shortcut will probably end in .url.

5. Save the document as you would if you'd made any other changes to it, using the familiar File ➤ Save or Save As feature you know so well.

In the future, when you open that Windows application document (whether it's a word-processed document, a spreadsheet document, or whatever), and you then double-click on the Internet shortcut you've created, Navigator will start and load the URL, taking you automatically to the Web page of interest.

 If you have an e-mail program that uses OLE technology—the Windows 95 Inbox, or Netscape Messenger, for example—you can drop one of these shortcuts into an e-mail message, and when the recipient of your message clicks on the shortcut (assuming he or she has Navigator), Navigator will do its thing, and the Web page of interest will appear.

Activating an Internet Shortcut

Any time you see an Internet shortcut, you can double-click on it, and Navigator will launch itself and display the page to which the shortcut points. Remember, your Internet connection must be active for this procedure to work.

What's Out There

Visit http://www.msn.com/ to find out how to customize the Microsoft Network's Start page.

Away We Go!

You now have basic Navigator browser skills, and you know a thing or two (or three or four) about keeping track of sites you've seen, too. Now let's take a look at how you can communicate with others (via discussion groups and e-mail) the Collabra way.

Discussion Groups and E-Mail the Collabra Way

Before the advent of the wonderful World Wide Web and its attending browsers, there was an Internet, and it was already a happening place. Much of what went on via the Internet then took the form of talk—typed talk, to be sure, but talk nonetheless—in newsgroup articles and e-mail. For a long time, many people thought newsgroups *were* the Internet—the whole Internet. Even today, e-mail is one of the most popular features of the Net, and newsgroups are a highly viable forum for discussion on all sorts of topics.

In earlier versions, Netscape provided a competent newsgroup reader and the ability to send and receive e-mail. Among the stellar accomplishments of Netscape Communicator is the combination of Messenger, a full-featured e-mail program that lets you send and receive e-mail, and Collabra, an improved newsgroup reader, in the Netscape Message Center. Let's take a look at this centralized Communicator feature.

◆ Accessing the Message Center

Netscape's Message Center is the area where you can work with both e-mail and discussion groups. There are three easy ways you can access this mini-application:

◆ From the Desktop or Start menu, click on the Netscape Messenger shortcut

◆ From the Netscape Communicator component bar, click on either the Mailbox or Discussions icon

◆ From the Netscape Navigator menu bar, select Communicator ➤ Discussions or Communicator ➤ Message Center

Doing any of these simple point-and-click operations will bring up the Netscape Message Center window (see Figure 5.1).

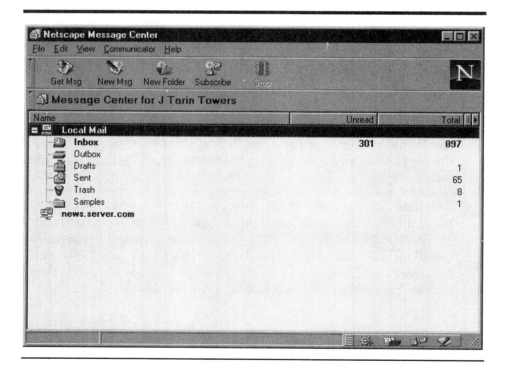

Figure 5.1: Netscape's Message Center window provides one easy interface to both e-mail and discussion groups.

In this window, as you'll see, there are several icons. The Mail icon, which looks like a little mailing envelope, has several folders indented beneath it, including Inbox, Outbox, Drafts, Sent, and Trash. Netscape Messenger lets you send and receive e-mail messages, and it includes a lot of enhancements to make your e-mail experience more fun and manageable. The Discussions icon, which looks like two word-balloons connected by a network, is where you access Collabra and Usenet discussion groups. This is where all the news reading takes place (hence the name *newsreader*, for software that reads news).

 Before you can start using e-mail or participating in discussion groups with Communicator, you must set up the software to work with the way you access the Internet, whether that's via an Internet service provider, an online service such as AOL or CompuServe, or whatever. This is a special aspect of installing Netscape that involves specifying your real name, your e-mail address, and your server information. See Chapter 11 for details.

◆ Participating in Discussion Groups with Collabra

Unlike many other Web browsers, Netscape Communicator provides you with fully workable access to discussion groups via Collabra. One aspect of online discussion groups is Usenet, a collection of topics called *newsgroups*. Usenet newsgroups are not "sites," exactly. A Web server is responsible for storing and delivering a relatively small amount of data in the form of Web pages and related files, and it's generally connected to a domain name server that stores addressing information about the rest of the sites on the Internet. In contrast, a news server stores information about every newsgroup in the Usenet system; this data includes the name of each Usenet newsgroup, as well as all the current messages posted in each of thousands of newsgroups.

Using Netscape Collabra, you can read and post articles (messages) to those Usenet newsgroups that interest you, and you can also access private discussion groups created using the Collabra server. You can even create and manage your own discussion groups.

The Collabra Server

Netscape's Collabra server (it doesn't come with Communicator) allows people who use intranets to create and manage their own private discussion groups. Collabra improves on the existing Usenet model by allowing discussion group owners to control who has access to their discussions server.

For information about getting and using the Collabra server, visit Netscape's page on the subject: `http://home.netscape.com/inf/comprod/server_central/ product/news/index.html`.

To find out about creating your own public Usenet Newsgroup, read "How to Write a Good NewsGroup Message," at `http://www.cs.ubc.ca/spider/ edmonds/usenet/good-newgroup.html`.

Starting Netscape Collabra

Netscape Collabra is quite easy to start up. Simply follow this single step:

1. From Netscape's menu bar, select Communicator ➤ Netscape Collabra. The Message Center window will appear.

That's all there is to launching the Message Center, which Collabra is a part of. Now you're almost ready to start participating in discussion groups.

You can also use the Netscape component bar to launch the Message Center and read news. Just click on the Discussions icon and voilà! The Message Center appears!

Reading Usenet News for the First Time

The first time you read Usenet News, you need to retrieve what's called the *news.rc file*. Don't panic—this is something that Collabra does for you. The news.rc file is a mini-directory of Usenet. It contains a listing of all the discussion groups available to you, and it's updated every time you go to read news. In order for it to be updated, however, it has to be created in the first place.

 If you're using Collabra to access private discussion groups created using the Collabra Server, the process is the same as the one described for participating in Usenet News.

What's Out There

To find out all about Usenet newsgroups get the FAQs. What Is Usenet is at `ftp://rtfm.mit.edu/pub/usenet/news.answers/usenet/what-is/part1`, MIT's RTFM (Read the Freakin' Manual) archive is at `ftp://rtfm.mit.edu/pub/usenet/news.answers`, and the Ohio State archive is at `http://www.cis.ohio-state.edu/hypertext/faq/usenet/`. Remember that accessing FTP URLs is the same as visiting a Web page—just type the address in the location bar.

This process can take several minutes, because Usenet is pretty big, but it's easy to start. Just follow this simple process:

1. With your Internet connection up and running and the Netscape Message Center open, click on the news icon. This icon generally bears the name of your own news server, which you specified when you installed Communicator.

2. From the Message Center menu bar, select File ➤ Subscribe to Discussion Groups.

   or

   Click on the Message Center's Subscribe icon. In either case, the Subscribe to Discussion Groups dialog box will appear, as seen in Figure 5.2.

3. At this point, Netscape will start putting together your news.rc file. It will contact the news server you specified when you installed Netscape, and you'll see the Subscribe to Discussion Groups dialog box begin to fill up with names of newsgroups. Hang on for a minute (or

several), until the status line at the bottom of the dialog box reads Document: Done.

4. Now your news.rc file is finished loading, and you're ready to choose a newsgroup or two to read. Don't close this dialog box yet—we've got some explaining to do first.

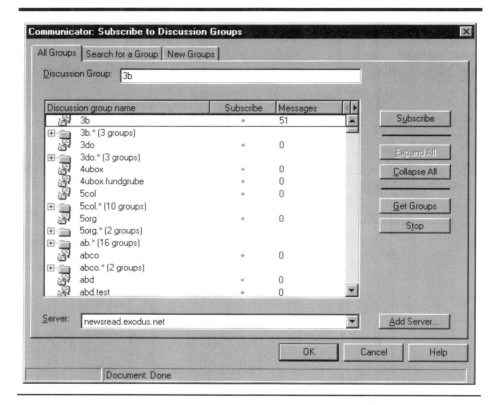

Figure 5.2: The Subscribe to Discussion Groups dialog box lets you browse through the list of all Usenet newsgroups and choose groups you'd like to read.

At first glance, you may find the Subscribe to Discussion Groups dialog box a bit confusing. Don't worry—we're going to tell you how to use it. Near the bottom of the dialog box, you'll see the selected Usenet news server (you told Netscape the name of your Usenet news server when you got Netscape working with your Internet connection). Clicking on one of the other news servers in the pull-down list (most likely you'll only have one server) will display the list of newsgroups located on that server—the news.rc file that we just loaded. This list is displayed in the main viewing area.

You may have cause to access more than one news server, particularly if you have more than one Internet service provider, or if you need to access private discussion groups for work or research purposes. Chapter 11 describes how to specify your news server. To add a news server, use the Message Center menu bar, and select File ➤ New Discussion Group Server. The New Discussion Groups Server dialog box will appear; in the text box, type the name of the news server you wish to add (the address will probably use the format news.server.com). Click on OK, and another Discussions icon will be added to the Message Center, which you can then use as described in this chapter.

The newsgroup list is divided into three columns: Discussion Group Name, Subscribe, and Messages. The first column, as you might think, lists the name of the discussion group or set of discussion groups. The Subscribe column will contain a bullet until you subscribe to a discussion group, at which point you'll see a checkmark displayed in that column, next to the name of the subscribed discussion group. The Postings column displays the number of articles, or posted messages, currently active in each discussion group. This column may not be filled for each and every discussion group; some discussion group headings signify a group of groups, rather than a single discussion group.

Let's subscribe to a newsgroup. This is the easiest way to learn about Usenet news.

What's Out There

For a complete list of ways you can search Usenet, visit Netscape's Usenet Destinations page at http://home.netscape.com/escapes/search/usenet.html.

Subscribing to a Discussion Group

Collabra lets you subscribe to groups you read or participate in regularly. When you subscribe to a discussion group, its name will appear in the Netscape Message Center window, indented beneath your news server folder. After you've subscribed to a discussion group, you can read the discussion group any time you're online just by double-clicking on its name. Let's subscribe to `rec.travel.usa-canada`, so you can see how easy it is to join a discussion group.

> Subscribing to a discussion group involves no money changing hands and no particular commitment. It's just a way of informally "joining up" to listen in or actually participate in the discussion group.

To subscribe to a discussion group, follow these easy steps:

1. You should still have the Subscribe to Discussion Groups dialog box open. If it's not already open, open it from the Message Center menu bar by selecting File ➤ Subscribe to Discussion Groups. The Subscribe to Discussion Groups dialog box will appear, looking something like it does in Figure 5.2.

2. Locate the newsgroup to which you want to subscribe, either by scrolling through the list of newsgroups or by typing part of the name into the Discussion Group text area. To subscribe to `rec.travel` `.usa-canada`, type **rec.travel.u**, and the list will automatically jump to the name of the newsgroup. You'll see a gray bullet next to the name of the newsgroup, in the Subscribe column. Click on that bullet, and it will turn into a checkmark, indicating that you have subscribed to that newsgroup.

3. To close the Subscribe to Discussion Groups dialog box, click on the OK button. The dialog box will close and return you to the Message Center, where you'll see the `rec.travel.usa-canada` newsgroup indented beneath the name of your news server.

> If you don't see the names of the newsgroups to which you've subscribed displayed immediately in the Message Center window, you may have to click on the + (plus sign) to the left of the Discussions icon in order to see the names of your subscribed discussion groups; this works just like it does in Windows Explorer.

In the Message Center window, the discussion group to which you've subscribed will appear as a discussion icon that looks like two word balloons connected by a network. Next to this icon you'll see the name of the newsgroup, and the number of unread messages in the Unread column.

Until you start reading this discussion group, this number will be the same as the number in the Total column, which indicates the total number of messages available to that discussion group. In Figure 5.3, you can see that we've subscribed to two other newsgroups: `comp.os.ms-windows.win95 .misc`, which is a hotbed of talk about Microsoft Windows 95, and `alt .stupidity`, which collects the inane yammerings of people with too much time on their hands.

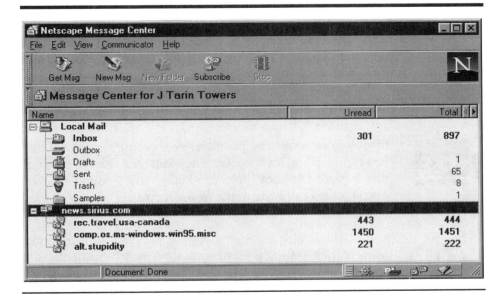

Figure 5.3: The newsgroups to which you subscribe will be listed in the Netscape Message Center window.

What's Out There

Some particularly good sites for finding discussion groups worth reading: DejaNews keeps a giant archive of past Usenet news articles that you can search at `http://www.dejanews.com/`. You'll find a no-nonsense, searchable, browsable listing of newsgroups at `http://sunsite.unc.edu/usenet-i/`. And Zippo Dot Com, at `http://www.zippo.com`, selects the best discussion groups for you, telling you, among other things, where there are messages about software you can get via FTP.

Getting into a Discussion Group without Subscribing

The URLs for discussion groups start with news: rather than with http:. Knowing this handy fact, you can access a Usenet newsgroup by selecting File ➤ Open Location from Navigator's menu bar and, in the window that appears, typing the discussion group's URL (which is just the name of the newsgroup preceded by news:) into the text box and clicking on Open. For example, to visit the sci.physics.relativity Usenet newsgroup, you'd type **news:sci.physics.relativity**. Collabra will open a Netscape Discussion window, from which you can read the articles posted. This is a quick way to get into a newsgroup, and Collabra generally assumes you want to subscribe to the newsgroup you specified, and does the job for you. You can also follow a link from a Web page that starts with news:.

Once you've accessed a particular newsgroup using this technique, you can read articles and, using the skills described in the sections that follow (check out "Posting a Reply" and "Posting a New Article"), you can write to the newsgroup.

Just as in Navigator, the right mouse button offers shortcut options for many of the tasks you want to accomplish in Collabra. Right-clicking on a newsgroup offers you options such as marking all messages as read or unsubscribing. Right-clicking on a single message brings up a plethora of options for that message, including opening, forwarding, filing, saving, or replying to it, as well as options for composing messages and managing threads.

Reading Articles in Subscribed Discussion Groups

To read articles once you've subscribed to a discussion group, double-click on that discussion group's name in the Netscape Message Center window. A new window will open, and the window's title will be the same as the name of the discussion group. All the "unread" articles in the discussion group will appear in a list in the discussion group window (see Figure 5.4). Boldface listings signify single messages, while plain headings indicate a thread that contains more than one message.

Unsubscribing from Newsgroups

You won't always want to remain a subscriber to a particular newsgroup. Your interests will change; the newsgroup may grow dull. You'll want to move along.

After awhile, you'll probably want to let them go. Unsubscribing is really easy. Click on the checkbox to the right of the newsgroup name to remove the checkmark. When you do this, the name of the newsgroup will disappear from the list of newsgroups to which you are subscribed. You can always resubscribe if you want to pick up that newsgroup again.

To read an article, simply click on it in the list. When you do this, Netscape transfers the contents of the article to your computer and displays it in a new newsgroup window as shown in Figure 5.5. To return to the list of articles, close the article's window, and you'll be returned to the newsgroup's primary window.

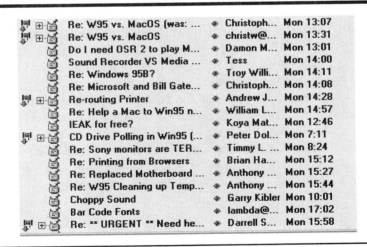

Figure 5.4: Some of the unread articles listed for a group called comp.os .ms-windows.win95.misc (a general discussion group about Microsoft Windows 95)

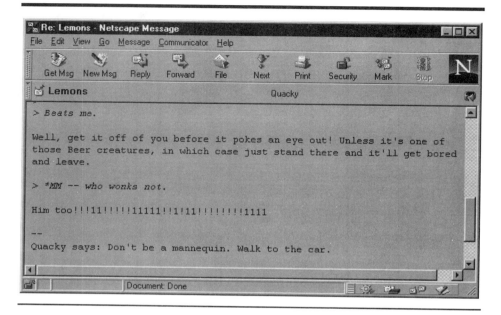

Figure 5.5: Reading an article from the `alt.stupidity` group

 You can view the list of articles and the articles themselves in the same window if you'd like. From the Message Center window, double-click on the name of a discussion group to open the Netscape Discussion window. Click on the blue arrow icon at the bottom of the Netscape Discussion window. This toggles the Hide Message status to Off, and displays a pane in the lower portion of the Newsgroup window in which you can read the articles while you're looking at the list of all articles for that discussion group. To hide the messages again and read them in separate windows, just repeat the process, this time toggling the Hide Message status to On by clicking on the blue arrow now marked Hide (message name).

Reading Along a Thread

Notice also in Figure 5.4 that articles are listed by authors' names and that some articles appear with plus signs next to them, in the style of Windows

Explorer. Some less-capable newsgroup readers display articles only in the order they were posted, but Netscape arranges articles by subject in the order they were posted.

 By ordering the messages in this way, Netscape allows you to read all the articles about a subject, one right after the other. Messages grouped by subject in this way are called *threads*, and reading messages this way is called *reading along a thread*. A thread is essentially a string of related articles—they're related in that they are usually responses that follow the original article.

After clicking on the plus sign to display all the messages in that thread, you'll see one message that's not indented, which often signifies the beginning of a discussion on a particular topic (or the oldest available message in the thread). A message that appears indented below another is a later message about the same subject; often it is a reply.

When you're done reading the first article, you can read the next article in the thread—this can be the next contribution to the discussion or a reply to the message you just finished—by clicking on the Next button. If you're in the middle of a thread, you can read the article posted prior to the one you're looking at by clicking on the Back button. This button and all the others you need are at the top of the Collabra window.

Which Buttons Do What

Let's quickly go over all the buttons Netscape Collabra provides for reading articles.

The Tool	Its Name	What It Does
Get Msg	Get Msg	Retrieves more messages from the news server
New Msg	New Msg	Posts a new message to the newsgroup you're reading
Reply	Reply	Sends a reply to the message you're currently reading, an e-mail reply to the person who posted the message, or both

The Tool	Its Name	What It Does
Forward	Forward	Sends a copy of the message you're currently reading to another person via e-mail
File	File	Saves a copy of the current article to your hard drive
Next	Next	Moves to the next article in the thread you are currently reading
Print	Print	Prints the current message
Security	Security	Displays security information about the news server, if any
Mark	Mark	Marks the current message as read, or to read later
Stop	Stop	Interrupts the transfer of an article to your computer

Watching and Ignoring Threads

If a newsgroup is really busy, or *high traffic,* in netspeak, you may want to choose which threads you follow and which threads aren't worth it. You can ask Netscape Collabra to watch or ignore a thread, so you can easily keep up with the news that's important to you.

Watching a thread is easy. Just follow these quick steps:

1. With the appropriate newsgroup window open, single-click on the name of the thread you want to follow. This highlights the thread.

2. From the window's menu bar, select Message ➤ Watch Thread, and a little sunglasses icon will appear beside the name of the thread.

3. Now that you've specified which threads to watch, you won't want to view the others right away. From the window's menu bar, select

View ➤ Messages ➤ Watched Threads with New (messages). The Discussion window will display only those threads that are being watched.

4. Collabra will save this View option until the next time you download new messages. To view all threads, select View ➤ Messages ➤ All. To toggle off the Watch Thread setting, simply reselect Watch thread (which you can also do by right-clicking on the name of the watched thread).

Ignoring a thread is simple, too. Click on the annoying thread that you want to ignore. From the Discussion window's menu bar, select Message ➤ Ignore ➤ Thread. That will mark the thread with a little "don't" icon (as it looks on No Parking signs). This will skip the thread and move your cursor and the highlight to the next message, and Collabra will continue to skip that thread as long as it's marked as ignored (for instance, when you're reading messages by using the Next button).

Ignoring a thread isn't permanent. You can always go back and read those messages if you so desire. Or you can choose to read only those threads you've ignored. To view only ignored threads, select View ➤ Messages ➤ Ignored from the Discussion Group menu bar.

Reading Usenet News Offline

You can select an entire thread and download it to read offline. To select a thread, click on any message in the thread and, from the Discussion window's menu bar, select Edit ➤ Select Thread. All messages in the thread will be highlighted. Once you've selected the thread, from the menu bar, select Message ➤ File Message, and from the menu that appears, choose a folder (such as your Inbox) into which to save these messages. Once you've filed the messages, you can go offline and read them at your leisure.

You can also highlight single messages or whole batches of messages, if you hold down the Ctrl key and click on messages or threads with the left mouse button. With these messages highlighted, just file them as described.

Posting a Reply

If you want to post a reply to an article you've read, follow these easy steps:

1. With an article open (presumably the one to which you want to reply), click on the Reply button. From the pop-up menu that appears, you have four choices:

   ◆ Reply to Sender

   ◆ Reply to Sender and All Recipients

   ◆ Reply to Group

   ◆ Reply to Sender and Group

   A Composition window will appear, as shown in Figure 5.6.

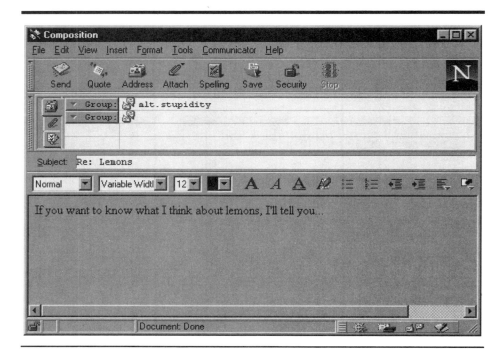

Figure 5.6:   This window is your door to writing newsgroup replies.

2. In the window's Subject box, the subject of your post (taken from the original article) will appear. In the To box (if you chose to respond to the person who posted the message), the name and e-mail address of the poster will appear. In the Group box(es), the newsgroups in which the original article appeared will be listed. You can add or remove recipients or discussion groups as you like by typing their names in the To or Group boxes.

3. The original message (the one to which you are posting a reply) will appear in the window; if you delete this original text, or if it doesn't appear, click on the Quote button at the top of the window to quote the original message. To make it easy for you to see what's what, each line in the original message will be prefixed with the | symbol (called a *pipe*). You can delete any part (or all) of the original message if you like.

The original message will be quoted automatically if you've checked the appropriate box. Use Collabra's menu bar, and select Edit ➤ Preferences. Click on the Mail and Groups category and then on the words *Mail Server* (indented below it). Place a checkmark in the box marked Automatically Quote Original Message When Replying, if that's what you'd like to have happen. You can remove the checkmark if you'd rather not automatically quote the original message.

4. Type your reply to the original message in the text box along the bottom of the window, and click on the Send button at the top of the window.

Your reply will be posted automatically to the groups in which the original article appeared. Your message will be conveyed via e-mail and then transferred to the person or discussion group you sent it to. If the latter is the case, it should become visible in the latest batch of messages for all to read within an hour.

You needn't feel compelled to quote the entire original article in your reply. In fact, you can assume that people have already read the message to which you're responding. It's considered good form to delete as much of the original message as necessary 'til you get down to the part that is immediately relevant to your response. Further, you can add or delete newsgroups listed in the Newsgroup text box as you wish. This is a simple matter of typing in the names of any newsgroups you want to add in an empty box (usually located at the end of the list of newsgroups) or of highlighting any you want to delete and then wielding your Delete key. For example, if you're responding to a message directed to both `rec.cooking.french` and `sci.physics.nuclear`, but your message only deals with crepes and not their radioactivity, you may want to reply only to `rec.cooking.french`.

Posting a New Article

You can post new articles to start new threads as well. Simply click on the New Msg button at the top of the newsgroup window. The procedure after this point is exactly the same as that for posting a reply, except that the subject of the article is not filled in and there is no text in the Message text box. Refer to the preceding section ("Posting a Reply") for more information.

Communicator's Profile Wizard

If more than one person uses the same computer in your home or office, you may want to give each user their own profile. This will let everyone who uses Communicator have their own individual bookmarks, history, cache, e-mail files, and discussion group folders, but the profiles are not password protected.

When you installed Communicator (see Chapter 11), you set up one profile. Setting up another with the Profile Wizard is just as easy:

1. If Communicator is open, you must exit the program.
2. From the Windows 95 Start Menu, select Programs ➤ Netscape Communicator ➤ Profile Manager. The Profile Manager dialog box will appear.

(continued on next page)

3. Click on New. The Profile Wizard will launch, and the New Profile dialog box will appear, offering an introduction to profiles. Click on Next, and the next panel of the dialog box will appear.

4. This is where you fill in your name and your e-mail address in the text boxes designated as such. When you're finished, click on Next to move on to the next panel of the dialog box.

5. The first text box in this panel of the Profile Wizard is for the name of the profile. The Wizard will suggest a name for the profile based on the information you entered in the last panel. You can change this name, if you like.

6. The next text box asks you to confirm the path name for the folder your personal Communicator files will be stored in. It's a good idea to use the path name Communicator suggests. Click on Next to go to the next panel.

7. The first two text boxes in this panel of the Profile Wizard ask you to confirm your name and e-mail address. The third is where you fill in the name of your outgoing mail server (your SMTP server, which you got from your Internet service provider). Type in the address of your mail server, and click on Next to go to the next panel.

8. The Username text box is where you fill in the dialup username you use to log into your server and check your e-mail. It's generally the first part of your e-mail address (the part before the @ sign). If it's different from what the Wizard suggests, correct this.

9. The next text box is for your incoming (POP) mail server, which you got from your Internet service provider. This machine may or may not have the same name as the outgoing server you specified in step 7. Type its name in the box. If your mail server is POP3, click on POP3; if it's of the IMAP type, click on IMAP. Click on Next to move on to the next panel of the Wizard.

10. This panel asks you to specify the name of your news server, which you got from your Internet service provider (you can call them and ask for any server names you're not sure about). That's all you need to do; click on Finish to close the Profile Wizard.

Closing the Profile Wizard also closes the Profile Manager and launches Netscape Communicator using the new user's profile. You can start using Communicator and any of its parts, or you can exit Communicator. The next time you start Communicator, the Select Profile dialog box will appear, from which you can choose to log in as any of the user profiles you've created.

(continued on next page)

You can repeat steps 1 and 2 above to launch the Profile Manager in order to delete or rename profiles. With the Profile Manager on screen, click on the name of the profile you wish to rename, and then click on Rename. The Renaming Profile dialog box will appear. Type in a new name, and click on OK, and the dialog box will close. You'll see the new profile name in the Profile Manager window.

Deleting a profile is similar. Click on the profile name you want to delete, and then click on Delete. A warning dialog box will appear; click on Yes to delete the profile. A warning dialog box will appear again, letting you know that while the profile has been removed from Communicator's list of available profiles, the files within it have not been deleted. If you want to delete them, you can use the Windows Explorer to go do that.

Editing the information you input during the creation of a profile is no more difficult than using Communicator's Preferences dialog box to make the changes. From just about any Communicator menu bar, select Edit ➤ Preferences, and find the information you want to change; preferences for Messenger and Collabra are in the section called Mail and Groups.

◆ Sending and Receiving E-Mail with the Message Center

Communicator offers a full-featured e-mail program, Netscape Messenger, that allows you to send and receive e-mail using the Netscape Message Center. This is relatively new to the world of Web browsers and is quite a nifty feature. Heretofore, most Web browsers allowed you to send e-mail but not to receive it. That was because receiving e-mail involved much more complicated issues of, for example, storing messages 'til you read them. Netscape licked this challenge in Navigator version 2, and now you have the improved e-mail capability in Netscape Communicator to prove it.

Before you can use Netscape Mail, you must set up Netscape to use your Internet service provider's POP3 mailbox and SMTP mail server. This is not difficult; turn to Chapter 11 for more information.

Starting Messenger

To start Messenger, take these simple steps:

1. With the Netscape Message Center window open, and the Local Mail icon highlighted, click on the Get Msg button. The Password Entry dialog box will appear (see Figure 5.7).

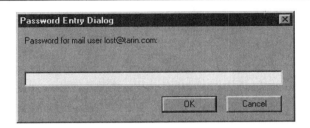

Figure 5.7: In the Password Entry dialog box, you must enter your e-mail password.

2. Type the password assigned to you by your Internet service provider, and click on OK. In a few seconds, the Getting New Mail dialog box will appear, informing you of the status of your mail retrieval.

3. When Netscape has retrieved all of your new mail, click on the Inbox icon to open the Inbox window, which is where your incoming mail will arrive. You can see it in Figure 5.8.

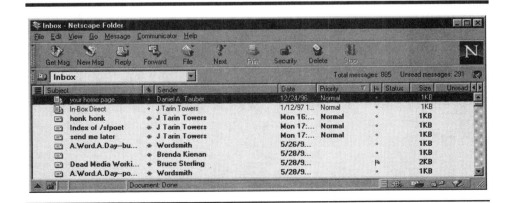

Figure 5.8: The Netscape Inbox window allows you to read and send e-mail to anyone on the Internet.

With the Netscape Inbox window open, you can receeive and send e-mail.

 Messenger will save your password during each Message Center session, and you must re-enter it each time you open a new Messenger session.

Reading Your Mail

The Netscape Inbox window is organized the same way the other mail folder windows are. The drop-down list below the toolbar lets you select which folder you want—it should include Inbox, Outbox, Drafts, Sent, and Trash. Messages within these folders are listed chronologically in the main window pane below the message header columns. We'll find out what these other folders are for in a minute; for now, let's look at the Inbox.

Opening E-Mail Messages

To read a message, you double-click on the name of the message, and the message will appear in the large window in the Inbox. You can read messages in the Inbox window or in a separate window for that purpose. Click on the blue arrow marked Hide to hide the message box, and then a new window will pop open when you click on the name of a message. To go back to reading messages within the Inbox window, click on the blue arrow again to reopen that panel of the Inbox window.

What's Out There

A delightful mailing list is A.Word.A.Day. Every day, an interesting, odd, or obscure word is sent to your e-mail box. To find out how to sign up, visit A.W.A.D.'s home on the Web at http://www.wordsmith.org/awad/.

Using the Mail Button Shortcuts

The buttons that appear on the toolbar at the top of the mail folder windows are shortcuts to many commonly used and popular features.

The Tool	Its Name	What It Does
Get Msg	Get Msg	Retrieves mail waiting on the mail server
New Msg	New Msg	Writes and sends a new e-mail message
Reply	Reply	Replies to the author of the current message
Forward	Forward	Forwards the current message to someone else
File	File	Stores the current message in a Messenger folder
Delete	Delete	Deletes the selected message
Next	Next	Moves to the next message
Print	Print	Prints the message that's currently on screen
Security	Security	Provides information about the security of an outgoing message
Stop	Stop	Stops transmission or whatever activity is occurring

NOTE When you click on the Delete button to get rid of a message, it doesn't actually vanish. Instead, it's moved to the Trash folder. To permanently dispose of messages in the Trash folder, select File ➤ Empty Trash Folder from Messenger's menu bar.

Sending a Message

Sending a message with Messenger is easy. You can do it while you're connected to the Net, or you can write up a bunch of messages when you're not connected and send them along later, which is a boon if you're not near a phone line or are interested in saving online time.

Writing and Sending a Message Online

So you're already connected and just want to dash off an e-mail or two? Just follow these steps:

1. On the Message Center (or Inbox) toolbar, click on the New Msg button. The Message Composition window will appear. In Figure 5.9 you can see one into which we've entered all the necessary info, but when this window appears it will be empty, waiting for you to fill it in.

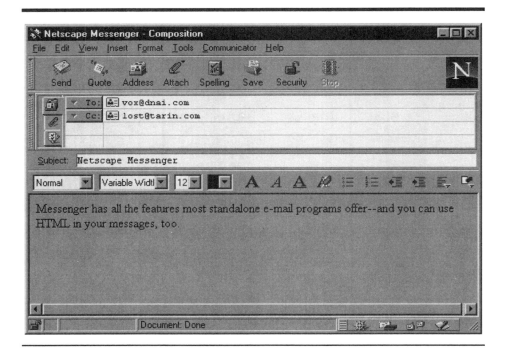

Figure 5.9: In the Message Composition window, you'll enter all the stuff that makes up your e-mail message.

2. In the To text box, type the e-mail address of the person to whom you want to send an e-mail message.

You can also use a nickname or get the e-mail address from your Address Book: from the Message Center menu bar, select Communicator ➤ Address Book. See "Creating Your Very Own Address Book" (later in this chapter) for more details about these handy features.

3. Now in the Subject field, type a subject for the message you are about to write.

4. Click in the big text box (called the *body* of the message) along the bottom of the window, and start typing your message.

5. When you are done typing your e-mail message and are ready to send it, click on the Send button along the top of the window. Your message will go off in a matter of seconds, and you will be returned to the Netscape Message Center (or Inbox) window.

Copies of all the messages that you send are stored in the Sent folder. If you want to see what you said, just open the Sent folder and open the message like you would any other. You can also move the messages in your Sent folder to other folders; see "Filing Messages," later in this chapter, for details on creating folders and filing messages.

What's Out There

Find your favorite star's e-mail address with the listings at http://oscar .teclink.net/~chip1120/email.html.

Writing a Message Offline and Sending It Later

Sometimes, especially if you're using a laptop that's nowhere near a phone line and you'd like to write e-mail, it's convenient to be able to compose your messages while you're offline (not connected to the Internet). Luckily, Netscape Messenger is flexible enough to let you do this by following these simple steps:

1. On the Netscape Messenger toolbar, click on the New Msg button. The Message Composition window will appear.

2. Compose your message as you normally would. When you're finished, don't hit the Send button. From the Message Composition window's menu bar, select File ➤ Send Later. Messenger will save this message in your Outbox.

3. When you exit the Message Center, Messenger will open a dialog box that reminds you that you have unsent messages and ask you if you'd like to send them now. If you want to send your batch of queued messages, click on Yes. If you aren't ready yet, click No to return to the main Message Center window.

4. To send this and other queued messages later on, connect to the Internet; then from the Netscape Message Center window, select File ➤ Send Unsent Messages.

At last, all your queued e-mail messages will be on their merry way.

All the messages that are queued and ready to be sent are stored in your Outbox. You can open your Outbox before you send these messages and edit them.

Using Drafts for Sending Delayed Messages

If you're working on a particularly long or important message, you may want to save it and send it after you've had a chance to revise it. You could queue it in the Outbox, as we've just described, but then you couldn't send any other messages until you were finished writing the important one—the one you really don't want to send right now. The Netscape Message Center has devised a way around this dilemma; it's called Drafts. You can save a message as a draft, and it won't be sent until you graduate it from lowly draft to outgoing message. Drafts are stored in the (guess!) Drafts folder. It's

easy to create and send drafts, and you can do this either online or offline.
Just follow this simple process to create a draft message:

1. Start typing your new message as you normally would. If you want to
   check this out, go to the Netscape Message Center and click on New
   Msg. Fill in whatever fields you'd like (you can fill in the rest later).

2. Click on Draft. This saves a copy of the message, as is, to the Drafts
   folder, but it doesn't close the Message Composition window.

3. Close the message without sending it. You are returned to the
   Message Center window.

 You can continue working on the open draft message instead of
closing it. If you complete and send the message, the draft will
disappear from the Drafts folder, while a copy of the message you
actually sent will appear in the Sent folder.

If you close the message you saved as a draft without sending it, it's easy to
open it later and continue working on it. Just follow this easy procedure to
send the revised draft:

1. In the Message Center window, open the Drafts folder by double-
   clicking on its icon. The Drafts folder will open, and you should see
   the name of the message you just drafted.

2. Double-click on the name of the message to open it. Finish whatever it is you have to say, and when you're done, click on Send. The
   message will be sent, and it will disappear from the Drafts folder and
   reappear in the Sent folder.

Pretty cool, eh?

 You can send a message using Navigator without even opening the
Message Center. One way to do this is to click on a link to an e-mail
address; a Message Composition window will appear with the
address you clicked on filled out in the To field. Another way is to
use Navigator's menu bar to select File ➤ New ➤ Message, which
will also open a Message Composition window.

Replying to a Message

Replying to a message is very much like writing a new message. Just follow these steps:

1. With the message to which you want to reply on screen, click on the Reply button. From the pop-up menu that appears, choose either Reply to Sender or Reply to Sender and All Recipients. (Reply will address your reply only to the person who sent the message; Reply All will address your message to everyone involved—including all the people who were "Cced.") Regardless of what you choose, the Message Composition window will appear.

2. In the Message Composition window, you'll see that the Mail To, Cc, and Subject fields are already filled in, based on information that came from the message to which you are replying. You can modify any of these fields if you like, or you can leave them as is.

3. In the text area near the bottom of the window (the message body), type your message. You can include the contents of the original message in your reply by clicking on the Quote button.

 If you want messages to be automatically included in your new message when you're replying or forwarding, you can set this as a default. From the Message Center menu bar, select Edit ➤ Preferences. When the Preferences dialog box appears, click on the Mail and Groups category and then the word "Messages". The dialog box will change to reflect your choice. Place a checkmark in the box marked "Automatically quote original message when replying" by clicking on the box. Click on OK to close the Preferences dialog box. The next time you reply to a message, the original message should be quoted automatically.

4. After you type your e-mail message, click on the Send button. In a matter of seconds, your message will be transferred from your computer to your Internet service provider's mail server—it's on its way!—and the original message will reappear on your screen.

5. Close this message by clicking on the × in the upper right-hand corner to return to the Message Center.

Now you know how to send a reply.

Forwarding a Message

Occasionally, a message will arrive in your Inbox that is important, profound, or funny enough that you'll want to send a copy to your boss, your old college roommate, or your mom. Forwarding a message is almost the same as replying to a message, except that you need to choose a new recipient. Just follow these steps:

1. With the message to which you want to reply on screen, click on the Forward button. The Message Composition window will appear.

2. In the Message Composition window, you'll see that the Subject field is already filled in, based on the subject header of the message that you're forwarding. You need to fill out the recipient; you can type the e-mail address of the person to whom you're sending the message, or you can type a nickname of your friend from your Address Book (see "Creating Your Very Own Address Book," later in this chapter).

3. If the main text area is empty, click on the Quote button to paste the original message into it. You can edit this message if you only need to forward a part of it to your friend.

4. After you edit the e-mail message you want to forward, click on the Send button. Your message will be on its way over the wires, lickety-split, and the original message will reappear on your screen.

5. Close this message by clicking on the × in the upper right-hand corner to return to the Message Center.

Now you know how to forward all those jokes, recipes, and top-secret corporate memos.

Enhancing E-Mail Messages with Attachments

Sending e-mail messages usually means that you're writing plain, vanilla text and sending it to someone. But what if you want to send something besides text? Suppose you want to send someone a word-processed document, a spreadsheet, a sound or video file, or an image? That's what e-mail *attachments* are for—with Netscape Messenger, you can *attach* a different kind of file to an e-mail message, and the person who receives the message will download the attachment (the other file) along with the e-mail message when they check their mail. And you can receive attachments with Messenger, too.

Attaching a File to an Outgoing Message

Suppose you want to send Aunt Susie a picture of your new house. Of course, the file, regardless of what type it is, has to reside on your computer before you can attach it to your outgoing message. Assuming that you have a GIF file on your hard drive ready to send, let's see how you can attach the file to an e-mail message. Attaching a file is a simple process:

1. From the Netscape Message Center window, click on New Msg. The Message Composition window will appear as a blank message ready to be filled in.

2. Click in the To text box and fill in the recipient's e-mail address, and then click in the Subject text box and fill in a subject, such as *Our New Home*. Click in the message body text box and type a message as you normally would. When you're all done writing your message, you're ready to attach the file.

3. Click on the paper clip tab (near the subject line fields). The address area will change to become the file attachment area.

4. Click the cursor anywhere within the text box shown on the paper clip (Attachments) tab. The Enter File to Attach dialog box will appear. This dialog box is quite similar to an Open dialog box. Browse through your files until you find the file you want to attach. When you're ready, click on Open, and the Enter File to Attach dialog box will close.

There are several ways you can access the Enter File to Attach dialog box; read on for more options.

5. The Attachments tab will now display the path and name of the file you just chose. If you'd like to attach more than one file, you can repeat the attachment process as often as you'd like.

6. When you're finished attaching files, and assuming you've already filled out the To, Subject, and Body fields of the message, the message is ready to be sent. Click on Send to send the message, Save to save the message as a draft, or select File ➤ Send Later to queue the message to send at a later time.

When your message has been sent, you'll be returned to the Message Center. Sending the message will probably take more time than the second or two you're accustomed to, because you have to send both the message and the file to your outgoing mail server, where they will be sent to Aunt Susie.

 Most e-mail programs automatically print a note at the top or bottom of the incoming e-mail message that tells the recipient there's a file attached, but it couldn't hurt to mention the name and nature of the attachment in your message.

There are a few ways to attach a file to a message, all of which produce the same result:

◆ Click on the paper clip tab, and then click in the text field. The Enter File to Attach dialog box will appear.

◆ On the Message Composition toolbar, click on the Attach button, and from the pop-up menu that appears, select File. The Enter File to Attach dialog box will appear.

◆ From the Message Composition menu bar, select File ➤ Attach ➤ File. The Enter File to Attach dialog box will appear.

The process is the same as described previously in this section once the Enter File to Attach dialog box pops up.

Attaching Links and HTML to an Outgoing Message

Using links in an e-mail message is easy as pie. If you embed a Web page URL in an outgoing message, and the person to whom you send the message has Netscape Messenger (or a few other mail programs, including Eudora and Microsoft Exchange), they can click on the link that appears in the message body to automatically launch their Web browser and locate the Web page. The same goes for e-mail addresses, FTP sites, and Telnet addresses.

Inserting a link into a message is easy. Just follow this single step:

1. Open the Message Composition window by clicking on New Msg from any Message Center window. From the Message Composition menu bar, select Insert ➤ Link. The Character Properties dialog box will appear, with the Link tab visible, as seen in Figure 5.10.

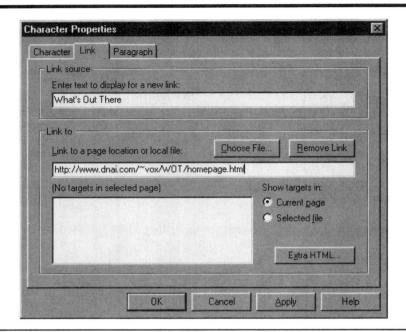

Figure 5.10: The Link Properties dialog box allows you to place links in your outgoing messages.

2. Click in the Link Source text box, and type the text you wish to display as an underlined link. This can be the URL itself, or another word or phrase.

3. Click in the Link To text box and type (or paste in) the URL of the Web page you want to link to.

4. Leave the rest of the fields alone. When you're finished, click on OK to close the Link Properties dialog box and return to the Message Composition window.

5. Click on Send, and the HTML Mail Question dialog box will appear; you have three choices:

◆ Send in Plain Text and HTML (best if you don't know whether your friend is using an HTML-capable mail reader)

◆ Send in Plain Text Only (best if your friend doesn't have an HTML-capable mail reader)

◆ Send in HTML Only (best if you're confident your friend is using Messenger to read their e-mail)

The outgoing message that you send will include a clickable link to a Web page or other Internet address.

 Unless you're really certain that your friend is using Messenger to read their mail, you'll probably want to send the URL as plain text. Otherwise, your messages will appear as a bunch of HTML code— which is quite unsightly in non-HTML mail readers.

 You're probably aware that Web addresses need to start with `http://` in order for them to be recognized from program to program as URLs. E-mail addresses, when used as links, must start with `mailto:`, as in `mailto:user@site.com`. Telnet addresses must start with `telnet://`, as in `telnet://site.edu`, and FTP addresses must start with `ftp://`, as in `ftp://ftp.archive.org`.

Mailing a Page While Using Navigator

If you see a Web page that can't be beat while you're using Netscape Navigator, there's an easy way to send it—not just a link to it, but the whole thing—to a friend. Remember that this process works best when you're sending the page to someone with an HTML capable e-mail reader. Just follow this quick process:

1. With the page you want to send in view in the Navigator window, use Navigator's menu bar and select File ➤ Send Page. The Message Composition window will appear, with the subject line filled in with the title of the page, the page's URL in the body field, and the page's address indicated in the attachments field.

2. Fill in the To field by clicking in the text box and typing the e-mail address of your intended recipient. Add any notes you want to the body text field by typing them in.

3. When you're finished, click on Send, and the message will be on its way.

The person who receives the message will get both the link and a copy of the Web page in their Inbox.

You can embed HTML (hypertext, images, and more) into your e-mail messages—effectively transforming your messages into documents. To see an example of such a message, click on the Samples folder and read the documents inside. See Chapter 9 to find out how to add HTML to your messages.

Receiving an Attachment

When someone sends you a message with a file attached, you need to save the attachment on your hard drive and then open it. This is simple to do with the Netscape Message Center—it even opens some attachments for you.

◆ If the attached file is an image such as a GIF or JPEG, Netscape will display the image in the body of the e-mail message.

◆ If the attached file is a sound file, video, or multimedia document that Netscape recognizes, the message will display a link to the file. Click on this link, and a Netscape window will launch and play the sound, video, or multimedia clip.

◆ If the attached file is a word-processed document, a spreadsheet, a program, etc., Netscape will display a link to the file. Click on this link to open the Save As dialog box and save the attachment to your Desktop or to another folder on your hard drive. You can then open or launch this document or program by opening the appropriate folder and double-clicking on the file's icon.

◆ If the attached file is an HTML document, Netscape Mail will display the HTML within the body of the e-mail message, just as though you were looking at a Web page in the Navigator window. You can click on links to follow them, and Communicator will open them in the Navigator window.

You may want to save an image or HTML file for later use rather than just looking at it in Netscape Mail. To do this, open the message with the image or HTML file in it. From the message's menu bar, select View ➤ Attachments ➤ As Links. Now you can click on these links and save the image or HTML file somewhere else on your hard drive.

 There are two styles of links on the Web: *relative* and *absolute*. Unfortunately, Messenger only seems to understand the absolute kind. If you're surfing an attached HTML file from within the Messenger environment, and you get a lot of "file not found" errors, try right-clicking on the link and, from the pop-up menu that appears, select Open in New Window. This act will launch a Navigator window, and because Navigator can read just about any kind of link there is, that should resolve the problem.

Creating Your Very Own Address Book

Netscape provides you with the convenience of keeping an address book in which you can organize and store the e-mail addresses of all the people with whom you correspond. Netscape Communicator's Address Book, seen in Figure 5.11, works and is useful both in Netscape Messenger and Netscape Collabra, as well as Netscape Conference—any time you need to enter an e-mail address, you can use your handy Address Book. But first you have to get the addresses in there.

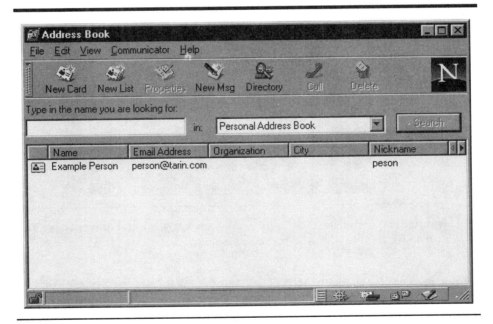

Figure 5.11: Communicator's Address Book simplifies sending e-mail.

One Way to Add People to Your Address Book

Adding new e-mail addresses to your Address book is as simple as most other Netscape tasks. Usually, you'll find you want to add the e-mail address of someone to whom you're replying. To do this, you'll of course start with either an e-mail message or a Usenet article from the person whose e-mail address you want to add to your book appearing on screen.

1. Open the e-mail message or Usenet article from the person you want to add to your Address Book. From the message's menu bar, select Message ➤ Add to Address Book ➤ Sender. The Card For "User" dialog box will appear, with the e-mail address and name of the person you just added filled in (see Figure 5.12).

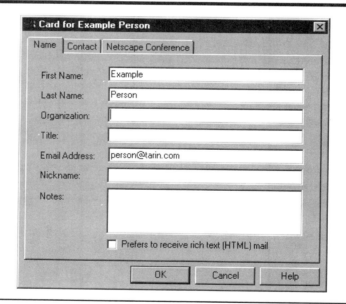

Figure 5.12: The Card For "User" dialog box lets you enter and change information about people with whom you correspond.

 You can also select Message ➤ Add to Address Book ➤ All if you want to add not only the person who sent the message, but all the recipients, too. This might be useful if you regularly send and receive mail from a large group of people at work, for example.

2. If you'd like to add (or correct) more information about this person, you can type it in the text fields, such as Title and Organization. You can edit the name by clicking in the First Name and Last Name fields and typing their name. You can also pick a Nickname for that person, and type a description of who they are in the Notes field.

The Nickname field can be really handy. In the old days, we called this a "handle." You can just use the person's given name if you like, or you can choose a short nickname, such as their initials or the first part of their e-mail address. Nicknames should be single words in lowercase letters. Once you assign a nickname to a person in your address book, you can type it in the To field, and Netscape will automatically use the corresponding e-mail address for that person when you send the message.

3. Click on the Contact tab of the Card User dialog box. Here, you can enter physical address and phone number information about this person, as well as information about where they work.

The other tab in the dialog box deals with Netscape Conference. For information about Netscape Conference, see Chapter 6, "Communicating via Conference."

4. Now, finish up by clicking on the OK button to add the new user information to your Address Book. The Card For "User" dialog box will close, and you will be returned to the e-mail message or Usenet article you were viewing.

Next time you open the Address Book window you'll see the new e-mail address listed.

Another Way to Add People to Your Address Book

If you know someone's e-mail address and you just want to add it to your Address Book without being in mid-reply to a message, follow these steps:

1. From the Message Center (or any Communicator window's) menu bar, select Communicator ➤ Address Book. The Address Book window will appear, as seen in Figure 5.11.

2. From the Address Book window's menu bar, click on New Card. The New Card dialog box will appear.

3. This dialog box is exactly the same as the Card For "User" dialog box we just talked about, except its text boxes are all blank. Use these text boxes to type information about the person you are adding to your Address book. In the Nickname text field, type a nickname ("alias" or "handle") for the person, or just use the person's given name. Nicknames must be single words and can contain only lowercase letters.

4. In the Notes text box you can enter a description or notes about the person whose e-mail address you are adding. For example, you might want to make notes about how you met this person, why he or she is of interest, or what you mean to contact him or her about in the future.

5. In the Name and E-Mail Address text boxes, type the name and e-mail address of the person whose address you're adding to your book.

You can make aliases for groups of e-mail addresses, too. Maybe there are several people you always send jokes to, or perhaps you have a group of coworkers that you usually send memos to all at once. To create a mailing list alias, open the Address book and click on New List. The Mailing List dialog box will appear, in which you can enter a name and nickname for the list, as well as the e-mail addresses (or nicknames) for all the people you want to include.

6. If you'd like, click on the Contact tab in the New Card dialog box, and type in their physical address, their phone number, and the like.

7. Now click on the OK button to add the e-mail address to your Address book. The Add User dialog box will close.

Now you'll see the new entry you just created in the Address Book window.

What's Out There

Lost track of old pals? You can track down friends and lost relatives using Yahoo!'s People Search gizmo. Pop over to http://www.yahoo.com/search/people/ and type in a name to find that person's snail-mail address and phone number, their e-mail address, or the URL for their home page.

Using Your Address Book for Sending Mail

In the "Sending a Message" section earlier in this chapter, we told you the basics for sending e-mail, but it can be even more convenient. Once you've got people listed in your Address Book, you can start using it to make sending e-mail easier. To send e-mail to someone who's listed in the Address Book, follow these steps:

1. From the Message Center menu bar, select Communicator ➤ Address Book to open your Address Book.

2. In the Address Book window, locate and single-click on the name of the person to whom you want to send mail. Click on the New Msg button, and the Message Composition window will appear, with your intended recipient's name and e-mail address filled in.

3. Go ahead—write and send an e-mail message as you usually would.

That's all there is to using Netscape's multifunctional, convenient Address Book.

Find Your Long Lost Pals with the People Search

If you've ever wondered whether an old friend you've lost touch with has an e-mail address, now is your chance to find out. Netscape Communicator has included a search mechanism in its Address Book that lets you search five different e-mail directories for e-mail addresses. These directories get addresses from Usenet posts, personal entries in the database, and lists sold by some companies to the directories. Try searching for your own name—you might be surprised. Conducting the search is easy; just follow these steps:

1. Open the Address Book by selecting Communicator ➤ Address Book from any Netscape menu bar.

(continued on next page)

2. Click on Directory. The Search dialog box will appear, as seen here.

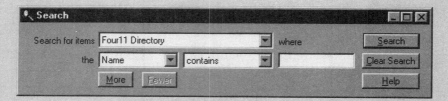

3. The topmost pull-down menu lets you choose which directory to search. Select either Four11, Infospace, WhoWhere, Switchboard, or Bigfoot.

4. The first pull-down menu on the second line allows you to decide what kind of information to search for. You'll probably want to search by name, but you can also search by e-mail address, phone number, organization, city, or street address. Click on the menu box to select one of these categories.

5. The next menu box allows you to choose how strict a match you want. Contains is probably your best choice, but you can also choose Doesn't Contain, Is, Isn't, or Sounds Like. Click on the menu box to make your choice.

6. Click in the text box to type in the name or other information you're looking for. It's best to choose either a first or last name to search by, rather than a full name.

7. When you're ready, click on Search. After the search site is contacted and it does the look-up, the Search dialog box will expand to show the search results, if any.

8. If you don't find the results you're looking for, try another directory, or try searching on the full name or just the last name. You'll probably have a harder time finding John Smith than you will finding Zbigniew Plotznik.

9. To search on more than one criteria at a time, click on the More button. The search dialog box will expand, and options similar to the ones discussed in steps 4–6 will be revealed. You can exit the dialog box by clicking on the × in the upper right-hand corner.

Once you find your friend's e-mail address, send a note introducing yourself. You can't be sure that this is the same person you went to summer camp with—you never know, there might be two Zbigniew Plotzniks lurking around the Internet.

To visit the Web sites of these people searchers, visit http://www.Four11.com/ for the Four11 directory; http://www.bigfoot.com/ to try Bigfoot; http://www .infospace.com/ for Infospace, http://www.whowhere.com/ to visit WhoWhere, and http://www.switchboard.com/ for Switchboard. You'll find other search options there, and these home pages are also the starting points for entering or editing your own directory entry.

You can also open Netscape Navigator and click on the Guide button. From the menu that appears, click on People to visit Netscape's People Search page. The URL of that page is http://guide.netscape.com/guide/people.html.

◆ Managing Your E-Mail

Netscape Messenger provides you with several tools to help you sort through the heaps of e-mail you're bound to get, either over time or every day. You can use folders and filters to file your e-mail, so your Inbox isn't crowded with every message you've ever received. Or you can mark messages as read or unread, or use priorities and flags, so you can read the important stuff first and save the rest for later.

Creating a New Folder

After you've had your e-mail account for a while, you may notice that the messages start to pile up rather quickly in your Inbox. Rather than keeping all your incoming mail in one folder (Inbox), you may want to create separate folders for different kinds of messages. You may have a folder called Business and one called Personal, or you may want to break it down even further into folders called Jokes, Aunt Susie, and Old Projects.

Creating a new folder is easy; just follow this short process:

1. Make sure the Message Center is open and ready to go. Select File ➤ New Folder, or click on the New Folder icon. The New Folder dialog box will appear.

2. Choose a name for your new folder, and type its name in the text box provided. The name should be fairly descriptive so you don't need to open it up in order to know what kind of messages are stored there. (We'll transfer messages there for storage in a minute.)

3. If you'd like, you can create this new folder as a subfolder, which means that it will be stored inside an existing Message Center folder. Click on the pull-down menu labeled Create as a Subfolder Of, and choose an existing folder from the list.

4. When you're finished, click on OK. The New Folder dialog box will close, and you'll be returned to the Message Center window. There you'll see the folder you just created.

Creating new mail folders is easy as pie. Now that we have a new folder, we're ready to transfer some mail into it. Read on!

Filing Messages

If you want to store mail in folders besides the Inbox, you can create as many folders as you'd like, but then you need to transfer, or file, the messages into the folders created for that purpose. Don't worry; this process is as easy as it gets:

1. From the Netscape Message Center window, open the Inbox by double-clicking on its icon or by going to the menu bar and selecting Communicator ➤ Messenger Mailbox.

2. Highlight the message you'd like to file by clicking on its name.

 You can select multiple messages to transfer into the same mailbox by holding down the Ctrl key while you're clicking the left mouse button.

3. From the Message Center Inbox menu bar, select Message ➤ File Message ➤ Folder Name, where Folder Name is the name of the folder into which you're stashing your message. The name of the message you just filed will disappear—don't worry, you haven't deleted anything. This is exactly what you wanted to happen.

The message you just filed has been transferred into the folder you selected. The next time you open that folder, whether it be Grandma's Recipes or Project Buzzard, your message will be filed safely inside. Now you know how to create folders and file messages into them, and you can read or delete their messages later as needed.

 You can sort your outgoing mail into these same folders if you'd like. From the Message Center, simply open the Sent folder by double-clicking on its icon. Now you can transfer messages that you've already sent into any folder you've created.

Copying Messages to Multiple Folders

You might have occasion to want a copy of a single message to appear in two different folders. If you save every single message from your girlfriend in a single folder marked Chelsea, but she sends you a joke you want to keep in your Jokes folder, you might want to make a copy of it. Or if you like to keep a copy of all your outgoing mail in your Sent folder, but you want to file your mail about Project Buzzard in the Project Buzzard folder, you can make a copy of it, and it will appear in both places at once.

Making a copy of a message is easier than boiling water. Just follow these simple steps:

1. With the folder open that contains the message you want to copy, highlight the message by clicking on its name.

2. From the folder's menu bar, select Message ➤ Copy Message. From the pull-down menu that appears, choose the name of the folder you want to copy the message into.

The next time you open the mail folder you chose, a copy of that important message will be filed safely inside, while the original message stays in the folder it calls home.

Changing the Look of Netscape News and Mail

Netscape Communicator lets you change the look of the Message Center to suit your taste. Here's how:

1. With the Message Center open, pull down the Edit menu and select Preferences. The Preferences dialog box will appear.

2. Click on the Mail & Groups category, and the contents of the dialog box will change to display options for changing the fonts, quoted text style, and window options for the entire Message Center (both mail and discussion groups).

3. To use a fixed-width font for displaying messages and articles, click in the circle next to Fixed Width Font. (You can adjust which fonts these are by clicking on Appearance in the category box, and then on Fonts.) Alternatively, to use a variable-width font, click in the circle next to Variable Width Font. (Most of the time it's advisable to use a fixed-width font for displaying messages and articles because this ensures that you'll see the whole message in the most legible layout. But maybe you have your own reasons for changing this.)

4. To change the style (appearance) of text you've quoted from other e-mail messages and articles in e-mail messages and news articles you write, click on the Style menu box. You have four options here: quoted text can be Regular, Bold, Italic, or Bold Italic (bold and italic at the same time).

5. You can also adjust the size of quoted text. Click on the Size menu box, and choose Regular, Smaller, or Bigger.

6. To change the color of text quoted in e-mail messages and news articles, click on the Choose Color button, and the Color dialog box will appear. Click on a color you like, and click on OK. The color box will display the color you just chose.

7. For both discussions and mail, you can choose to use a different window for every thread or message, or to reuse windows and change the content when you open a new message or discussion group. Place a checkmark in the boxes labeled "Reuse message list (thread) window" and "Reuse message window if you want a minimum of windows popping open." If you prefer to use a new window for each message or thread, leave these options unchecked.

8. When you're finished adjusting your preferences, click on OK to close the Preferences dialog box and return to the Message Center.

Presorting Your E-Mail with Filters

Wouldn't it be nice if you could have every e-mail message from Aunt Susie filed automatically into the Aunt Susie folder, or any e-mail with Project Buzzard in the subject line automatically transferred to the Project Buzzard folder? That's what e-mail filters do, and they're a snap to set up and use. Once you provide an e-mail address, a name, or other keywords to a mail filter, all messages henceforth that meet your criteria will be prefiled so you can read them in context.

Creating a New Filter

Before you can use a filter, you have to create it. Making a new filter entails telling Messenger the criteria for what kind of messages to filter and what actions to take when messages that meet these criteria arrive in your incoming e-mail. Setting it up is a piece of cake:

1. You should have the Message Center window open, but you don't need to be online for this. From the Message Center (or Inbox) menu bar, select Edit ➤ Mail Filter Rules. The Mail Filters dialog box will appear, as shown in Figure 5.13.

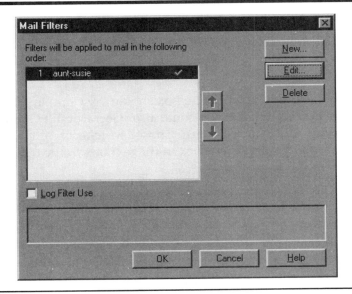

Figure 5.13: The Mail Filters dialog box lets you create filters to file your mail automatically.

2. Click on the New button. The Filter Rules dialog box will appear, as shown in Figure 5.14.

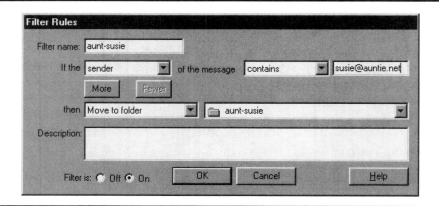

Figure 5.14: The Filter Rules dialog box is where you type in the nitty gritty of the filter.

3. Choose a name for your filter. This name should remind you what the filter is for or why you created it. For example, if we want to filter mail from Aunt Susie, we'll call our filter Aunt Susie. Type the name of your filter in the Filter Name text box.

4. Now you're going to set the rules for your filter. Click on the pull-down menu box marked If The. This box selects which field of the e-mail message your filter is going to check.

5. The next pull-down menu box should say Contains. This is usually the best choice, but you could also select Doesn't Contain, Is, Isn't, Begins With, or Ends With. Choose whichever option you feel is appropriate, and then click in the text box to the right of the pull-down menu.

6. The next text box is the most important part of your filter: It's the section where you get to type a name, an e-mail address, a subject keyword, or some other variable that would appear in the From, Subject, or Body field of an incoming message. Type your keyword or address in this box. For example, we'd type **aunt susie**.

7. If you'd like to set more than one criteria for your filter, click on the More button, and the Filter Rules dialog box will expand to reveal another row of boxes and menus. You can use these boxes as we described in steps 4-6. For example, you could set instructions that say, "If the message is from Aunt Susie, and the subject is recipes..."

8. The next pull-down menu box is the action part of the filter; this is what the filter does with your instructions. Your choices are Move to Folder, Change Priority, Delete, Mark Read, Kill Thread, or Watch Thread. Make your choice.

9. If you chose Move to Folder or Change Priority, there will be an additional pull-down menu box that enables you to choose a folder to move your message into, or a priority with which to mark the messages.

10. You can also type a description of your filter in the Description text box to remind you why or when you created this mail filter.

11. Should you decide to put your filter on hiatus, click on the Off button.

11. When you're done setting the rules, click on OK to close the Filter Rules dialog box and return to the Mail Filters dialog box.

12. In the Mail Filters dialog box, click on OK to return to the Message Center window.

The next time you check your e-mail, any messages that correspond to the filter or filters you just created will be sorted using the criteria you described.

Editing an Existing Filter

If Aunt Susie's e-mail address changes, your old filter won't do you much good. You don't need to start from scratch, because it's easy to edit a filter that you've made:

1. You should have the Message Center window open, but you don't need to be online for this. From the Message Center (or Inbox) menu bar, select Edit ➤ Mail Filter Rules. The Mail Filters dialog box will appear.

2. Highlight the filter you wish to edit by single-clicking on its name. Click on Edit, and the Filter Rules dialog box will appear.

3. Change whatever you need to change, be it the e-mail address to filter, the action you wish to take, or the mailbox you want the filtered messages to go to.

4. When you're finished editing your filter, click on OK, and the Filter Rules dialog box will close, returning you to the Mail Filters dialog box.

5. Click on OK to close the Mail Filters dialog box and return to the Message Center window.

The next time you check your e-mail, the filter will use your new instructions to handle your incoming messages.

 The up and down arrows in the Mail Filters dialog box are for moving the order of your filters up and down. That means if you think that it's more important for an Aunt Susie message to go to the Aunt Susie mailbox than for the filter to consider whether it's about Project Buzzard, you'll want the Aunt Susie filter to have first dibs on your incoming mail. Simply click on the name of any of your filters, and then on the up or down arrow, to move it through the list. Filters are listed in descending order, with the filter at the very top taking action first.

Deleting a Filter

If you decide you don't want or need a filter you've created, it's easy to get rid of it. Maybe you've changed jobs, quit a mailing list, or decided you'd rather have a certain kind of message arrive directly in your Inbox. Remember that you don't need to be online to do this. Just follow this simple process:

1. From the Message Center (or Inbox) menu bar, select Edit ➤ Mail Filter Rules. The Mail Filters dialog box will appear.

2. Select the filter you want to delete by clicking on its name.

3. Click on the Delete button, and the name of the filter will disappear.

4. Click on OK, and the Filter Rules dialog box will close, returning you to the Mail Filters dialog box.

5. Click on OK to close the Mail Filters dialog box and return to the Message Center window.

Your old filter is gone, although you can recreate it if you ever want to by following the same steps you used in "Creating a New Filter."

Instead of deleting a filter altogether, you may want to temporarily turn it off. To do this, open the Mail Filters dialog box and select the filter you want to turn off by clicking on its name. Click on the checkmark next to the filter's name, and it will turn into a bullet, signifying that the filter is turned off. You can return to the Mail Filters dialog box and click on the bullet, once again making it into a checkmark and turning it back on. Or you can double-click the filter's name to open the Filter Rules dialog box, where you can access the On and Off radio buttons.

Getting Free Subscriptions to Mailing Lists

One reason to have a mail filter is a mailing list. Okay, mailing lists are good for a lot more than giving your filters something to do. A mailing list is like a subscription to an interactive newsletter. Topics of mailing lists range from elementary education to computer security, and just about anything else. Once you sign up, you get e-mail automatically, either weekly, daily, or several times a day, depending on how much traffic the list gets.

Subscribing to a mailing list is almost always free. To join, you need to send a message to a specific e-mail address with a few words of instruction in either the subject line or the body of the message. You'll find information on subscribing to mailing lists as you search the Web, or through word of mouth. Or you can search a Web service like Lizst to find a mailing list on a specific topic.

If the list has a moderator, that person decides which messages are worthy of sending to everyone who subscribes. Some moderated lists don't even let the readers send in contributions—they're more like newsletters than interactive discussion groups. Unmoderated lists let anyone who reads a list send a message to the hundreds of readers following the discussion.

The Netscape Message Center has a couple of features that help you manage the way you read mailing lists. One, as we've mentioned, is the mail filter. Once you join a mailing list, you can create a folder for a mailing list, and then set up a mail filter that places all posts to this mailing list in the designated folder.

Another feature is the great thread sorting. Mailing lists, like Usenet newsgroups, often feature discussions in which several people respond to the same topic or post. You can sort the mail in whatever folder you like by thread—all messages that seem to be on the same topic (as indicated by the subject line) will be grouped together, with the original post at the top. To sort by thread, open the folder you want to sift through and click on the field button that looks like a stack of black lines (it's the first field button next to the name button).

What's Out There

A very nifty list of mailing lists, Liszt (cute, eh?), is at http://www.liszt.com/. Liszt grows like a weed, and it offers descriptions of the mailing lists, so you can easily pick those of interest. Subscription instructions are usually included. Once you subscribe to a mailing list, you'll get messages on the topic of interest delivered to your Inbox on a daily or even hourly basis.

Sorting the Messages in Your Inbox

If you get a lot of e-mail, you might find yourself wishing there was an easy way to sort the mail you've already gotten. Filters are great, but if your e-mail piles up before you put a filter to work and you need to locate that message your boss sent you last week, or if you want to find all the messages sent back and forth about Project Buzzard, sorting may be a bigger help than prefiling your mail with filters. Fortunately, Messenger makes it ridiculously easy to sort your mail by thread, subject, sender, date, flag, and read/unread status.

Just follow this single step:

1. Open the folder (or mailbox) that you want to sort. The row of column headings marked Subject, Sender, etc., just above the body text area are all you need. Click on one of them to sort by that category. For example, to sort by Sender, click on the word Sender. Or you can use the Messenger menu bar to select View ➤ Sort. Your options are

    ◆ By Date

    ◆ By Flag

    ◆ By Priority

    ◆ By Sender

    ◆ By Size (file size, usually in K)

    ◆ By Status (read or unread)

    ◆ By Subject

    ◆ By Thread (uses the name of the subject to determine threads)

    ◆ By Unread (similar to status)

That's all there is to it. Sorting only affects one mailbox at a time; you can sort all of your mailboxes in different ways, as often as you like. There are a couple other tricks to help you sort your mail:

◆ Highlight a message before you sort the mailbox. The message will stay highlighted afterwards. For example, if you want to find all the e-mail from your boss, select any message from your boss by single-clicking on it and then click on the Sender button. All the messages from your boss will appear on screen.

◆ Sorting messages by Sender puts the messages in alphabetical order by sender, and multiple messages from the same person will be listed in chronological order.

◆ Sorting once puts the messages in ascending order (A to Z, chrono-logical, etc.). Sorting twice with the same button puts the messages in descending order (Z to A, or reverse chronological).

◆ When you're finished doing whatever it was that made you need to sort your mail, you can sort it by date to put the mail back in its regular old chronological order.

You can sort your mail whenever you want, as often as you like, but you can only sort by one criteria at a time.

Searching Your Old E-Mail and Discussion Group Messages

Okay, so you've sorted your mail half a dozen times and transferred some of your messages into other folders you've created. You've set up several mail filters to help you file your mail into folders. You've got your e-mail super-organized, and you still can't find that message that Aunt Susie sent you about how to prepare her famous stuffed quail. Messenger to the rescue again! The Message Center Search function can help you find that impor-tant message in a jiffy, no matter what mail folder you've tucked it into.

1. From the Message Center menu bar, select Edit ➤ Search Messages. The Search dialog box will appear, as seen in Figure 5.15.

2. From the pull-down menu box, choose a folder to search in. You can choose Local Mail to search all your mailboxes; you can choose any single mailbox; or you can choose the name of a discussion group to search current messages posted to that group.

Figure 5.15: The Search dialog box lets you search for text in any message in the Message Center.

3. The next pull-down menu box allows you to choose the matching criteria. Contains is usually the best choice, but you could also select Doesn't Contain, Is, Isn't, Begins With, or Ends With, although these will take much longer to complete successfully.

4. The third box is where you type in the word you want to search for. This must be a word or phrase exactly as it appears in the e-mail message you're looking for. If we want to find *quail*, we'd be best off searching for *quail* instead of *stuffed quail*, just in case she doesn't refer to it as stuffed quail.

5. If you make a mistake, press the Clear Search button to clear what you've selected and typed. When you're ready to search, press the Search button to begin your search. The Search dialog box will expand to show you the search's progress and (hopefully) its results.

6. When the search is complete, the lower portion of the Search dialog box will expand to display all e-mail messages that met the criteria you entered. This display area is similar to a mail folder window, in that it shows all the message headers and allows you to sort the messages by Sender, Subject, and Date. You can also see the location of the message (which mail folder it's stored in).

7. To open a message, double-click on its name. The Message window will appear, but the Search dialog box will remain open. You can search as many times as you'd like in the Search dialog box, although your old results will not be stored anywhere.

8. When you're finished, close any messages you've opened by clicking on the × in the upper right-hand corner. You can close the Search dialog box the same way.

Using one word, especially a word that you think will only appear in a few messages, usually produces better results than using multiple words or phrases. Now you can find that elusive stuffed quail recipe, or the joke your brother sent you about the pink and purple Ping-Pong ball, with minimal effort.

 You can keep the Search dialog box open until you're done with it; with it open, you can switch between it and the Message Center as you would between two different windows.

Marking Your Mail

Sometimes you may check your mail when you're on your way out the door or otherwise limited by time. If you only have a few minutes, but you download 50 new messages, you need to find a way to figure out which ones are important and which can wait for later. There are several ways to mark your incoming e-mail messages as important or unimportant.

 The Message Center dialog box's default size is pretty small and takes up very little screen real estate. This means that not all the available feats you can accomplish with Messenger are visible to the naked eye at that size. To make more message descriptors visible, you can click on the arrow at the far left of the row of message headers, or you can resize the window by maximizing it or by clicking and dragging the lower-right corner until it's the size you like.

Flagging Important Messages

One way to make a note to yourself that an e-mail message is worth noting is to flag it. This means you mark certain messages in your Inbox (or other mail folder) with a little flag so you can easily tell them apart from the crowd. There are two easy ways to flag a message. Here's the first way:

1. With the mail folder that your message is in open, highlight the message you want to flag by single-clicking on its name.

2. From the Inbox menu bar, select Message ➤ Flag. A little flag icon will appear near the date of the message, in the column with the flag at the top (how about that?).

An even easier way to flag a message is like this:

1. With the mail folder that your message is in open, highlight the message you want to flag by single-clicking on its name.

2. In the Flag column, click on the gray bullet. A flag icon will appear.

Now your message is marked with a colorful flag that denotes importance, or that it needs a response, or whatever you choose.

 You can flag several messages that you'd like to read first and then, from the Inbox menu bar, select Go ➤ Next Flagged Message. Other options under the Go menu include Next Unread Message and Next Unread Thread.

Unflagging a message once you've dealt with it is just as simple. Highlight the message and single-click on the flag icon, and it will turn back into a gray dot. Or, from the Inbox menu bar, select Message ➤ Unflag, and the little flag will go away.

Prioritizing Incoming and Outgoing Mail

Another way to mark messages in order of importance is with Priorities. You can mark an outgoing message with priorities, or you can change the priorities of messages you've already received. Mail priorities, from lowest to highest, are standard in most e-mail readers, so if you mark your outgoing messages as highest priority, your friend who receives the message will see the message marked in red or flagged in some way as being important. In Netscape Messenger, different priorities are marked in different colors, so you can mark the mail you've already received as being of different priorities to organize your mail using Messenger's priority color scheme.

To denote a priority in an outgoing message, just do this:

1. Click on the Composition window's Message Sending Options tab (the one with the itty bitty checkmarks on its icon), and choose from the options in the Priorities menu, Lowest through Highest.

2. Finish typing your message as you normally would, and send it away.

If the message recipient has an e-mail program that can read priorities, that person will see your message marked with the priority you indicated before you sent it.

For your own benefit when reading your mail, you can change the priority of a message you've received. Since you have five levels of priority to choose from (Lowest to Highest), you can rate some or all of your messages according to importance. Think of priorities as reminders as to which messages are urgent, which messages are extremely urgent, and which messages denote nuclear war.

All you have to do to change priority of the messages in your mailboxes is right-click on the name of the message. From the menu that appears, select Change Priority To, and from its submenu, select a priority from Lowest to Highest.

Once you've marked your messages, you can sort your messages by flag or by priority, if you like.

What's Out There

Travel a lot? You can check your mail from any Web browser on any computer by using HoTMaiL, a free Web-based e-mail service. You won't get all the bells and whistles of Netscape Messenger, but you'll be able to check your e-mail for free. Try it out at http://www.hotmail.com/.

Marking Messages as Read or Unread

Occasionally, when you're short on time, you'll open a message that turns out to be long, unimportant, or otherwise postponable. Or you may glance at a message's title and decide it isn't worth reading. In these instances, what you want to do is mark a message as unread when you have opened it but haven't really read it yet, or mark a message as read if you have no intention of ever reading it.

So why would you want to mark a message as read? Well, sometimes we e-mail ourselves with copies of things we've seen online, or with record-keeping things of one kind or another. Or sometimes we get e-mail that we don't feel like reading right now, but we don't particularly feel like having its bold name shouting "read me!" at us. So we mark these kinds of messages as read, and we file them away or get around to reading them later on.

It's simple to mark a message read or unread. Just follow these simple steps:

1. With your Inbox open, highlight the message you want to mark as unread.

2. From the Inbox menu bar, select Message ➤ Mark ➤ As Read (or Unread). The name of the message will become bold, and the little gray dot next to the message (in the Unread column) will turn into a big green dot, which connotes a message that hasn't yet been opened.

    or

    Click on the green bullet or the gray dot in the Read/Unread column (that's the one with the green bullets and gray dots—how clever!). Green dots turn into gray bullets when you click on them, and vice versa. Now you can toggle messages as read or unread until the cows come home.

Often, when we're short on time, we'll open a message that we want to save for later, so we mark it Unread to remind us that, well, we haven't read it yet.

 You can mark all your messages as read from the Inbox menu bar. Just select Message ➤ Mark ➤ All Read. Or, if you've been away for a while, you can mark all messages before a certain date as read. From the Inbox menu bar, select Message ➤ Mark ➤ By Date. When the Mark Messages Read dialog box appears, choose a date by typing in the text box or clicking on the up and down arrow buttons. Click on OK, and all the messages before the date you indicated will be marked as read.

Quitting the Message Center

When you're finished reading and replying to your mail, quitting Netscape Message Center is a quick, standard procedure you can accomplish in just one step.

1. From the Message Center menu bar, select File ➤ Exit.

    or

Click on the × in the upper-right corner of the Netscape Message Center window. Either way, you'll return to whatever it was you were doing before you opened the Message Center, whether that's Navigator or another program.

The Advantages of Secure Mail

As the next generation of Netscape servers become more widely used, certificates and other secure mail features are becoming increasingly necessary. Netscape Messenger now has the ability to encrypt e-mail transmissions so they can't be peered into while they're traveling the wires to their destination. Netscape Messenger uses the S/MIME protocol, a security-enhanced version of one of the most widely accepted standards for sending outgoing mail.

You can create your own personal certificate and use this certificate to attach a digital signature to your message that verifies that it came directly from you. One interesting thing about digital signatures is that court precedents are being set that consider digital signatures to be binding in the same manner that the pen-and-ink kind are: They're beginning to be seen as solid proof that you yourself wrote and/or signed an electronic document.

Your personal certificate can also include an encryption key, or code, that allows ultra-private conversations to occur between you and selected recipients. If your recipient has a decryption code, they—and only they—can read the mail encrypted using an encryption key. You hold both parts of the key (the public key and the private key), and you give out the public key to those people with whom you want to exchange encrypted mail. Your friends then use the public key to decode the encrypted mail you send them.

When this book went to press, Netscape had not yet finalized the way that personal certificates and encrypted mail were going to work. To get a certificate, visit Verisign at http://www.verisign.com/. You can get a free certificate for use with e-mail, and you can also purchase various levels of security (the most expensive requiring a private meeting with a Verisign representative). To find out more about security in your Messenger e-mail (and the rest of Communicator), click on any Security button in the Communicator environment. You'll find helpful information there as well as steps for arranging to use certificates and digital signatures. You can also select Help ➤ Security from the Navigator or Messenger menu bar to read more about Internet security (and Communicator security in particular).

Now you can practice any of the skills you picked up in this chapter, or if you're done for now, you can quit Communicator altogether.

 If you'd like, you can download new mail and messages in one fell swoop before you disconnect from the Internet (or directly after you sign in). To do this, select File ➤ Go Offline from the Message Center menu bar. The Download dialog box will appear. There, you'll see checkboxes marked Download Mail and Download Discussion groups; check or uncheck these, as you see fit. You can also click on the Select Items for Download button to choose exactly which of your subscribed discussion groups you'd like to get messages for. You can then disconnect your Internet connection and read these new messages at your leisure. You can select Go Online to accomplish the same thing.

We're on Our Way!

Now that you know how to use Communicator's basic features, the discussions reader, and the e-mail program, let's turn our attention in Chapter 6 to Conference, Netscape's program for interactive communication, and then, in Chapter 7, to live content on the Web.

Do You Need Help?

For answers to your questions about using Netscape, call 800/320-2099 or e-mail client@netscape.com. Keep your credit card handy if you haven't paid for Netscape just yet.

Communicating via Conference

Netscape Conference, the program formerly known as CoolTalk, is plenty cool. It makes communicating about as interactive as it can be without seeing or sitting in a room with other folks. Conference lets you use the Internet as a telephone, "chat" with your friends via interactive typed messages, and collaborate using a whiteboard on which you and your compadres can draw or write material while you can all see it. Other Conference features include direct file transfer with the File Exchange tool and synchronized Web surfing sessions with the Collaborative Browsing tool. Conference is simple to use and doesn't require sophisticated hardware, so you don't have to be Joe Megabucks Genius to make it work for you.

 When you download Netscape Communicator, you have the option of getting the standard version, which includes Conference and Live3D, or a more stripped-down version that doesn't. See Chapter 10 before you download.

What's Out There

Kevin Savetz maintains a Net telephone guide at http://www.northcoast
.com/~savetz/voice-faq.html.

◆ Using Conference to Talk

Turn on your speakers and microphone and fire up that computer so you
can talk, talk, talk. You can yak with a pal (it's usually best to set up an
appointment beforehand to make sure you're both online), or you can
find a friendly and, presumably, talkative stranger.

What's Out There

The Virtual Voice offers news and reviews in the field of Internet telephony.
The URL is http://www.virtual-voice.com/.

If you haven't installed or set up Conference yet, turn to Chapter 11
for all the details.

Start Talking to a Friend

Here's how to start yakking it up:

1. Connect to the Internet as you usually do. (See Chapter 10 if you
   don't know how.)

2. From the Windows 95 Start Menu, select Programs ➤ Netscape
   Communicator ➤ Netscape Conference. The main Conference
   window (see Figure 6.1) will appear.

3. If there's someone in particular you'd like to talk with, you can type
   their e-mail address directly in the text box marked E-Mail Address. To

talk to your friend I. M. Smart, type her address, `imsmart@mensa.com`, in the text box. (Your friend has to have Conference, of course.)

4. Click on Dial to start the connection, and the Pending Invitation dialog box will appear:

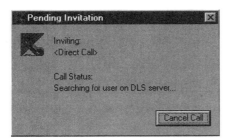

This means that Conference is ringing your pal, and assuming she answers and that your equipment is configured properly, your repartee can begin. (To use your Address Book to make this call, see "Using Your Address Book with Conference," later in this chapter.)

As they say, now you're talking (well, almost). Now that you're dialed in, you're free to use not only the Internet phone aspect of Conference (just step up to the mike), but the rest of the fancy features as well, which we'll get to later in this chapter.

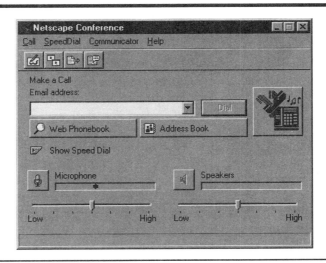

Figure 6.1: The Conference window is your first stop in live communication.

If you're having trouble hearing each other, first fiddle around with the volume settings on your speakers and microphone. You can adjust the volume levels from the Conference window by sliding the volume slide controls back and forth with your mouse pointer. Sometimes just finding the right volume level does the trick. If not, while you're talking, slide the Silence Sensor slide control (above the microphone volume control) to the left or right until you find the optimal setting for your computer. The Silence Sensor determines at what volume Conference will automatically pick up your voice. Finally, try leaving the present conference (see "Ending a Call") and opening Call ➤ Preferences. Click on the Audio tab and make sure your audio preferences are configured correctly for your sound card—you do have one, right?

What About Video?

When we wrote this book, Netscape Communications indicated that video conferencing would be available in the final release of the Conference that's included in the full version of Communicator. Video conferencing should either be included as part of the software or as a third-party plug-in. Either way, video conferencing requires a video card and, of course, a video camera. The dialing and speaking process will be pretty much the same, although the program itself might look slightly different from what you see in these pages. When video conferencing becomes available, the Conference Help files (select Help ➤ Help Contents from the menu bar) should cover any-thing else you need to know. Keep your eyes peeled, too, for other features like compatibility with other Internet phone programs and even regular old telephones!

Talk to Strangers (and Make New Friends)

Suppose you want to meet a new person who uses Conference—after all, that's what the Internet is all about: meeting new people and interacting with them. To meet a new person using Conference, follow steps 1 through 3 in the previous section. From there it's easy:

1. If you'd prefer to talk to a stranger, click on the Web Phonebook button in the open Conference box. A Netscape Navigator window will appear, which, in a few seconds, will display a page listing other

Internet phone users who are currently connected to the same server you are (see Figure 6.2).

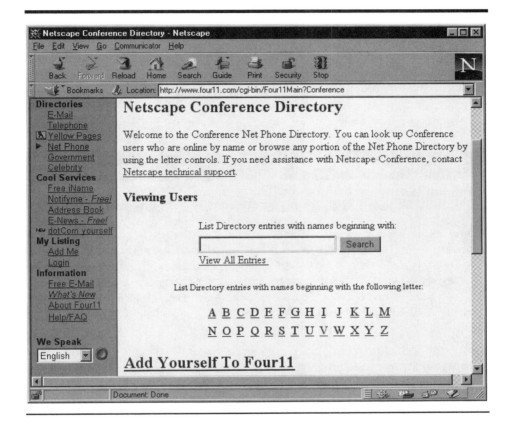

Figure 6.2: Netscape's Conference Phonebook lets you use Navigator to find calling partners. Just click and dial!

2. To ring someone, double-click on his or her name. This will return you to Conference, where you'll see the Pending Invitation dialog box.

3. If the person you've contacted accepts your invitation to talk, you're ready to go—introduce yourself!

Be nice to the people you meet—the duck may be somebody's mother. Be aware that you may be rejected, but if you don't succeed, try, try again—it's a free-for-all and someone out there will want to talk to you. If you'd like to see the business card of the person you're talking to (this is especially useful if you're talking to a stranger), pull down the Conference menu and select Participant Info. The caller's business card will appear, so you can see who he or she claims to be.

Conference comes set to use a DLS directory server provided by Netscape. You can change to a different directory server (some corporations run their own directory servers for their employees, for example) by selecting Call ➤ Preferences to display the Preferences dialog box. Click on the Network tab, and type the server's name in the DLS Server text box.

Using Your Address Book with Conference

If you've set up your Address Book as described in Chapter 5, you're probably thinking, "Hey, I have all those e-mail addresses typed in over in that other place. Do I really have to type them in here?" No! You can use your Address Book with Conference easily. With your Internet connection running and Conference open, click on the Address Book button. When your Address Book appears, select the person's name by clicking on it. Then click on the Call button. Conference will reappear and start dialing the person you picked out of your Address Book.

You can also dial people directly from your Address Book, and of course, you can add new people to your Address Book and then call them.

1. To make sure your friend's name is ready to go using Conference, use any Netscape menu bar to select Communicator ➤ Address Book. When the Address Book window appears, double-click on your friend's name. The Card for "User" dialog box will appear.

2. Click on the Netscape Conference tab, and the dialog box will change to reflect your choice (see Figure 6.3). Now click on the menu box to choose between Netscape Conference DLS, Specific DLS, or Hostname or IP Address. For the latter two choices, a text box will appear. Type in the IP number or machine name for the DLS server or networked machine.

3. When the settings for your friend are A-OK, click on OK to close the Card For dialog box and return to the Address Book.

From there, you can highlight your friend's name and click on Call, which will automatically launch Conference and start dialing for you. You can do this for new Address Book entries, too: just click on the New Card button and go from there. No muss, no fuss.

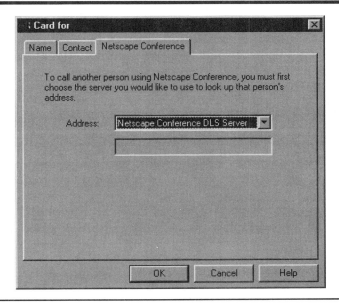

Figure 6.3: The Netscape Conference tab of the Card For dialog box

Ending a Call

When you're finished talking, say good-bye. Then, in the Conference window, click on Hang Up (it's where Dial used to be before your call got connected). Your call will be terminated, and you can exit Conference by selecting Call ➤ Exit from Conference's menu bar.

Handling Incoming Calls

To accept an incoming call, click on the Accept button on the dialog box that pops up when somebody rings you. When you accept a call, Conference will maximize and tell you who you're talking to automatically. To reject an incoming call, just click on the Reject button on the same dialog box. The person who was ringing you will simply go away.

You must have Conference running if you want to receive incoming calls. Unlike CoolTalk, Conference will *not* launch automatically when you receive a call. Your best bet is to run Conference (and minimize it, if you wish) whenever you're online and wish to accept calls.

The Bandwidth Follies

The primary problem with Conference can be summed up in a single word: bandwidth. Especially if you're connecting to the Internet through a modem rather than a network with a fast line like a T1, you'll notice that transmission quality could be a lot better, and it often takes several seconds for your computer to produce what the person you're talking to has just said. Until more of us are working with equipment that can keep up with the immense data flow necessary to support real-time voice communications, there will be problems with sound quality and voice lags. At times, this can be frustrating, which is one reason why the phone companies don't seem to feel overly threatened by Internet phone services quite yet. Telephony on the Net is still in its infancy…watch (or listen) for improvements in the future.

Setting Up Speed Dial Buttons

Most likely, there will be a few people that you'll call with Conference more often than others. You can assign up to six of these frequently called numbers to work with Conference's Speed Dial buttons. Before you can use Speed Dial buttons, you have to set them up. This is a snap:

1. From the main Conference window, click on the blue button marked Show Speed Dial. The Conference window will open up to show the speed dial area of the window.

2. Click on any of the buttons (numbered one through six) to open the Speed Dial Edit dialog box.

3. Type the full name, nickname, or username of the person you want to call in the Name box.

4. You need to choose either a direct address OR an e-mail address for the Speed Dial preferences. If the person does not have a direct address, type their e-mail address in the E-Mail box. If the person does have a direct address, type the address in the Direct Address box. This can be either an IP number or a resolved hostname (such as server3.home.com).

Make sure you type in either a direct address or an e-mail address, but not both. Otherwise, Conference will become confused, and you probably won't reach your party.

5. If the person to whom you're assigning a Speed Dial button is listed with a DLS directory server other than the default, type the server's address in the DLS Server text box. Otherwise, leave it alone.

6. When you're finished, click on OK to close the Speed Dial Edit dialog box and return to the main Conference window.

After you've assigned a person and an address to a speed dial number, the Speed Dial button you just edited will display the name of the person you entered, rather than "Speed Dial Button #1." All you have to do to reach them via Conference is click on the appropriate Speed Dial button.

If you want to change the information of a Speed Dial button, use the Conference menu bar to select Speed Dial ➤ (*Name*) ➤ Edit. The Speed Dial Edit dialog box will appear; follow steps 3 through 6 to edit the Speed Dial button.

To delete all the information on a Speed Dial button and reset it, use the Conference menu bar to select Speed Dial ➤ (*Name*) ➤ Clear. The Clear Speed Dial dialog box will appear. Click on Clear to clear the button and return to Conference.

You can also keep the speed dial area of the Conference window closed. (To close it, click on the blue arrow button labeled Hide Speed Dial). To use speed dial with this area of the window closed, use the Conference menu bar and select Speed Dial and then the name or number of the person you want to call.

Blocking Unwanted Calls

If you'd rather not make yourself available to be phoned by others through the DLS directory server, you can block incoming calls. Just follow these steps:

1. From the Conference menu bar, select Call ➤ Preferences. The Preferences dialog box will appear.

2. Remove the checkmark next to the label List My Name in Phonebook.

3. Click on OK to save your settings. This will return you to the main Conference window, from which you can access any of Conference's features.

If you want to *temporarily* stop accepting calls, you can block them without adjusting your preferences by using the Conference menu bar, select one of the following choices to adjust your call status:

Select	If You Want
Call ➤ Do Not Disturb	All incoming calls rejected
Call ➤ Auto Answer	All incoming calls accepted
Call ➤ Always Prompt	To be asked whether you're accepting calls

You can adjust your incoming call status as often as you want using Conference's menu bar.

What's Out There

Netscape maintains a Conference phone book that lists all the Conference users who are online at any given time. The URL for this handy service is http://home.netscape.com/comprod/products/communicator/conference/phonebook/.

◆ When Talking Won't Do: Chat

Talking is all well and fine, but while Conference is a great concept, it's not always as good in the execution as it was in the planning. You may prefer the more reliable method of interactive conversation known as Chat, which involves conversing in real time via typed messages rather than via actual talk. Conference's Chat feature lets you communicate with others in print (either to type what you're "saying" or to share text files). You can even work on documents together and then save your results. Let's take a look.

Using Chat to Communicate

To use the Chat tool, first follow steps 1 through 4 in the "Start Talking..." section to connect with a chat partner. Then,

1. Click on the Chat button on the Conference toolbar. (It's the one with the little cartoon message balloon on it.) The Conference Text Chat window will appear (Figure 6.4).

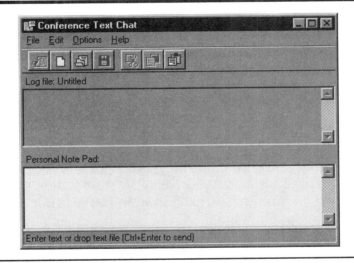

Figure 6.4: Type whatever you want to say in the Personal Note Pad text box.

2. To start chatting, type whatever it is you want to "say" in the Personal Note Pad text box, then click on the Send button on the Chat tool's toolbar (or press Ctrl+Enter) to post what you've typed to the conference. You have these tools at your disposal during your chat:

The Tool	Its Name	What It Lets You Do
	Send	Send whatever you've typed (or a text file you've included) to the person you're chatting with
	New	Start a new chat log
	Include	Send a text file to both the chat log and the person you're chatting with
	Save	Save the contents of your "conversation" to a file called a chat log
	Cut	Cut selected text
	Copy	Copy selected text
	Paste	Paste selected text

3. When you're finished chatting, make sure you say good-bye. Then, from the Chat tool's menu bar, select File ➤ Close. This will terminate your Conference chat session and leave you at the main Conference window.

What's Out There

For group chats, tune your Web browser (Navigator, not Conference) to SonicNet Chat Central (http://www.sonicnet.com/sonicore/chat/), or to HotWired's Club Wired celebrity schedule (http://www.hotwired.com/club/), or to Parents Place (http://www.parentsplace.com).

Using Chat to Send Files

If you'd like to try sending a text file to your chatty pals, follow these steps:

1. Create a text file using your favorite text editor. If you're running Windows 95, you can use NotePad, WordPad, or your favorite word processor (don't forget to save the file as text only, rather than as an MS Word .doc file).

2. When you're ready to send the text file you've created, click on the Include button on the Chat toolbar. The Include File into Pad dialog box will appear.

3. Browse through folders until you find the file you want to send. Click on Open and the contents of the text file will appear on the Chat Tool Personal Note Pad.

4. Click on the Chat toolbar's Send button to send the text file you've just included to the person you're talking to. The file will be included in your and the other person's log file.

Once the text file appears in the log window, you can both edit it, add to it, and save it.

Saving Your Log File

Now that you and your friend have uploaded a text file and edited it to perfection, you need to save it for later use.

1. Before you close your chat session, click on the Save button. Or, to ensure you're saving the file where you can find it later, use the Conference menu bar and select File ➤ Save As. The Save As dialog box will appear.

2. Name your file, and when you're done, click on the Save button. You'll return to the Conference Text Chat window, where you can continue or sign off.

That's really about all you need to know. Happy chatting!

◆ When You Need to Present Visuals: The Whiteboard

Sometimes it's convenient to be able to eyeball the thing(s) you're hearing about, and sometimes you just have to draw a picture (which is, after all, worth a lot of words). Conference's whiteboard lets you and anyone you're talking to via Conference share images and even mark on them. If you like, you can use Conference's whiteboard while you're talking to someone, but using it while you're chatting with someone is tough because you have to keep switching back and forth between the Chat and Whiteboard windows. And, just in case you're interested, it's possible for both people talking to mark up the whiteboard at the same time. Sometimes there's a lag when you're doing this, but so what if it takes a few seconds for your mark-ups to appear?

The Conference whiteboard (Figure 6.5) resembles many PC paint programs.

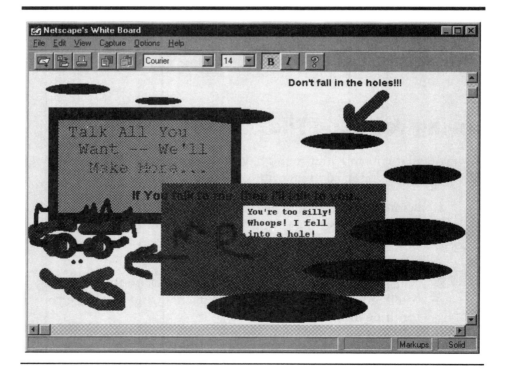

Figure 6.5: The Conference whiteboard offers a drawing area that can be seen by others thousands of miles away via the Internet.

Using the buttons on the toolbar at the top of the Whiteboard window, you can import graphics files (scanned photos, logos, etc.) and save and/or print the contents of the whiteboard. Here's a quick overview of the tools on the whiteboard's toolbar:

The Tool	Its Name	What You Can Do with It
	Open File	Open a graphics file so the person you're talking to can see it on the whiteboard
	Save File	Save the contents of the whiteboard
	Print	Print the contents of the whiteboard
	Copy Bitmap	Copy a Windows bitmap file to the whiteboard
	Paste Bitmap	Paste a Windows bitmap file to the whiteboard
Courier	Font Box	Change the typeface of text on the whiteboard
18	Point Size Box	Change the size of text typed onto the whiteboard
A	Bold	Make text on the whiteboard appear in boldface
A	Italic	Make text on the whiteboard appear in italics

Using the markup tools in the whiteboard's toolbox (we'll introduce you to these shortly), you can mark up an existing image by drawing or painting on it, adding text to it, or pointing to a part of it. You can also draw on the whiteboard, doodling to your heart's content.

Getting the Whiteboard Up and Running

Getting the whiteboard up and running will seem quite natural if you've already checked out Conference's telephone and chat features.

1. Connect to the Internet as you usually do.

2. From the Windows 95 Start menu, select Programs ➤ Netscape Communicator ➤ Netscape Conference. The main Conference window (Figure 6.1) will appear. If you'd like to use the Conference whiteboard while you're talking to someone, first start talking to him or her. (See the section called "Start Talking to a Friend" earlier in this chapter.) Or, you can doodle for your own amusement.

3. On the Conference main window's toolbar, click on the Whiteboard button (the one with the picture of a sketchbook) to kickstart the whiteboard.

4. Doodle away, using these nifty tools:

The Tool	Its Name	What It Lets You Do
✏️	Freehand Line	Draw a line in any shape you like
▱	Eraser	Erase the area specified by your click-and-drag motion
▢	Rectangle	Draw a rectangle
▣	Filled Rectangle	Draw a filled rectangle
◯	Circle	Draw a circle

The Tool	Its Name	What It Lets You Do
	Filled Circle	Draw a filled circle
	Pointer	Point to something in particular on the whiteboard
	Text	Type text onto the whiteboard
	Line	Draw a straight line
	Vertical/ Horizontal Line	Draw a straight (vertical or horizontal) line

Especially if you've used a PC paint program, these controls probably feel pretty natural under your fingers.

Importing and Marking Up an Existing Image

If you've got a graphics file on hand that you'd desperately like your Conference buddy to see, you're in luck—it's no sweat to import an existing image and then, if you like, mark it up. The whiteboard is comfy with these graphics file formats: Windows bitmap (.bmp), CompuServe GIF (.gif), Zsoft Paintbrush (.pcx), TIFF Revision 5 (.tif), JPEG (.jpg), Sun Raster, and TARGA. If your image is in another format, convert it to one the whiteboard supports before importing it.

Follow these steps to share your favorite images:

1. Start the whiteboard by following steps 1–3 in "Getting the Whiteboard Up and Running."

2. From the whiteboard's menu bar, select File ➤ Open. The Open dialog box will appear.

(continued on the next page)

3. Locate the graphics file and click on Open. The file will appear in the Conference window, first as a dotted-line image.

4. Click and drag the outline to where you'd like the image to appear and then click the left mouse button. (Alternatively, you can press Shift to preview the image where it will appear, or you can click the right mouse button to cancel this operation altogether.)

Feel free to use those handy markup tools to alter the image (your friend probably will).

Closing the Whiteboard

When all is said and done, to close the whiteboard, follow this simple step:

1. From the whiteboard menu bar, select File ➤ Close.

You'll still have Conference open—you can talk or chat or close up shop.

◆ Surf Together With Collaborative Browsing

There's a lot of stuff on the Web. Wouldn't it be nice if you could get a guided tour of just Web sites you're likely to be interested in? Or, if you're on your way to being a Web guru, you might like to show someone your new Web page, or a series of sites you're interested in. It's all well and good to ask the guy in the next cube to show you some stuff, but what if your daughter in Paris is the one with all the know-how? Netscape Conference's Collaborative Browsing tool lets two or more users connected via Conference surf the Web together, no matter how far apart they are.

Getting Collaborative Browsing going is easy:

1. Make sure that you have your Internet connection going and both Conference and Navigator open. From the Conference window, call a friend as you normally would.

2. On the Conference toolbar, click on the Collaborative Browsing button (it shows two little identical Navigator windows). The Collaborative Browsing tool will appear, as shown in Figure 6.6.

3. If you want to lead the browsing session, click on Control the Browsers. If not, make sure that you've unchecked this option so that your friend can run the session.

Figure 6.6: The Collaborative Browsing tool lets you sync your surfing with a friend.

4. To make sure you're both starting in the same place, click on Sync Browsers.

5. To start your browsing session, click on Start Browsing.

6. Now, for the browsing part, you need to switch back and forth between the Netscape Navigator browsing window and the Netscape Conference Collaborative Browsing tool. This is easy: Just open a Web page in the Navigator window by typing its URL into the location text box, using a bookmark, or clicking on a link. Every time you move to a new Web page, so will the friend you're connected with via Conference. If your friend is the one leading the session, they'll do the clicking, while you do the watching. All you have to do then is keep Navigator open—you can hide the Browsing tool if you like.

7. When you're ready to end the session, display the Collaborative Browsing Tool window and click on Stop Browsing. You can start another session, or you can click on Close. The Collaborative Browsing tool will close, returning you to the main Conference window, where you can talk, chat, or use the whiteboard. Or, you can hang up entirely.

That's all there is to it.

◆ Share Files with Minimal Effort

Generally, sharing files with people to whom you can't easily hand a floppy disk requires placing the files on an FTP server. That's all well and good, if you want to make the files public to the whole world, or if you have the system administration know-how to assign accounts and privileges (you don't really want to give away your own password). Now, we wouldn't just taunt you and tell you that you can't share files over the Internet, because you can. Netscape Conference includes a File Exchange tool that makes sharing files easier than making toast.

Making Your Own Files Available

Not only do you not have to know much about FTP to use the File Exchange tool, you only have to transfer the file once. With normal FTP, first you have to upload the file to a server, and then your friend needs to download it from the same server. Using File Exchange, you can transfer the file directly to your friend's computer. This is a breeze:

1. With both your Internet connection and Netscape Conference up and running, dial the person with whom you want to share your files.

2. From the Conference toolbar, click on the File Exchange button (it's the one that shows a little file with an arrow whisking it over the wires). The File Exchange Tool window will appear, as seen in Figure 6.7.

3. First thing you need to do once the File Exchange tool is open is set up the transfer. If the document you want to send is just text, select Options ➤ Ascii from the File Exchange menu bar. If the document you want to send is anything other than plain text, including a word-processed document, select Options ➤ Binary from the File Exchange menu bar. This will keep the blips from becoming blops.

4. To choose the file you want to send, click on the Open button. The Add File to Send List dialog box will appear.

5. Browse through your hard drive and select the file you want to send. When your file is selected, click on Open. The Add File to Send List dialog box will close, returning you to the main File Exchange Tool window. You should see the name of the file listed in the Files to Send area of the window.

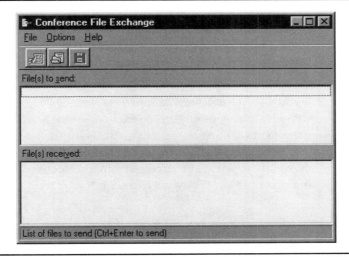

Figure 6.7: The File Exchange tool lets you send a file directly from your computer to your friend's.

6. Repeat steps 4 and 5 until you've selected all the files you want to send to your friend. When you're ready to actually transfer the files, click on the File Exchange Tool window's Send button. The Sending File dialog box will appear, informing you of the progress of the transfer.

When the transfer is complete (and it may take a while, depending on the size of the files), the Sending File dialog box will close and return you to the File Exchange Tool window. You may want to ask your friend (via the Conference phone or the Conference Chat tool) to confirm that he or she received what you sent.

Receiving Files with the File Exchange Tool

If you're the one receiving files rather than sending them, your role in the procedure mainly involves being online and waiting. Just follow this simple step:

1. Make sure you're online and running Conference. You'll receive a call from your friend, who will probably tell you one way or another that he or she is going to send you a file. Just open the File Exchange tool.

When your friend starts sending the file, you'll see a Receiving File dialog box. When you're finished, you'll see the name of the files you've received in the Files Received area of the File Exchange tool.

What could be easier? You didn't even have to click anything!

 If you want to receive files sent your way while you're busy doing something else, open the File Exchange tool and, from its menu bar, select Options ➤ Pop Up on Receive. This way, as long as you're running Conference when the file is sent your way, the File Exchange tool will automatically open to receive and inform you of the names of the files you were sent.

What's Out There

If you still have questions about Conference, see Netscape's helpful Conference FAQ page: `http://help.netscape.com/faqs/conference.html`. This handy tipsheet includes detailed information about troubleshooting audio and networking problems.

Talk, Chat, Draw!

Now that you know how to use Conference's telephone capabilities and you've been introduced to its Chat tool and whiteboard, collaborative browsing, and file sharing tools, it's time to take a look at another plug-in that comes with the standard version of Netscape: Live3D. Hold onto your hat, because we're off to explore the wild world of virtual reality. VRooM.

Experiencing Live Content

There's a lot more to Web pages these days than text and images. We remember when making fonts different sizes and colors was the height of cool; these days, a Web page can practically balance your checkbook and cook dinner for you. Okay, maybe not quite. A lot of the biggest hype about the Internet has to do with the non-Web aspects of the Web: live content that makes your browser dance, sing, roll over (and sometimes play dead). For our purposes, live content is stuff that moves. You've heard of Java, and we're going to try to explain to you *why* it's so cool and what you can expect from it. We'll also talk about the difference between client-side toys and server-side toys (er, we mean technologies). And last, but not least, we'll give you the skinny on navigating virtual worlds with VRML, the closest thing to three dimensions that you can get on a computer screen.

 Multimedia stuff like Shockwave, QuickTime, and RealAudio can be every bit as cool as Java and VRML. In this chapter, we're going to cover the bleeding edge technologies that make your browser window into something else entirely: a host for other mini-programs that enable you to interact with other computers (and other computer users) with so much movement, you'll get motion sickness.

◆ Types of Live Content

Java, JavaScript, ActiveX, client pull, server push, VRML—sounds like the recipe for some Top Secret government documents that could compromise national security. Don't worry, those are just the latest technologies that make your Web browser a remote control for active technologies all over the world. We'll take a look at each kind, and explain what the difference is between them. Hold onto your hats—your Web experience will never be the same again.

Client Side, Server Side: What's the Diff?

First we have to slow down a little bit and explain what these things do and how they work. We learned a little bit about clients and servers in Chapter 2. The server, as you may recall, is the computer elsewhere on the Internet or your company's intranet that stores and delivers data (data being Web pages and all the wonderful things attached to them). On the other end of the chain, the client is the piece of software on your own computer that you use to request this data (i.e., you click on a link, and the client, a.k.a. Communicator, goes and finds the server and asks it for information).

Client-side applications are programs or processes that take place locally, on your machine. In this way, your machine does much of the work involved in an animation or other live content, thus letting the server do its thing and deliver Web pages to other people. *Server-side* technologies, on the other hand, take place on the Web server out there in cyberspace. The same machine that spends much of its day delivering Web pages all over the world can also perform many other functions you may request, such as searching, processing information, or delivering additional data to a Web page. This data can be in the form of animation, multimedia, sound, and the like, in addition to text and numbers, which is usually how we think of data. Figure 7.1 shows a face created in a server-side program.

It's not a difficult concept: If an application is client-side, your PC does the work. If it's server-side, the Web server does the work and delivers it to your computer as soon as it can. Some kinds of data are better done by the client, and some by the server. For example, search engines (as described in Chapter 8), require a lot of computing power—in some cases, the combined efforts of several large computers at once. The kind of hard work involved in searching the entire Internet is best done by big computers that can handle the job. In comparison, small-scale tasks such as those performed by news tickers, calculators, and clocks are frivolous. This kind of small fry work can be done by a junior computer like the one you have on your desk—these are client-side tasks that you can try at home.

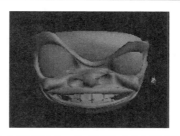

Figure 7.1: FaceMaker lets you design your own monster heads.

To give you some context for some client-side and server-side programs you may run into: RealAudio is a server-side program that pushes streams of audio to your computer a bit at a time. Shockwave, on the other hand, is a client-side application that downloads an entire program (in the form of a Shockwave file) to your PC before it becomes operational. Once you've downloaded it, you can click on it, play games with it, and hear sounds without the server having to do another blooming thing (until you click on the next link).

 One kind of server-side programming is called CGI, or Common Gateway Interface. CGI programming is incredibly versatile and can be used for anything from updating guest books to running interactive games to creating new text or live content based on a computer program. A common use of CGI is the "whatever server," which dishes out randomly selected content at the touch of a button. CGI programs generally work behind the scenes (on the server side); sometimes you can tell you're experiencing a CGI program if your URL ends in .CGI or .PL, or if the URL contains the phrase CGI-BIN.

What's Out There

If you want to see just how far server-side programs can go, pay a visit to FaceMaker, at http://zeppo.cs.ubc.ca:5656/ (see Figure 7.1). This online program lets you edit and create new faces based on 3-D models. You can make the faces as pictures or VRML environments.

To experience some of the nuttiest randomization this side of reality, visit the Surrealism Server, at http://pharmdec.wustl.edu/juju/surr/surrealism.html.

Pushing the Envelope: Netcaster and Push Media

The word of the hour on the Internet these days is "push." "Server push," in terms of Web content and interactivity, can mean anything that's delivered by the server without an explicit request on the user's part before each delivery event. "Push media," on the other hand, refers more specifically to interactive content that's delivered in chunks, on a schedule, according to the user's preferences.

In the regular Web model, people who are interested in certain topics need to seek them out independently in order to find what they're looking for. For example, imagine that Sheila is interested in physics, affirmative action, and Antonio Banderas. She will probably conduct several Internet searches on her areas of interest, and bookmark the best or most relevant pages. Every so often, she checks these pages to see what, if anything, has been added to them.

Sheila also checks general news sites to find any new stories about affirmative action. This entails visits to a few big news sites—say, CNN and FOX News—in which she must open the home page and then comb the site for any relevant information. Sheila regularly checks the home pages of the most active university physics programs for new developments, and the Web sites of major entertainment magazines for any pictures or stories on Antonio Banderas.

Now, Sheila has to spend a lot of time searching the Web to find what probably amounts to a few news items a week. Wouldn't it be nice if she could program a little Web VCR to record only those items of interest? Each time Sheila logged onto the Net, her little Net butler would tell her how many new items were available about her stocks, her favorite stars, and the issues that are important to her. Enter the "push" model of content delivery. (Well, actually, it's more like "scheduled pull," but everyone's calling it "push" and we bow to the swell of public opinion.)

(continued on next page)

Many push delivery programs, such as Pointcast, Intermind Communicator, and Netscape's Netcaster (an upcoming component of Netscape Communicator), ask the user to register a profile that specifies a number of details, including personal and financial interests, demographic information, and favorite Web sites. These programs then venture out onto the Web while the user is busy doing other things, and retrieve only those items that are relevant to the user's specified preferences. Many such programs call their delivery methods "channels," because they're based on the premise that people would like to be able to design their own television channels that would show only stuff that they wanted to see.

Netcaster's final design is in development as we write; you can see what a public beta of Netcaster looked like when this book went to press in Figure 7.2. Currently, Netcaster is comprised of channels customized for delivery by popular Web sites. Rather than surfing through an entire site every time you log onto the Web, these channels only load items that have changed since your last visit.

Although few programs available today get as specific as Sheila (and we) would like, the idea is that people would rather have a personal robot fetch or send items of interest than track these things down on their own. Some argue that this will in effect make the Web more like television (and thus, less interactive), but "push" is definitely a field to watch.

What's Out There

Find out all about Netscaster, including how to install it if your version of Communicator doesn't include it, by visiting `http://home.netscape.com/comprod/products/communicator/netcaster.html`.

For updated information on the latest Netcaster release, go to the Sybex Web site at `http://www.sybex.com` and click on Updates.

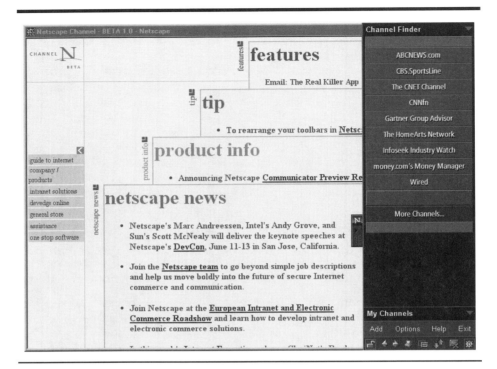

Figure 7.2:   This beta version of Netcaster is made up of channels customized for delivery by popular Web sites.

Client Pulls and Server Pushes

Client pulls are written right into the code of the Web page, and they are used to automatically request information from a Web server without the person using the browser having to do anything. Pages that automatically reload, or that automatically load a new image or send you to a new Web page, are using client pull.

Server pushes, on the other hand, operate on the Web server's end. The server sends some data to the Web browser, but instead of closing the connection, as it does for regular old Web pages, it leaves the client-server connection open and sends more data whenever it feels like it. Server pushes are used for a variety of functions, with animation being one highly visible use. Server push animation isn't used as often now that

GIF89 animation has become common (see "Dancing Puppies and Flying Envelopes," later in this chapter), but it's still a pretty versatile option available to innovative Webmasters.

What's Out There

To see an example of client pull in action, take the LA Rock & Roll Slide Show Tour, which we found at `http://net101.com/rocknroll/index.html`. For a continuous client pull demo and a bunch of giggles, try the Punchline Server, at `http://www.paranoia.com/~sorabji/blink/punchlines/`.

Two great examples of server push animation are the incredibly creative Word, found at `http://www.word.com/`, and Razorfish, at `http://www.razorfish.com/` (the Blue Dot is especially nice). Many of the zany animations on both of these sites wouldn't be possible without server push.

For some great examples of animations of all kinds, pay a visit to the Micro Movie Mini Multiplex (MMMM), which we found at `http://www.teleport.com/~cooler/MMMM/MMMM.html`.

Dancing Puppies and Flying Envelopes: GIF89a Images

Back when CompuServe invented the GIF (Graphical Image Format), they intended it to be an image type that could be compressed into a fairly small filesize, print easily, and still hold a lot of image information. When the specifications for the GIF format were updated to version GIF89a, the capabilities were expanded to include things such as transparency, layering, and animation, but until the advent of the Web, no one had much use for GIFs as anything other than static pictures on the screen.

GIF89s, as they're often called, support the transparent images that allow a picture to seamlessly blend into a colored background. They also support animated GIFs, which are basically a mini slide-show, or a stack of digital images, that Netscape "plays" like a flipbook. The images that dance over and over are generally "looped" GIF89s that are set to play the same animation over and over again. You can see three frames of a GIF89 in Figure 7.3.

(continued on next page)

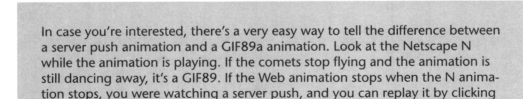

In case you're interested, there's a very easy way to tell the difference between a server push animation and a GIF89a animation. Look at the Netscape N while the animation is playing. If the comets stop flying and the animation is still dancing away, it's a GIF89. If the Web animation stops when the N animation stops, you were watching a server push, and you can replay it by clicking on the Reload button.

Figure 7.3: This puppy dances because it's an animated GIF.

What's Out There

Our favorite gallery of animated GIFs is Addicted to Showing Off With Animated GIFs, at `http://www.morestuff.com/anima/a2anim.htm`. That's where we got the puppy shown in Figure 7.3.

You can find out how to build your own GIF89a animations at Royal Frazier's GIF Animation page, which is the one that started the whole craze. It's at `http://members.aol.com/royalef/`.

Client Side: Java, JavaScript, OLE, and ActiveX

As we told you earlier, client-side applications, once downloaded, are completely functional without having to talk to the server they came from. These applications range in power and function, and they do need to have network access for some of the more interactive features like person-to-person communications. Perhaps the best thing about client-side Internet technologies is that they're small—and they're fairly close to platform-independent.

Get a Jolt from Java

You've doubtless heard lots about Java and how it's going to revolutionize the Web. Java isn't any one program or tool; it's a programming language developed by Sun Microsystems that enables a vast new frontier of interactivity. Using Java, developers can create little applications, called *applets*, that can be embedded in HTML documents or launched by Communicator to run alongside your Web browser. The reason why everyone's so excited about Java is that most of these applets don't take more than a minute or two to download and, once they're on your computer, they don't need to talk to the server in order to run (although they might talk to the server during the course of an especially interactive process).

Okay, so what does that mean for you? Let's say a programmer creates a Java calculator. Once you download this calculator, you can punch in all your figures and the calculator doesn't have to ask the main server what the answer to 2 plus 2 is: All the information it needs is right there in that little tiny program. We found a Java abacus that not only adds up numbers, but animates the beads of an abacus while it's doing so (see Figure 7.4). The potential of Java applets is almost boundless, especially given the fact that Java is theoretically platform-independent, which means that a Windows user, a Macintosh user, and a Unix user can all use the same program, and its appearance and performance will be exactly the same.

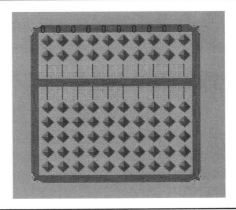

Figure 7.4:   This Java abacus is somewhat of an anachronism, but it does the math.

Aside from calculators, programmers create dazzling effects such as animation that might be used in games or for illustrations; ticker tape feeds for news, sports, and stock data; real-time interactivity that can be used for anything from crossword puzzles to the sharing of medical data; and handy gadgets such as mouse pointers that change shape when you drag them over something. Java can also be used to create interfaces to database servers—which are used in almost every Internet shopping environment. Creating Java applets requires a fairly high level of programming knowledge and, as such, is beyond the skill level of most non-programmers.

What's Out There

Everything you ever wanted to know about Java you can find at Gamelan (`http://www.gamelan.com/`).

Take a visit to Sun, the home of JavaSoft, to read the latest: `http://java .sun.com/`. If you want to see groovy applets and you couldn't give a pickle for how they work, try the JavaSoft gallery, at `http://www.javasoft.com/ applets/`, or head to Yahoo!'s Java Applets directory at `http://www.yahoo .com/Computers_and_Internet/Programming_Languages/Java/Applets/`. That's where we found the Java Abacus, whose URL is `http://www.ee.ryerson .ca:8080/~elf/abacus/`.

JavaScript Acts Up, No Downloading Required

JavaScript is *not* the same as Java, although the uninformed often confuse the two because the names are so similar. They are not, in fact, the same thing at all. *JavaScript* is nothing more than a means for writing macros, while *Java* is a fully developed programming language. (This means JavaScript can be used by mere mortals.) Netscape Communications Corporation developed JavaScript under another name before the birth of Java, and when Sun invented Java, Netscape renamed what they were working on to align it in the minds of millions with Java, which was a very hot property.

While Java allows programmers to create applets that users like you download via Navigator, JavaScript lets folks embed JavaScript code within the code for the Web page itself. This means there is no extra download time involved in experiencing JavaScript stuff beyond the time it takes to load the Web page itself. JavaScript can do lots of nifty things that aid in navigation and page design.

For example, people have used JavaScript to make pop-up menus within a Web page that take you to another part of a Web site; to control the way a page loads within a site that uses frames; to change colors as you move through a site; to create buttons that move you from place to place; and to make messages appear when you perform certain actions while surfing. Many of the best uses of JavaScript are like this—they enhance or improve the way you navigate through a site.

 JavaScript can also be used for creating applets such as clocks and calculators, just as Java can. Once the task gets much more complex, however, it generally exceeds JavaScript's capabilities.

One clever use of JavaScript can be seen in *kiosk* mode. When you load a Kiosk page, a new Navigator window launches that has a specific size and shape determined by the designer; it often doesn't use scrollbars, status bars, or toolbars; or it might have its own toolbars for navigating the Web site. A kiosk window (see Figure 7.5) can contain pictures, links, Java, or plug-ins—in short, anything a standard Web page can include.

What's Out There

Two sites that make excellent use of JavaScript for the kiosk effect are Entropy8, at `http://www.entropy8.com/`, and the Triple W Ranch, at `http://ubinfo.pub .buffalo.edu/Chuck/`. Both of these sites are quite beautiful.

Another clever use of JavaScript is the site at `http://www.homepages.com/ fun/1040EZ.html` that helps you fill out your EZ tax form using JavaScript.

If you want to make some of your own JavaScript tools, Netscape's JavaScript Authoring Guide resides at `http://home.netscape.com/eng/mozilla/ Gold/handbook/javascript/index.html`. You can find a lot more JavaScript sites in Yahoo!'s JavaScript listings: `http://www.yahoo.com/ Computers_and_Internet/Programming_Languages/JavaScript/`.

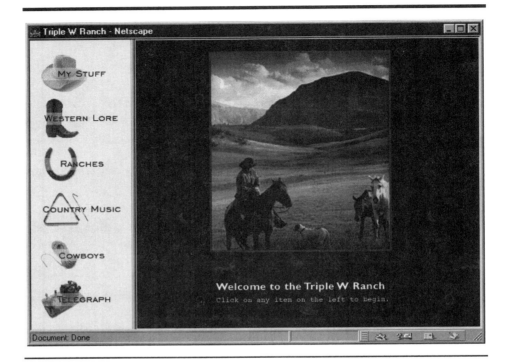

Figure 7.5: The Triple W Ranch launches a gorgeous kiosk to aid your navigation.

Ye Olde OLE Gets a Boost From the Web

OLE stands for Object Linking and Embedding—and that sounds kind of like Web pages, doesn't it? Microsoft invented OLE a few years ago, and it may be best known as what makes dragging and dropping work in Windows 95. Until OLE was developed, it was nearly impossible to use a piece of information (such as a pie chart or a spreadsheet) that was created in one program available in another program (such as a word processing document). Now it's possible to click on something in one program and have it automatically launch another program, or even to have a document include data created in several different programs.

What this means to Web pages is that it's theoretically possible to embed not only Java programs, but pieces of OLE-compatible programs, such as spreadsheets, databases, charts and graphs, word processing documents, and other such things you just can't do with straight HTML. If your Web browser is OLE-compatible, in theory you can put other OLE-type data into HTML documents that will be read by your browser (in this case, Netscape Navigator), *no matter what platform you're using.* Other possible applications include sharing networked data on an intranet using Web browsers as the go-between, as well as automating tasks using your browser. The concept of using OLE Internet-wide is fairly new to the world of computing; the most widespread use of it so far is ActiveX, another Microsoft child. That brings us to the next section, which covers ActiveX.

What's Out There

There isn't much on the Internet right now about OLE that isn't written for programmers, but if you want a brief overview, read "What Is OLE?," which we found at `http://www.microsoft.com/oledev/olemkt/oleis.htm`. That page is a part of Microsoft's OLE Development site, which is at `http://www.microsoft.com/oledev/` if you're interested in learning more.

Activate Your Browser with Active Platform

Active Platform is the new breed of OLE technology that's being used for everything from games to graphics to data processing—all on the Web. Microsoft, which started pushing Active Platform in a big way with the introduction of Internet Explorer 3, is touting Active Platform as a platform-independent engine for multimedia and Internet transactions. Active Platform can be programmed to work with Java, but it's more of an extender to existing programming languages than a standalone programming tool.

There are two primary components of Active Platform. ActiveX controls are like Java applets or Netscape plug-ins. They're the little programs that can be embedded in Web pages or launched to run in tandem with your Web browser. Active Platform documents are OLE documents, such as Microsoft Word documents or Excel spreadsheets, that can be read and even edited through a Web browser. The other pieces of the Active Platform family are tools that allow programmers to string together applications and documents using Active Platform (written in Visual Basic and Visual Studio) as the connecting tissue.

Okay, so why should you care? Because Active Platform is being used right now to create dynamic and colorful multimedia content that you can look at right in the Netscape window. Using Active Platform, you can play chess head-to-head over the Internet, watch movies or listen to music in your browser window, create your own Web pages with an Active Platform Web authoring tool, or analyze corporate data with a point-and-click interface. Most any control you'll find useful can be downloaded from ActiveX.com.

What's Out There

The best site out there for both learning about Active Platform and downloading ActiveX controls is ActiveX.com, which, as you might figure, is at `http://www.activex.com/`. This great site is another gift to you from CNET, the Computer Network. Of course, you'll also want to check out Microsoft's ActiveX Resource Area, at `http://www.microsoft.com/activeplatform/`.

Interacting with Live Content

There isn't much to interacting with live content. In the case of animations, for example, you just watch them (although you can click on the Stop button to halt some of the particularly tenacious ones). In the case of server push and client pull, you don't even need to click your mouse to enjoy the interactivity. CGI sites can be really creative in their participatory content; you may be asked to type some text into boxes, click on buttons or check checkboxes. There will generally be a clearly marked button called Send or Post or Get Info or something similar that indicates that, if you push it, something will happen.

Java and ActiveX may or may not be obvious. Scrolling text isn't always Java, and miniature spawning windows could be Java, JavaScript, Active Platform, or all three in action. Often, if a site uses technology you can't figure out at first glance (as in, it involves more than links and buttons), there will be a clearly marked help file that you can refer to that often appears in the form of a "download our new toys" link.

Java and ActiveX Controls: What's the Risk?

In the buzz surrounding new Internet technologies, one word continues to surface as both a boon and a risk: security. While new measures ensuring secure transactions are being perfected, some of the new interactive technologies are adding new risks to plain vanilla Internet surfing.

Both Java and ActiveX pose some risks to the sanctity of your personal computer (or your office network). The very versatility that makes Java applets and ActiveX controls able to work their interactive magic leaves your computer vulnerable to attacks from evil applets and conniving controls. It is even possible for JavaScript to retrieve some information about you and the files on your computer and send it back to the server from whence it came.

So what's a concerned netizen to do in order to protect not only the privacy of their personal data, but the viability of their computer itself? Nefarious programmers could theoretically write executables (another word for programs) that can open a DOS window and systematically replace or delete system files, or plant viruses that launch and do pretty much the same thing.

Two means of easing your mind and protecting your computer are being implemented. Chances are that companies like Netscape and Microsoft are more reliable than Joe Schmoe from Boise. (For one thing, Joe Schmoe might be hard to track down and sue.) What these large companies want to do is use *digital signatures* that cannot be tampered with. These signatures would let you know that this applet was created by a certain company on a certain day using certain safety measures. You can tell Netscape that you only want to accept *signed applets;* so when you begin to download an applet or an ActiveX control that's requesting write access to your computer (or another risky behavior), up pops a warning message (see Figure 7.6) that lets you choose whether to allow this risk, er, program, onto your computer.

Of course, you always have the option of saying no. If you want to disable Java or JavaScript, open Navigator, and from the menu bar, select Edit ➤ Preferences. In the Category area, click on Advanced, and from there, you can deselect Java or JavaScript (or both) by unchecking the relevant checkboxes with a click of the mouse.

You can read more about security and certificates in Chapter 5.

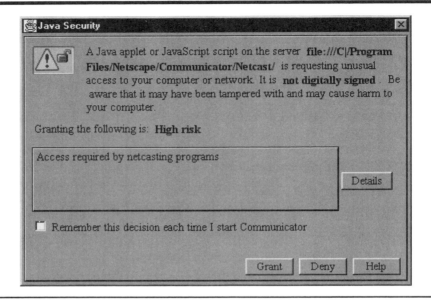

Figure 7.6: The Security dialog box allows you to refuse Java applets from unknown sources.

Netscape and Sun Duke It Out with Microsoft: The Battle of the Browsers

Okay, so Sun Microsystems, a large workstation and network computing company, invented Java in 1995. This was followed shortly by Netscape's launch of JavaScript, which had a disconcertingly similar name. Please note that Netscape, the software, was invented by Marc Andreessen, who was part of the team that originally developed Mosaic, the first graphical Web browser. By this time, Microsoft realized that their fingers weren't in the Internet pie, so they launched Internet Explorer. Both Netscape Navigator and Microsoft Internet Explorer then integrated Java capabilities into their browsers, which made HotJava, Sun's Java-equipped Web browser, all but obsolete. Version 3 of Internet Explorer incorporated JavaScript and two other Netscape inventions, plug-ins and frames (as well as other Netscape-specific HTML tags). That same browser also launched ActiveX,

(continued on the next page)

which made Microsoft's OLE technology Internet-capable. Now it's Round 4 in the battle of the browsers, and this go-round has Netscape incorporating Active-Platform into their browser. Where will it all end?

If it sounds confusing, that's because it is. The whole darned computing industry is confused, wondering about the difference between browsers and gawking at the speed with which new versions are released. Meanwhile, Sun and Netscape are both trying to figure out how to get around Microsoft's dominance of the desktop computing industry. Microsoft Windows 95 is on about 80 percent of the world's desktops, and nobody's happy about that but Microsoft. Sun has released a prototype of a desktop machine that would be entirely network-based and would use Java for all its applications, thus circumventing the need for a memory-intensive operating system such as Windows. And Netcaster, from Netscape, is another intriguing step into the desktop arena (see "Pushing the Envelope: Netcaster and Push Media," earlier in this chapter). We don't know if there are going to be winners or losers in this game, but we do know that there must be an awful lot of exhausted programmers out there. In the meantime, just sit back and start clicking, because nobody's going to have any exclusive technologies for very long.

◆ Navigating Virtual Space with Live3D: VRML

Imagine, if you will, entering three-dimensional worlds in which you can interact with what's happening on your screen, perhaps by walking through a representation of a house you're considering buying. Imagine playing a multiuser online game that's not just visually stunning but navigable—imagine that in this game you traverse a three-dimensional universe. Imagine virtually touring the inside of your computer!

Okay, now stop imagining, and get real, because the standard version of Netscape Communicator comes with Live3D, a happening VRML viewer. Take a look at Figure 7.7 to see a freeze-frame representation of a VRML site.

We'll show you around VRML in coming sections, and we'll define terms so that you'll understand all the technical jargon that goes along with virtual reality. By the time we're through, you'll be able to amaze and amuse your friends with your knowledge of the spaciest thing in cyberspace.

What's Out There

One really exciting VRML 2.0 site is Square USA's Dungeon of VRML, in which you walk a character through a maze in search of the magical sphere (see Figure 7.7). The URL is easier to find: `http://www.sqla.com/~shiro/VRML/`.

One of the first VRML sites, Virtual SOMA, is still one of the best. Stroll through the streets of San Francisco's South of Market district by visiting `http://www.planet9.com/vrsoma.htm`. Incidentally, this part of San Francisco is where a good portion of the multimedia content on the Internet is produced.

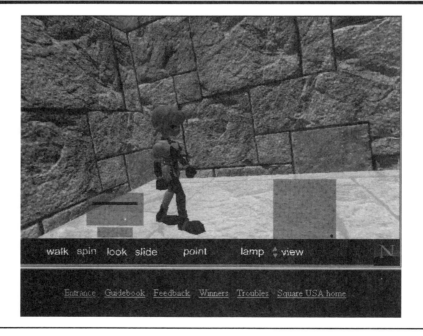

Figure 7.7:   Follow Tina on her quest through the Dungeon of VRML.

 If a site asks you to choose between several versions of its VRML world, fear not. Live3D supports both VRML 1.0 and VRML 2.0, so you can visit either. Of course, you can also choose the worlds that are optimized for Live3D, if that choice is offered.

◆ A Short Lowdown on Virtual Reality

Live3D is your ticket to the amazing world of virtual reality. But what is virtual reality? Virtual reality, or VR, is what you get when programmers use computers to model, or re-create, reality as we know it. This results, of course, in 3-D images. The thing is, those wacky virtual reality programmers don't just confine their efforts to re-creating reality—they sometimes create alternative realities. Fans of the latest Star Trek series are undoubtedly familiar with holodecks, which are places where members of the crew can go to unwind by living out a fantasy of their choice. Well, virtual reality is supposed to be the same kind of thing, and although Live3D can't yet equal the experience of being in a holodeck (where you're surrounded by the sights, smells, and sounds of your fantasy), it's as close as most of us are likely to come, at least for now.

Actually, virtual reality philosophers would say that virtual reality is much more than cool 3-D images—that it represents a fundamental change in the nature of a computer's user interface, moving it to a more human-centered design. They believe that the space around the user should become the computing environment and that the entire *sensorium* (a fancy word for all five senses) should be engaged in the interface. They go on to say that virtual reality was created in an effort to make computers more responsive to the humans who used them and that it focused around a basic realization: if something is represented sensually, it is possible to make sense of it. Perhaps this is true; we'll let you be the judge of that once you've had a chance to experience virtual reality for yourself.

 Let the browser beware: VRML sites, like all Web sites, vary widely in quality. A badly coded VRML site may crash your browser inexplicably, and unfortunately, you may not know that a site is unwieldy until it has started loading. As a safeguard, you shouldn't try surfing VRML sites unless you have 16MB of RAM or more.

◆ Just What Is VRML?

In the words of its creator, Mark Pesce, VRML (Virtual Reality Modeling Language) is a language for describing multiuser interactive simulations. Say what? Put in terms that we can all understand, VRML is the computer language used by clever programmers who've got lots of time to fiddle around (and lots of expensive computer equipment for fiddling) to create the 3-D images that characterize so-called virtual worlds. In Web-speak, a virtual world (sometimes just called a "world" by those in the know) is a Web site that contains 3-D images of places and/or things created using VRML. Some virtual worlds also include an audio component that you can access if you've got a compatible audio plug-in, but at the moment, these sites are relatively few and far between—sound, as we say elsewhere in this book, takes mucho memory and the amount of information necessary to provide both 3-D images and sound is incredibly huge.

What's Out There

You can catch Mark Pesce all over the Net. He moderates the VRML mailing list. To join, send mail to www-vrml-request@vag.vrml.org with the command subscribe as the only word in the body of your message. Mark's home page is at http://www.hyperreal.com/~mpesce/. And he's got lots to say about VRML in the VRML Hypermail Archive (http://vag.vrml.org/www-vrml/arch/).

As long as we're defining terms, let's add one more to the mix: a WRL (pronounced "whirl") file is the collection of data (that is, of VRML code) that describes a virtual world. That's enough technical mumbo-jumbo for now; let's get on to what VRML and virtual worlds are good for.

Netscape Communicator 4 uses Live3D 2, which complies with the VRML 2.0 specifications. What this means is more animation, more interactivity, and enhanced movement capabilities. These worlds are more colorful than VRML 1.0 worlds, and they can also incorporate embedded textures and video. Some VRML 2.0 worlds allow the user to "walk" and "fly" in addition to spinning and clicking. For a demonstration of how VRML 2.0 works, fly on over to the VRML Consortium.

What's Out There

If you do want more in the way of tech talk, as well as a bunch of virtual places to visit, then check out the VRML Consortium (a.k.a. VRML.org), a resource page at (guess what?) `http://www.vrml.org/`. Or try the VRML Repository at the San Diego Supercomputer Center, one of the premier resources for VRML. The central URL there is `http://www.sdsc.edu/vrml/`.

Techies who want lots o' links on this topic should hop on over to 3DSite's VRML Links page, which we found at `http://www.3dsite.com/cgi/VRML-index.html`.

What VRML Is Good For

Okay, so VRML is terribly cool, the freshest idea since word processing, but what the heck can you actually do with the thing? Let's take a look at areas of human endeavor that lend themselves easily to this new medium.

Education   Simulations of objects or situations that are otherwise difficult to see may become an important component of education. For example, medical students can brush up on their anatomy and "practice" surgical procedures using 3-D images of the human body. And let's not forget flight simulators and even driver education!

What's Out There

A visit to `http://www.nas.nasa.gov/NAS/Vislab/` (not a VRML site per se) will clue you into different kinds of visualization techniques now being developed by the science community. For an outstanding example of VRML in chemistry, examine `http://ws05.pc.chemie.th-darmstadt.de/vrml/`.

Design, Architecture, and Art   Rather than making models out of paper and wood, architects, industrial designers, and the like are already likely to use CAD (computer-aided design) programs to model their creations on the computer. VRML offers them the opportunity to take this to the next (three-dimensional) step. And although virtual art is still in its infancy, there are some highly creative people out there (see Figure 7.8).

What's Out There

An illuminating site highlighting both lighting design and architecturally inspired art, Lightscape's Walkthrough Library, is at http://www.lightscape .com/VRML/. Be aware, however, that these WRL files are enormous—they range from 2.5–10MB apiece, so they won't move at the speed of light.

WaxWeb (Figure 7.8) demonstrates how art and technology can be yoked to create an interactive and thoroughly enjoyable educational experience. This site, which is located at http://bug.village.virginia.edu/, contains a VRML version of David Blair's feature-length independent film WAX, or the discovery of television among the bees.

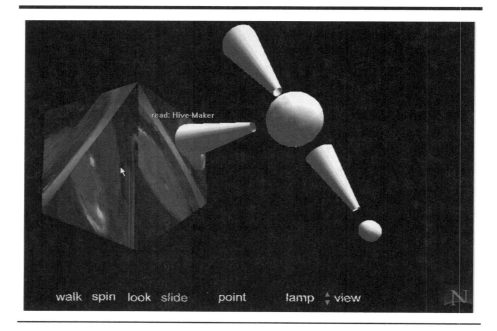

Figure 7.8:   Join the hive and give WaxWeb a try.

What's Out There

For a different kind of 3-D environment, look into AlphaWorld. Worlds, Inc., which you'll find at the URL http://www.worlds.net/, claims that Alpha-World is the first true online society. You can even build your own site in this multiuser virtual reality land. Visit Worlds, Inc. to download AlphaWorld, WorldsChat, and other trendy interactive stuff, including product demos in Java and VRML.

Entertainment   For those who are looking for yet another way to procrastinate, or those who are looking to unwind through new gaming experiences, VRML is a revelation. Interactive virtual reality games are becoming increasingly popular and may ultimately prove to be big business too.

Marketing   Advertising has already become part and parcel of the Internet. It's everywhere, just as it is in the print and broadcast media. And it's expected to pay for a lot of otherwise free content. Whatever your own feelings may be about the issue of advertising on the Internet, it seems likely that advertising and sales companies will seize on virtual worlds to create virtual showrooms and 3-D advertising. You may be able to preview a home for sale, a certain model of car with various interior options, or a vacation resort, all from the comfort of your computer screen. Figure 7.9 gives you a glimpse into Intel's clever use of VRML.

What's Out There

Intel's Intel Inside site combines a slick advertising gimmick with actual education by leading you on a tour of your computer's insides. Look for this computer innerspace wonder at http://www.intel.com/procs/ppro/demos/stepinto.htm.

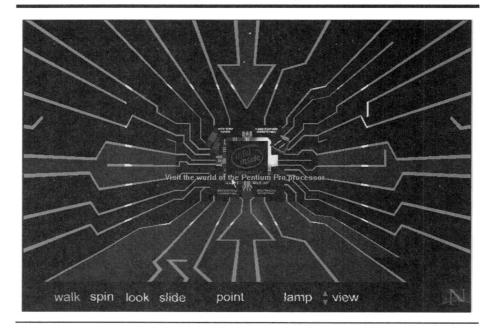

Figure 7.9: Intel takes you on a virtual reality tour of the inside of a computer.

If you're connected to the Internet via modem, you'll have to be patient while viewing VRML sites. As with all the other nifty multimedia gadgets on the Web, the problem is bandwidth. That is, if you're using a modem (even a fast one), it may take a good while for the huge amount of information necessary to create 3-D images to get from a remote machine to the computer on your desktop.

◆ Getting Live3D Going

You must have the full version of Netscape Communicator installed to use Live3D (that's the version we recommend you download in Chapter 11). If you're unsure whether or not you've got Live3D installed on your system, follow these steps (it doesn't matter whether or not you're online when you do this):

1. From the Netscape menu bar, select Help ➤ About Plug-Ins. A list of the Netscape plug-ins that are installed on your computer will appear (Figure 7.10).

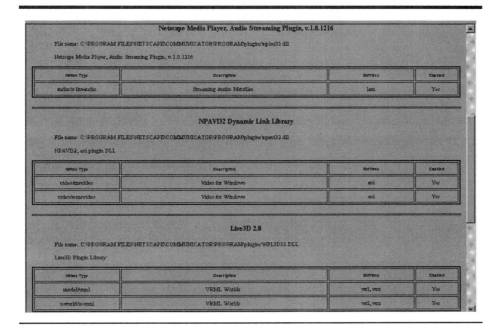

Figure 7.10: These are the Netscape plug-ins on our machine

2. Scroll down the list to see if you see an entry that lists Live3D or something called Cosmo; the description says that the mime type (file type) is x-world/x-vrml, and that Live3D or Cosmo files end in the suffix WRL or WRZ. If the entry is there, proceed to step 3; if it isn't, you probably haven't installed Live3D. To remedy this, use Navigator to open the URL `http://home.netscape.com/comprod/products/navigator/live3d/download_live3d.html`, and follow the download and installation instructions on that page.

3. After figuring out that you have Live3D, click on Netscape's Back button to get back to what you were doing or looking at.

The Cosmo VRML player was developed by Silicon Graphics for Netscape and is included in Communicator 4. If both Live3D and Cosmo are installed on your computer, Navigator will decide which plug-in to use when you access a VRML site.

Now that was easy, right? Let's move along to using Live3D.

Plug-Ins and Helper Apps

While Netscape Communicator and its browser component, Navigator, offer plenty of functionality, they can't do everything. Plenty of media types can be delivered over the Web, and some can't be handled by Communicator alone.

Helper applications, or *helper apps*, as they're called, are external programs that launch and work alongside Navigator; for example, to help it perform tasks such as viewing Adobe Acrobat (PDF) document files and connecting to Telnet sites.

But helper apps alone don't solve the problem of handling other media in the context of the Web. One of the advances Navigator 2 offered when it was released was the ability to extend its capabilities through the use of *plug-ins*. These are mini-applications that, when installed to work with Navigator, allow the browser to read (and play or display) file formats that work as inline Web page extensions. Live3D, for example, works as a Navigator plug-in.

While Navigator 4 is famed for easy streaming media, some sound and video formats offered on the Web can't be handled directly by Navigator. These can be handled via plug-ins. If you click on a link to one of these files, Navigator 4 will simply display the video within the browser window. The file formats Navigator can handle this way include WAV, AU, AIFF, and MIDI for sound files, and AVI and MOV for video files. You must, however, download QuickTime drivers to make MOV files really go—some of them "go" in 3D!

Navigator 4 will automatically download and install plug-ins it doesn't already have on hand whenever it encounters pages that require them. There are some plug-ins and helpers you may want to seek out, however, to broaden your Web experience:

- ◆ RealPlayer, Streamworks, VivoActive, and VDO Live, for playing live and on-demand audio and video content
- ◆ Shockwave, for experiencing CD-ROM quality multimedia
- ◆ Adobe Acrobat, for viewing high-design documents
- ◆ PNG Live, to load rich graphic files
- ◆ The Pointcast Network, for another push media experience

What's Out There

To soup up Navigator with plug-ins and helper apps (and take them for a test drive) visit these sites for downloads, instructions, and sample galleries:

- ◆ The Real Player: http://www.real.com/
- ◆ Xing Technologies' Streamworks: http://www.streamworks.com/
- ◆ VivoActive: http://www.vivo.com/
- ◆ VDO Live: http://www.vdo.net/download/
- ◆ Macromedia Shockwave: http://www.macromedia.com/
- ◆ Adobe Acrobat: http://www.adobe.com/prodindex/acrobat/main.html
- ◆ PNG Live by Siegel & Gale: http://www.siegelgale.com/
- ◆ The Pointcast Network: http://www.pointcast.com/
- ◆ Apple QuickTime (you must download QuickTime drivers to use the plug-in that comes with Navigator): http://quicktime.apple.com/

◆ Navigating through Virtual Space

Once Live3D is installed on your computer, you don't have to do anything special to activate it; it will start up automatically whenever you come across a virtual world. You'll visit some virtual worlds by following a link; some sites might include a mini VRML window on an otherwise basic Web page. Furthermore, navigating through virtual space is very easy because most VRML sites provide you with the same basic set of controls. When you enter a virtual world, you'll see a row of buttons appear at the bottom of your screen as the WRL file is loading.

Because Netscape is working extra hard to get WRL files and load them, you might find that clicking on that ol' familiar Stop button won't do what it's supposed to do until it's too late. Netscape may keep loading those huge files against your will—just grit your teeth and bear it.

Using VRML Navigation Buttons

At all the sites we've seen so far, you've got eight buttons at your disposal that you can use to examine all or part of a virtual world. Here's an overview of what each of the buttons can do for you.

 Not all VRML worlds include all eight options, depending on how they've been coded.

The Button	What It Does
Walk	"Walks" you closer to or farther from the object you're viewing (when you click and drag with the left mouse button)
Spin	Rotates the object you're viewing in the direction you indicate by clicking and dragging with the left mouse button (left = clockwise, right = counterclockwise, up = toward you, down = away from you)
Look	Allows you to activate a link (by clicking on it) whose presence is indicated by text that appears on or near the object you're viewing
Slide	Slides the object you're viewing in any direction you indicate by clicking and dragging with the left mouse button
Point	Zooms in on any part of an object you click on
Lamp	Adjusts the "lighting" of a virtual world; that is, the virtual light source within the world will get brighter (with the up arrow) or darker (with the down arrow) as you choose
View	Zooms in on or pans out to show different (fixed) views of an object; you can click on the object to stop these moves or progress from view to view with the green up and down arrows
?	Toggles this display of helpful information in the lower-left corner of the window

Point the rightmost button on your mouse at a virtual world on your screen and click. A pop-up menu will appear; select Navigate from that menu and you'll have quick access to navigation commands.

Navigating Your First VRML World

If you'd like to practice getting around before you encounter a full-fledged virtual world, follow these steps. (Note that you don't have to be online to test your navigational skills.)

1. From the Netscape menu bar, select File ➤ Open Page. The Open Page dialog box will appear. Here, in a moment, you'll specify the name and location of the file you'd like to open.

2. The file we're looking for is a 3-D rendering of the Netscape icon, which is stored in a file called vrmlui.wrl. To point Netscape at the proper file, in the Open Page dialog box's File Name text box, type the full path name: **c:\program files\netscape\communicator\ program\plugins\live3d\ui\vrm.wrl**. Once you've specified the file and pathname, click on Open. The dialog box will close and the file should appear on your screen.

Alternatively, you can browse through folders until you locate the file, by clicking on the Open Page dialog box's Choose File button, which will open the Open dialog box you're undoubtedly familiar with. If you choose this route, you may have to pull down the list labeled Files of Type (in the Open Page dialog box) and select VRML Worlds (*.wrl, *.wrz) to see the VRML files listed there.

3. Soon you should be looking at a big white 3-D N on a dark background, along with a blue cone and a desk lamp (see Figure 7.11). The buttons at the bottom of the screen are the controls to which we introduced you just a moment ago. Use them until you feel comfortable with what they do, then you're ready to begin your next journey.

There's no special action you should take to stop browsing a VRML world—it's just like any other Web document; you can take it or leave it. Now that you know how the VRML controls work, there's just the small matter of how VRML links work, and then we're off.

Figure 7.11:   Use Netscape's demo world as your first trip through VRML reality.

◆ Using VRML Links

Using VRML links couldn't be simpler, especially if you're already familiar with their cousins, HTML links. The main difference between VRML links and HTML links is that while HTML links usually appear underlined in a special color, VRML links appear as yellow text that appears and disappears depending on where on a virtual world you've positioned the mouse pointer. As soon as you move the mouse pointer to a place where yellow text appears, you're ready to use the VRML link. To follow a VRML link, just follow these steps:

1. While you're viewing a virtual world, move the mouse pointer until you see some light-green text appear on the screen, superimposed over the 3-D images. This text is a VRML link.

2. Click on the text. You should then be transported to the destination specified by the link you've chosen. It may take a while for you to see where you've been transported, so be patient.

Generally, VRML links lead to one of two things: another virtual world or a Web document containing information related to the virtual world you're currently viewing.

In the VRML world we were just visiting (the vrml.wrl file we found on your hard drive), there's a VRML link embedded that takes you to Netscape's Live3D Home Page. You have to have your Internet connection up and running to use the VRML links, of course. Let's check out the Live3D home page—make sure your Internet connection is up and running.

1. If you haven't done so already, follow the procedure outlined in the section "Navigating Your First VRML World." This will open the VRML world supplied by Netscape (the one we're going to use to follow a VRML link).

2. Move your mouse over the big N until the words "Live3D Home Page" appear, in bright yellow text.

3. Click on those words. In a few seconds, Netscape's Live3D Home Page will appear on your screen in all its glory. This page is all about VRML and how it works, and it also points you to some cool virtual places to visit on the Web.

What's Out There

Netscape's Live3D Home Page includes demo worlds that show off the VRML 2.0 technology. Live3D 2 includes one Netscape-only traveling technique called "Stay On Ground" that applies to walking through some virtual landscapes. If you want to get there without going through the demo we just described, surf on over to `http://home.netscape.com/eng/live3d/`.

 Links in a virtual world can take you any place links in a Web document can. For example, a virtual world can contain links to HTML documents, still images, sounds, and other virtual worlds stored on servers all over the world.

VRML links between worlds do tend to be a lot slower and more cumbersome than HTML links. VRML files tend to be quite a bit larger than HTML files and, as such, take much longer to load. Have patience. That's often the price you pay for living on the bleeding edge of new technologies.

What's Out There

See where it all began.... Silicon Graphics, Inc., known to those in the know as SGI, does VRML proud with a Web site called VRML Moving Worlds, at `http://webspace.sgi.com/worlds/`.

Construct's Web site, which evolved out of the Interactive Media Festival and the VRML Arc Gallery, is at `http://www.construct.net/links/projects .html#vrml`.

Netwatch's Top Ten Links site (`http://www.pulver.com/netwatch/topten/ topten.htm`) includes links to good VRML sites, electronic publications, and forums on VRML.

Terminal Reality, a cool 3-D "terminal" that can lead you all kinds of hip places, is at ZD3D, ZDNet's 3-D site (`http://www.zdnet.com/zdi/vrml/`). ZD3D includes all kinds of news and links about VRML and other 3-D technologies.

To find more VRML sites all over the Net, try searching for VRML with Hotbot. Go to `http://www.hotbot.com/`, and then click on Media Type. On the page that appears next, click in the checkbox marked VRML, and follow the instructions for a Web search. You'll read more about searching the Net in Chapter 8.

Next Stop: Starting Points

Now that you've got the skinny on Java, JavaScript, Active Platform, as well as VRML, virtual worlds, and all that good stuff, let's go out on the Web and explore some good and useful starting points that map the whole Internet.

Starting Places and Search Tools

You won't always want to *wander* the Web; sometimes you'll want to focus your travels or gather information in ways that aren't so willy-nilly. Fortunately, there are some great comprehensive starting points on the Web that can really help get you going. Many Web sites—Netscape's included—provide listings of interesting sites, usually by category. Several really terrific directories focus on organizing sites by specific subjects, while a growing number of search engines can be used to find facts and opinions on focused topics. There are even some nifty all-in-one search pages that gather up a lot of search options for your convenience.

 In this chapter, we'll cover comprehensive starting places and search tools. There are also plenty of starting places that focus on certain subject areas (biosciences, handicrafts, travel, etc.) or on certain Internet activities and experiences (audio, VRML, chat). But here we'll concentrate on the starting places and search tools that will get you started in an overall way, with a healthy portion of subject-specific engines and starting places at the end of the chapter.

◆ Directories and Search Engines: An Industry Is Born

Imagine TV without the benefit of those handy programming guides that come with your Sunday paper, or imagine a really huge library without a card catalog—whether it's in a file cabinet or on a computer. You wouldn't know what's where, when, or how to find anything.

...That's the Web without the tools you can use to show you around. An entire industry of Web indexing has arisen from this need, and today there are lots of well-known Web directories and search tools, all competing to be the biggest, the best, or both.

Let's start by defining terms. A *directory* in this context is really a large database filled with references to Internet sites; the organization of this database is overseen by editorial types who (presumably) keep it intelligently organized. Yahoo! is an *index* type of directory; its main feature is a browsable, subject-oriented listing of sites (though the listing is also searchable).

Some directories go further by also offering reviews and rating systems so you can pick and choose from what an "expert" thinks is best before you spend your time wandering around online. These days, directories generally are searchable, adding another dimension to their usefulness, and many are beginning to offer editorial content, including Best of the Web awards, articles, and informative material such as newsfeeds.

A *search engine* (in this context) differs from a directory in that it offers no editorial content, and its main feature is an enormous, searchable database of sites that has been gathered in an automated process using a Web crawler or robot, with little or no regard to any sort of indexing or reviewing. A search engine typically can perform faster searches of more stuff than the search aspect of an index or guide can do. However, search engines offer you uncategorized lists, which may be less useful in some circumstances (say when you're trying to find the "best" site on a given topic) or more useful in others (like when you want a comprehensive listing of everything available on your subject of interest).

In this chapter, we're going to cover the major directories (both the index type and the guide type), and the major search engines. We'll also show you some great all-in-one places that offer you the choice to search all these gizmos from one convenient location.

◆ The Big Picture

The first time you start Navigator, the Welcome to Netscape page will be the default home page—the page you see automatically. (Later, you can display a different home page on start-up, if you like.) The Welcome to Netscape page is a perfectly good place to start (we'll look a little more closely at what it has to offer in a second), and there are many other good starting places as well. Before we look at these in detail, let's go over some general information about Web sites and home pages.

What Is a Web Site? And a Home Page?

A *Web site* may be a single page or a collection of pages on the Web. Often you'll enter a Web site by starting at its *home page*. You can look at this in a couple of ways: To you, the user, the home page can be a starting point for exploring a single site or the whole World Wide Web. You can think of a home page as a kind of "main menu." This analogy breaks down a bit because the Web is neither hierarchical nor linear and is by no means menu-driven; but a home page does outline your options—at least the options for moving along the links from a site to other points of interest both within and beyond this site, as imagined by the site's producer. To whomever publishes it, the home page is a cross between a magazine or book's cover and its table of contents. Producers of a Web site's home page have to think through its construction completely to make clear what the site is about and what can be found there.

 Just to clarify a bit, a *Web site* may be a single page or a collection of pages. The main page among a number of pages in a Web site is the *home page*. (A *Web server*, by the way, is the machine and software that houses the Web site.)

In reality, a home page is any hypertext document that has links to other points on the Web and acts as a starting point. Your start-up home page, the one that is automatically loaded each time you launch Navigator, should be one that helps you get going. It may be the default Welcome to Netscape page, some other home page that provides a general starting point, or one that is specialized to your interests. You can even set up Netscape so it doesn't automatically access and display a home page, if you want to start your daily surfing without the distraction of seeing a page you've seen a thousand times before. Read on to find out how to choose any of these options.

Changing Your Start-Up Home Page

For new users and experienced users whose purposes are fairly general, the Welcome to Netscape page or another of those we describe in this chapter might be best. For example, you might find it handy to make your start-up home page a page that's deeper in the Netscape site, like the Net Search page, with its listings of comprehensive directories and search tools. Or you might want to use search.com (described later in this chapter), a compendium of search gizmos from the broad to the special interest. The search.com site will give you a good launch pad that's even more general and comprehensive than the Welcome to Netscape page, which is devoted primarily to Netscape and Netscape users. For those with more specific interests, such as cooking or computing, a home page geared to those interests might be better.

 To speed Web access, you might want to choose as your start-up home page one residing on a server that's near you—the closer the better. This is getting easier to do, with the Web's rate of growth. Or perhaps you work for a company that has its own home page. You can even construct your own custom home page using Netscape's nifty bookmark features, as described in Chapter 4, or using HTML, as you'll see in Chapter 9.

To change your start-up home page, you'll use Communicator's Preferences dialog box—this handy dialog box is your entrance way to changing many facets of Communicator's behavior on your machine.

Here are the steps for changing your start-up home page:

1. Start Navigator by clicking on its icon, without bothering to start your Internet connection. (What we're doing here is strictly a local operation.)

2. From the menu bar, choose Edit ➤ Preferences. The Preferences dialog box will appear.

3. From the Category column along the left of the Preferences dialog box, click on Navigator. The dialog box will change to reflect your choice.

4. At the top of the dialog box, find the Navigator Starts With option. Next to it are three choices: Blank Page, Home Page, and Last Page Visited. Click on Home Page to make it active. In the text box below this, you'll find the URL for the home page currently slated for display at start-up (see Figure 8.1).

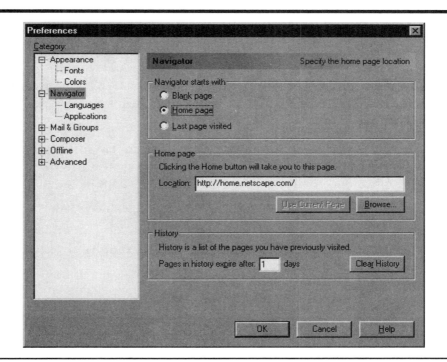

Figure 8.1: Enter the URL for the home page you want to appear at start-up. The URL shown here is the default Welcome to Netscape page.

5. Highlight that URL and type in its place the URL for the home page you want. You can choose any page on the Web, or even an HTML page stored on your hard drive. To choose the page currently loaded in the Navigator window, click on the Use Current Page button.

6. Click on the OK button. The Preferences dialog box will close, and the Navigator window will reappear.

If you do happen to have been connected to the Internet when you performed this procedure, you can check to make sure you typed the URL correctly by pressing the Home button on Navigator's tool bar.

When next you start Navigator, you'll see the page you just designated as your start-up page rather than the original default start-up home page. And from now on, every time you press the Home button on Navigator's toolbar, your new home page of choice will appear. You can change this page as often as you like.

Let's say you have some reason for not wanting to see any home page at all when you launch Navigator. Perhaps you have a slow Internet connection and you don't want to bother loading any given Web page on startup. The steps you'll follow to do this are similar to those for changing the start-up home page:

1. With Navigator running (you don't have to be connected to the Internet while you do this), select Edit ➤ Preferences from the menu bar. The Preferences dialog box will appear.

2. From the choices along the left of the Preferences dialog box, select Navigator.

3. In the area labeled Navigator Starts With, find Blank Page and click on its radio button.

4. Now click on the OK button. The Preferences dialog box will close, and the Netscape window will appear.

What could be easier? When you launch Netscape again, you should see absolutely no home page. Instead you'll see an empty document window.

You have one other option for Navigator's start-up view: using the last page you visited on your last surfing excursion to start today's session. Simply follow steps 1 and 2, above. Then, in the Navigator Starts With area of the Preferences dialog box, click on Last Page Visited. Click on OK to return to the Navigator window. Next time you launch the browser, you'll pick up where you left off, and the last page you loaded will load.

If you elected to have no home page appear, then decide you want to return to the home page you designated in the Home Page Location box (as described in the preceding procedure), click on Home on Navigator's toolbar, and voilà! You return to your chosen home page in a flash. And even if you've changed your start-up home page or arranged for none to appear at start-up, you can always access the Welcome to Netscape page. Simply click on the N icon in the upper-right corner of your screen.

What's Out There

You can always go home again. The URL for the Welcome to Netscape page is http://home.netscape.com/. You can bookmark it, as described in Chapter 4, or you can click on the N icon for even easier access.

Now let's look at some alternative choices for your start-up page, including a few all-purpose directories. We'll start with the default start-up home page you've heard so much about—Netscape's own wildly popular and very useful site.

You're certainly allowed to like more than one page. To find out how to create bookmarks, shortcuts, or toolbar buttons featuring your favorite sites, head over to Chapter 4.

◆ The Netscape Web Site

As might be expected, Netscape has one of the most frequently visited Web sites on the Internet. (Figure 3.1 in Chapter 3 shows the Netscape home page.) From the Netscape Web site you can always get the scoop on the company and its upcoming products. You can download the latest version of their software, get information about other software that enhances Communicator, and get general information about the Web and the Internet. Because the Netscape Web site includes so much important information, we talk about different aspects of it throughout the book. Here we'll talk about the resources on the Netscape site that are best suited as jumping off points to the rest of the Internet.

Netscape Guide

Netscape offers a jumping-off point for your Web travels called Netscape Guide, which is an index of Web sites hand-picked by the good people at Netscape and Yahoo!. You can get to Netscape Guide in a number of ways, including:

◆ Click on the Guide button on Netscape's toolbar, and from the pop-up menu that appears, select The Internet.

◆ Click on the <u>Guide to the Internet</u> link on the Welcome to Netscape page.

◆ Open the URL http://netscape.com/yahoo/guide/.

Registering Communicator

The first time you start Communicator, take the time to read the license agreement that appears on-screen and register the program. It's the honest, right thing to do, and it couldn't be easier. You can check out the license agreement and register via links on the Netscape site.

The agreement says that Netscape Communicator is free for the use of students, faculty members, staff of educational organizations, employees of non-profit corporations, and *individuals evaluating the program*. If you fall into the last group, you must pay a license fee once your evaluation period is up.

Filling out the registration form is terrifically simple; really it's just like filling out a paper registration card, except that you're doing it on screen.

Follow links on the Netscape home page or open the URL http://home .netscape.com/misc/quick_purchase to get to the Netscape Quick Purchase page. Here you can click on the link for the version of the software you have and fill out the simple forms to order and pay for a copy of the latest version of Netscape Communicator (including Netscape Navigator, the browser component of the suite) or any number of other software products Netscape offers.

Regardless of which method you choose, you'll see the Netscape Guide page on the screen. Each of the icons that appears in the Netscape Guide site links to a page listing more specific Web sites. For example, to see links to sites about Finance, just click on the Finance icon. When we clicked on the Finance link, we got the page shown in Figure 8.2.

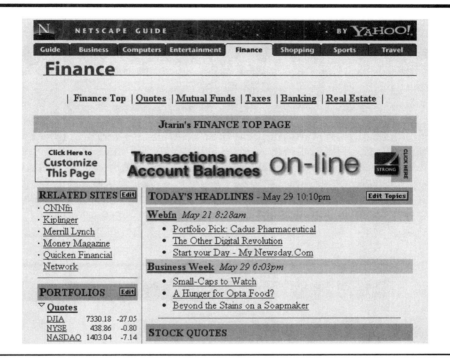

Figure 8.2: We clicked on the Finance icon and found all sorts of personal finance resources that appear on the Net.

Search Gizmos and More

The Netscape site also offers easy access to many search engines that are scattered throughout the Web. You can access the Netscape Net Search page in any one of many ways, including

◆ Clicking on the Search button on Netscape's toolbar

◆ Clicking on the Net Search link on the Netscape Guide page

◆ Opening the URL http://netscape.com/escapes/search

Regardless of how you bring up the Netscape Net Search page, you'll see something like what we saw, which is shown in Figure 8.3. Some of the premiere directories and search engines appear one at a time in a graphic at the top of the page—there are tabs labeled with the names of those directories and search engines at the top of the graphic. To select any of these featured search gadgets, click on the tab for the one that interests you.

Other Points of Departure

Many Internet service providers and online services are creating their own starting points for the Internet. If you have a version of Navigator that you got from your provider, it may be configured to load up their home page (instead of the Netscape home page) whenever you start it. You should take a look at the page and see what they have to say. Many providers put important announcements on the default home page that their version of Navigator loads.

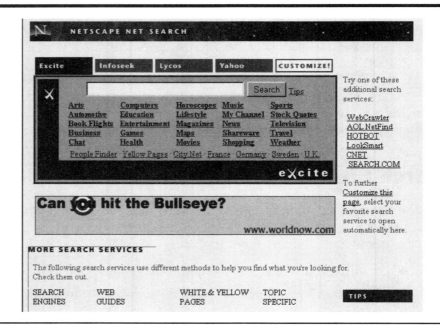

Figure 8.3: Netscape's Net Search offers you quick access to a gaggle of Internet directories and search engines. When we visited, Excite popped up first.

 Some other directories and search engines don't actually appear in the graphic. This is not because they are lesser options; it is because they did not pay for the privilege of appearing in the more eye-catching graphic at the top of the page. To use any of the non-featured search tools, click on a link (below the graphic) for the one that interests you; either its home page or its search page will appear. Or, if you're looking for a more specialized search tool, choose from some other categories, such as White Pages or Web Guides.

To actually use Net Search, just follow the bouncing ball:

1. Open the Netscape Net Search page by any of the methods listed previously.

2. Click on the tab for the search engine of interest, and the graphic will change to present it. (Or you can use whichever search engine popped up first.) Note that each search tool will organize and display the information in the graphic according to its own wisdom, but in general they'll all have a text box into which you can type a word or phrase for what you seek, and a button labeled Search, Find, or something similar, that you'll click on to conduct the search. (Some will also cram in the list of categories they cover in their browsable index, but that's another story.)

3. In the text area, type a word or phrase for what you seek.

 Later in this chapter, we cover the major directories and search engines in more detail, including tips for how to conduct a more exact search. Read on for more information.

4. Click on the Search button (or Find, or whatever this particular search tool calls it). In a few seconds you'll see the results of your search.

What actually appears on the results page varies from one search engine to another, but it will generally be some sort of a list, with links from which you can now jump to any of many resources that match your interest.

Once you've searched for an item of interest using one of the search engines, you can use the Back button or the Go menu to return to Netscape's Net Search page.

Here's a sneaky search trick you can use with Navigator. Just type a few words into the location bar and press ↵. Navigator will automatically treat these words as a search request and ask one of its favored search engines (on a rotating basis) to look up your query. Note that this doesn't work, however, if you type in only *one* word—as we've said before, when you type a single word into the location bar (*Disney*, for example) and press ↵, Navigator treats this as a domain name and looks for a corresponding Web site.

◆ About Search Tools

Let's say you work in the planning department of a large corporation, and you need to write a business report about "reengineering." Say you want to pepper your report with statistical data—productivity levels in American business over the past 10 years, unemployment levels, inflation rates, and so on. You also want to describe the viewpoints of financial, economic, and business experts and address forecasts for the future of business.

The Web is gigantic, webby, and *growing*. (We've said this before.) You just can't expect everything on the Web to be contained in any one place or to be searchable with any one tool. To do your Web research—on our example topic or on any other topic—you'll use a number of tools. You may use AltaVista, Lycos, or Infoseek to find a comprehensive listing of pages that contain some reference to your topic, then you may use Excite to find hand-selected, top-rate sites on some specific aspect of your topic.

 Just as each Web page you encounter bears the mark of its publisher (in the form of what's included and excluded and how information is presented), each search tool also has been affected by its publisher's knowledge and interest. For example, if you search for material on a specific topic in Yahoo! and don't find anything, that doesn't mean your topic is not represented on the Net. Search again, using AltaVista, search.com, or one of the other tools, and see what comes up there.

When you conduct your search, you'll have to describe the information that you want. In general, you will enter one or more words into a text box on screen. The *search engine* (the program or search tool that actually does the search) you're using will compare this text (called a *search string*) with some part of or all the text associated with all the Web pages this search engine knows. (Most search engines also employ a *Web crawler* to find out in an automated way what's on the Net. This is how they learn of the pages they then "know" about. See "What Web Crawlers Do," below.)

As we describe various search engines in upcoming sections, we'll show you how they compare through the use of examples. This should give you an idea of how best to use each search tool.

 A lot of sites and pages are known to any given search engine, but not every single one can be. Only those that have been discovered by the search engine's Web crawler will appear in that database. This is true of all search tools—the Web grows faster than they can catalog it, though all the search tools are expanding all the time.

Types of Searches

As mentioned, each search engine focuses on some part of or all the pages; sometimes you'll even be able to specify whether what you are searching for will appear in the Web page's

◆ Title
◆ URL
◆ Text

or

◆ In a description, abstract, or review of the Web page

or

◆ All of the above

The search engine will sift through the pages it knows of, looking for the text you specified, and it will return a list of all the pages that contain the text you specified. If you specified that the search engine look only in titles, URLs, or text, it will look *only* in those parts of the document(s). Thus, the exact way the search engine matches up what you are searching for with its database is partly controllable by you and partly dependent on the particular search gizmo you are using. Obviously, the searches that are most useful are those that search the text of the page along with the page's title and URL, turning up a list of the most relevant pages. Even then, some search engines search smaller portions of the text than others do.

Using Logical Operators in More Complicated Searches

To make your searches more specific, you can use *logical operators*—AND and OR, for example—which work kind of like conjunctions in English grammar. The way you use logical operators varies a bit from one search tool to another, but the ideas remain the same. In general, if you want to find documents that contain *all* the words in a search string, you can join the words with AND. If you want to find *any* of the words in a search string, you can join the words with OR.

Here's an example: If you want to find documents that discuss American business, simply entering *American business* as your search string will often result in a list of documents that contain either the word *American* or the word *business*. That would be an awful lot of documents, only a few of which would discuss *American business* per se. If you join the two words with AND, as in *American AND business*, the search tool will look for documents that contain both words rather than either word. If you joined them with OR, as in *American OR business*, you'd get all the documents that contain either word and all the documents with both words.

...Logical, eh?

What Web Crawlers Do

At the heart of most Internet search tools is a *Web crawler*, a program that "crawls" around the Web looking at page after page and site after site, bringing the address, the titles, and in some cases descriptive pieces of the pages' contents into a gigantic searchable database. More and more search engines these days store a compressed version of the *entire* text of the page (which brings up some interesting intellectual property issues). The speed and efficiency of these Web crawlers is what makes legendary the databases compiled using them. In Chapter 2, you can find out more about Web crawlers.

When a search engine offers you a list of pages, it has to put them in some type of order. It usually decides this order based on *relevancy*, which can include many different criteria. One of the most common is *frequency*, or the number of times a particular phrase is mentioned. For example, if you search on the word *widget*, the Web page that contains the most mentions of the word *widget* will appear first. The search engine—which, after all, is only so bright—has found what it thinks to be the most relevant page. Now, whether that page actually has any substantial information about widgets is another story....

When you encounter those text boxes into which you type the stuff you want the search engine to go looking for, it's important to know how much or how little text you are allowed to type and whether the search engine can make some basic distinctions. For example, the smartest search engines "know" enough so that you can type a phrase such as *pigeons for sale* and they will not bother matching the word *for* or will skip over words that include *for*. Other search engines will return everything that matches at all, without much discrimination; so you'd get not just all the sites that include the words *pigeons* and *sale* (the important words in this case) but also *format*, *fortune*, *before*, and every other instance of the combination of the letters *f*, *o*, and *r*.

While this is all pretty basic stuff, search engines are rapidly growing more and more sophisticated. All the search gizmos we discuss in this chapter include advanced settings so you can control how they look for documents and the scope of their searches, and they'll all undoubtedly add features to their already impressive capabilities as time goes on.

There are all kinds of search tools. We'll look at some of the big names in searching, and then we'll take a look at a terrific all-in-one search page that pulls in lots of options for searching the biggies and the more specialized. And last but not least, we'll look at some specialized search gadgets that help you find information from phone numbers to stock quotes.

Okey dokey—now let's find out how to use some of these directories and search engines.

◆ Yahoo!: A Subject-Oriented Index

Yahoo!, the big, beautiful index begun at Stanford University by a couple of (presumed) Yahoos, has since gone commercial, with not only a bunch of Web sites, but books and magazines bearing its name, and TV commercials blaring its existence. Yahoo! is very easy to use; it consists of a hierarchical list of a whopping number of sites on the Web, organized by subject (see Figure 8.4). (The number's growing at a phenomenal rate.) All you do is click your way from here to there along a logical path to find what you seek.

What's Out There

You can mosey on over to Yahoo! with the URL http://www.yahoo.com/.

Some categories we found when we looked were Art, Business and Economy, Computers and Internet, Education, Entertainment, Government, Health, Recreation and Sports, and plenty more.

 Yahoo! doesn't employ any crawlers or spiders to find Web sites. Instead, it relies on human beings—both Yahoo! employees and users of Yahoo!—to find links worth including and submit them for consideration. That means that Yahoo! is limited by human bandwidth, but it also means that it indexes only those pages with some modicum of actual content. You won't find Aunt Sally's Web site filled with snapshots of cousin Sue here—unless it's a work of art.

 If you know of a page that is not in the Yahoo! lists, click on Add URL on any Yahoo! page. A form will appear into which you can type the URL of the page you want included in Yahoo!. The people who run Yahoo! will review your submission, and, if they like the page, it will become part of Yahoo!'s list.

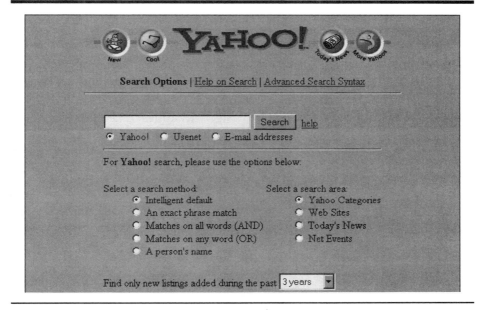

Figure 8.4: Yahoo!'s subject-oriented list allows you to click around until you find what you seek.

Searching through Yahoo!

Like many Internet directories, Yahoo! is not just clickable—it's searchable. To do a simple search of Yahoo! from its home page, follow these steps:

1. At the top of the Yahoo! home page, you will find a text box followed by a Search button. In the text box, type one or more words (separated by spaces) that describe what you seek. Yahoo! will find only entries that contain *all* the words you enter in the text box; so be careful about what you enter.

2. Click on the Search button. A page will appear showing a listing of Yahoo! categories and Web pages (all appearing as links) that contain all the words you set out for the search.

If Yahoo! doesn't find what you're looking for, your query will automatically roll over and search AltaVista. You can find out more about searching AltaVista directly in the section of this chapter called "Searching AltaVista."

You are not limited to searching Yahoo! based on a few simple words.
Yahoo! also has a search page that gives you much more control over
how it locates the information you want. To use this alternative Yahoo!
searching method:

1. Click on the Options link (it's to the right of the Search button,
which you'll find either at the top or bottom of any Yahoo! page).
The Yahoo! Search Options page will appear (see Figure 8.5).

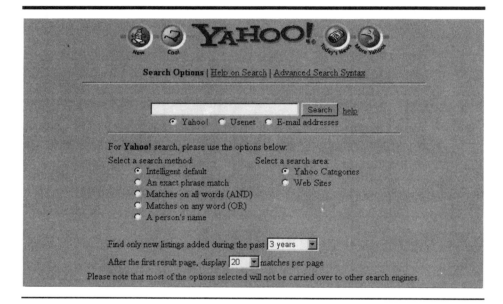

Figure 8.5:   Yahoo! is searchable!

2. In the text box, type one or more words (separated by spaces)
describing what you seek.

3. Make selections to indicate how and what you want to search:

◆ Where to search—in Yahoo! (the main database), Usenet (the
DejaNews Usenet archives), or E-mail Addresses (the Four11
e-mail directory)

◆ What search method you want to use—Intelligent Default
(Yahoo! knows best, presumably); an Exact Phrase Match
(when you know exactly what you're looking for); Matches

on All Words (the *and* button); Matches on Any Word (the *or* button); or a Person's Name (to find the home page or e-mail address of a friend)

◆ What parts of Yahoo! you want to search—Yahoo! Categories or Web Sites

◆ How far back in time you want to search (choices range from one day to three years)

◆ How many documents you want to see per page as the result of your search

4. Click on the Search button. A page will appear showing a listing of pages (all appearing as links) that match the criteria you set out for the search.

To check out the pages that appeared in the listing as the result of your search, simply click on their links. If you click around a while and get away from the page listing the result of your search, you can always go back to that page by selecting Go from Navigator's menu bar and then selecting Yahoo! Search Results from the list that appears.

Yahoo! boasts an obscene number of subsidiary directories. These range from Yahooligans! (a directory just for kids), to a couple of phone directories and an amazing mapping server, to news, stock quotes, sports scores, and a truckload of other specialized data gizmos. You'll also find quite a cosmopolitan array of city- and country-specific directories. The first was for the San Francisco Bay Area, and now they've got Boston, New York, Japan, and France covered, among others. You can link to any of these places from the Yahoo! home page.

◆ Excite: More Than a Directory

Excite offers a whole passel of features and services that make it an ideal starting point for your Internet exploration. From Excite, you'll be able to search a large database of Internet resources, browse a subject-oriented catalog of Web pages, or read current news articles and columns.

What's Out There

You can access Excite at http://www.excite.com/.

You can access all of the different areas of Excite right from its home page. Along the top of the page you'll see a number of colorful icons. Click on one of the icons (they're links, too) and a new page related to the subject of the icon will appear.

In addition to its search functions, Excite offers Channels By Excite, a topical directory of Web sites, news stories, feature articles, chat areas, and other special features. Other Excite offerings include PAL, a real-time messaging system, and City.Net, a travel directory of the world.

Searching Using Excite

Excite will search through its database of Web sites and give you a brief description of those that might interest you based on the topic of your search. To use this feature:

1. Open the Excite home page. You can conduct your search from here, or you can click Options to broaden Excite's horizons. In that case the Excite Search Options page will appear.

2. In the text box, type a word or phrase to describe what you seek.

3. You can specify which parts of the Internet you want to search. Your options are

Select	To Search
Search the Web	The entire Web (or at least the part of the Web that Excite's Web crawler has encountered)
Search Current News	Current news articles
Search Selected Web Sites	Reviews of Web sites produced by Excite's staff
Search Newsgroup Postings	Usenet news articles and classifieds
Search City.Net Travel Guide	Articles about travel destinations worldwide

5. Click on the Search button. In a few seconds, a page will appear listing sites that correspond to the criteria you set.

6. If you find a site that's just like what you're looking for, click on the <u>More Like This</u> link to locate sites that are similar to the one you found.

To view any of the pages that appeared in the listing as the result of your search, simply click on their links. If you click around for a while and get away from the listing of your search results, you can always go back to that page by using the Back button on the Netscape toolbar.

 As Excite's crawlers and human surfers find sites and categorize them, they work into their database a list of "concepts" for each site. This list is used in a way that echoes a thesaurus—it enables you to find a site based on what it's about as much as by the words or phrases it contains. Let's say a site is about coffee but the word *coffee* is never used in the site—maybe it's always called *java* or *joe* instead. If you search Excite for *coffee* sites, you'll find this one, because someone was smart enough to apply the concept *coffee* to it. This is what concept searching is. You can learn more about Excite's search methods by clicking on <u>Search Tips</u> or find more detailed tips by clicking on <u>Advanced Search</u>.

Now, with starting-point basics under your belt, let's take a wider look at the big, powerful search engines available to you on the World Wide Web.

◆ Searching with AltaVista

AltaVista is well known as a very *fast* search engine, with an incredible number of Web pages documented in its database. If it's on the Web, you'll probably find it in AltaVista, and the list AltaVista returns when you search will appear at lightning speed. The trouble is, when you search for something in AltaVista, you don't get a list of *sites* that have something to do with the subject of your search, you get a list of *pages*. Thus, a hundred Web pages in a single site might appear in the list of stuff AltaVista finds matching your search string.

The advantage of AltaVista is that it excludes nothing; the disadvantage is that AltaVista does not engage in any selection or ranking process. AltaVista is your best choice if you're trying to find some relatively obscure piece of information, but if you want to find all the "best" sites on your topic, AltaVista (like any other huge search engine) is going to leave you with lots of hand sifting to do.

What's Out There

You'd think it would be easy to find AltaVista because the URL would include something like `altavista.com`, but it ain't so. The URL for AltaVista is `http://www.altavista.digital.com/`, because Digital Equipment Corporation operates the search engine. Fortunately, the nice people at `http://www.altavista.com/` do include an AltaVista search box.

To perform a search using AltaVista, follow these steps:

1. Start up your Internet connection, launch Navigator, and open up AltaVista's home page.

2. In the Search text box on the AltaVista home page, type a word or a phrase that describes what you want to find. AltaVista works best when you give it a number of words.

You may have to try a number of variations on the words you use to describe what interests you before you find the exact resource you need (*auto*, *vehicle*, and *car* will all turn up different pages). Try to be specific, but not too specific. Using the plural *books*, for example, will omit instances of the singular *book*. Also note that AltaVista is partially case-sensitive. If you search for *Photoshop*, AltaVista will ignore any records in which *photoshop* is not initial-capped.

3. Click on the Submit button to begin the actual search. The Netscape N icon will become animated. In a few seconds, a new page will appear, listing everything matching your search criteria that was found in the database. (Figure 8.6 shows some of the results of a search for *personal finance*.)

AltaVista lists only the first 10 records per page that meet your criteria, ranking them by relevancy. You can click on the links along the bottom of the page (they look like page numbers) or the Next link to get any additional pages of links, or start again by entering new search criteria and clicking on the Submit button. You can also adjust your existing search criteria, since they appear automatically in the search box after you submit your query.

 If you're using the simple (regular) search option, the words AND, OR, and NOT in your search string will be ignored. Instead, you can use plus (+) and minus (–) signs to accomplish something similar. If you search for *Charlie+Brown*, for example, your results will find only those pages that include both *Charlie* and *Brown*. Alternately, if you search for *Dylan Thomas–Bob*, any pages that feature the word *Bob* will be excluded from your search for pages that do contain *Dylan* and *Thomas*. (Thus, you'll get the *Dylan Thomas* pages and not the *Bob* Dylan pages, but here's a quiz: will you get some *Thomas* Jefferson pages?)

Word count: finance:1062422; personal:3436690

Documents 1-10 of about 400000 matching the query, best matches first.

L. Ross Gott III Professional Services - Personal Finance - What you should kn
What you should know about money market funds. Americans have more than $380 billion invested in money-market mutual funds. And, contrary to popular...
http://www.gottnet.com/client/persfin/what_to_.htm - *size 3K - 17 May 96*

Personal Finance Advisor
Deloitte & Touche Personal Finance Advisor, with tips and information on investing, taxes, insurance and retirement planning.
http://www.dtonline.com/pfa/pfa.htm - *size 5K - 2 Dec 96*

DICTIONARY OF PERSONAL FINANCE
Title: DICTIONARY OF PERSONAL FINANCE Author: Siegel; Shim; & Hartman Price: $ 20.00 Publisher: SIMON & SCHUSTER Year: 1992 ISBN: 0-02-897394-1 Pages: 391.

Figure 8.6: Here you see some of the results of searching AltaVista for personal finance.

 If you have a home page or some sort of Web presence, try typing your own name into the AltaVista search box sometime and see what comes up. You may be surprised. Or, if you want to find something amazingly specific, try not just names, but a lyric from a song, or one of your favorite quotations.

Performing More Complicated Searches with AltaVista

You don't have to limit yourself to entering simple text such as we've described as your search criteria. You can use the Advanced Search page to do more sophisticated, complex searches.

To use the Advanced Search page, follow these steps:

1. From the AltaVista home page (or any AltaVista results page), click on the words Advanced Search in the AltaVista banner graphic along the top of the page. A page will appear that has a number of different searching options (see Figure 8.7).

2. Choose whether to search the Web or Usenet. AltaVista catalogs not only Web pages, but an extensive back library of Usenet articles.

3. In the Selection Criteria text box near the top of the page, type a word or a phrase to describe what you want to find, just as you did in the simpler search. You can type multiple words into the Selection Criteria text box, and also special words that describe how the words relate to what you are searching for.

Use	Like This Example	And It Will
AND	Adobe AND Photoshop	Find all records that contain both the word Adobe and the word Photoshop.
OR	Photoshop OR CorelPaint	Find all records that contain either Photoshop or CorelPaint, or both.
NOT	NOT Macintosh	Find all records that do not contain the word Macintosh.
NEAR	Macintosh NEAR Clone	Find all the records that include the word Clone, within 10 words of the word Macintosh.
" "	"Image Pals"	Find all the records that include the phrase Image Pals.

To get a lot of very helpful advice about using these search options, click on <u>Help</u> in the AltaVista graphic banner. The AltaVista Advanced Search page offers a slightly different Help page than the regular Help page; click on Help when you need it, and you'll see the page that applies to the search you're using.

Figure 8.7:   Click on AltaVista's <u>Advanced Search</u> link, and a number of more sophisticated search options will be yours. Here we are searching for *women near film*.

4. In the Results Ranking Criteria area of the page, you can control the order in which documents that meet the criteria you specified in step 3 will appear when they are listed. Enter words that are in the documents that you wish to appear at the top of the list. If you leave this area blank, the results of the search will appear unordered.

5. If you're searching Usenet, you can specify start and end dates for the posting of Usenet articles. Only articles that were posted between these two dates will appear in the search results. In the Start Date and End Date text boxes, type the earliest and/or latest dates you want to search between.

6. Once you've entered the text you want to search for and have filled in any of the other options described in the preceding steps, click on the Submit Advanced Query button. The famous N will become animated, and in a few seconds a new page will appear, listing everything matching your criteria that AltaVista's search engine found in the AltaVista database.

The listings that appear will follow AltaVista's policy of providing those sites that most closely match your criteria at the top of the list.

 You might notice that one of several handy search tips appears under the AltaVista search box. (The tips appear in rotation.) You can find a whole bunch of these tips (for tasks like searching within certain domains, finding images or other specific types of files, or finding links to your own home page) by clicking on <u>Help</u> at the top of any AltaVista page.

◆ Searching with Lycos

Lycos was developed by a group at Carnegie Mellon University as a tool for cataloging enormous amounts of Internet material. Currently operated by a private company, Lycos has (as of this writing) more than 10 million pages listed in its database. Like other search tools, Lycos is actually composed of two pieces:

◆ A Web crawler that seeks out and catalogs pages on the Web, logging everything it finds into a database

◆ A set of Lycos Web pages with which you can access and search the database

Unlike some others, the Lycos Web crawler records a site's URL and title in the database, *and it records the first 20 lines of the page*—not the whole web thing.

What's Out There

You can call on Lycos using the URL http://www.lycos.com/.

Lycos's great strength is that its database is so huge you're bound to find something about your topic listed there. Let's take a look at how to search Lycos:

1. From the Lycos home page, go to the I Want To Search pull-down menu and select The Web, Sounds, Pictures, or Top 5% Sites (best for broad topics).

2. In the text box of the Lycos home page, type a word or phrase that describes what you want to find.

3. Click on the Go Get It button. Lycos will start searching, the Netscape N icon will become animated, and in a few seconds a page will appear with a detailed list describing the stuff Lycos found that matched your criteria.

After Lycos brings back some search results, you can look for other kinds of sites, too. Right beside the search box, you'll see buttons labeled The Web, Search Top 5% Sites, Search Pictures, Search Sounds, Search Sites by Subject, and Need Help?. Click on one of these buttons to get different kinds of information or help on your search.

In this list, you'll get the title and URL of each Web page that matched your criteria. You'll also get the very beginning of each page (generated automatically). Figure 8.8 shows the results of a search for *Fela Anikulapo Kuti*, a popular Nigerian musician.

PointReview

When you're dealing with a database of Web sites the size of Lycos, it might be hard to find a *good* site about the subject you're looking for. PointReview is a directory that reviews Web sites, naming them "The Top Five Percent of All Web Sites." While we don't know about *that*, it is true that the sites in Point's directory are rarely content-free. Point is especially useful for finding good sites about popular subjects, like children's sites or entertainment. You can browse Point by subject, or you can use the handy search box. Another nifty feature of Point is its featured articles, which focus on popular topics like online games and paranormal phenomena. To visit Point, click on the Top 5% Sites link on any Lycos page.

What's Out There

Get to the Point by opening `http://point.lycos.com/`.

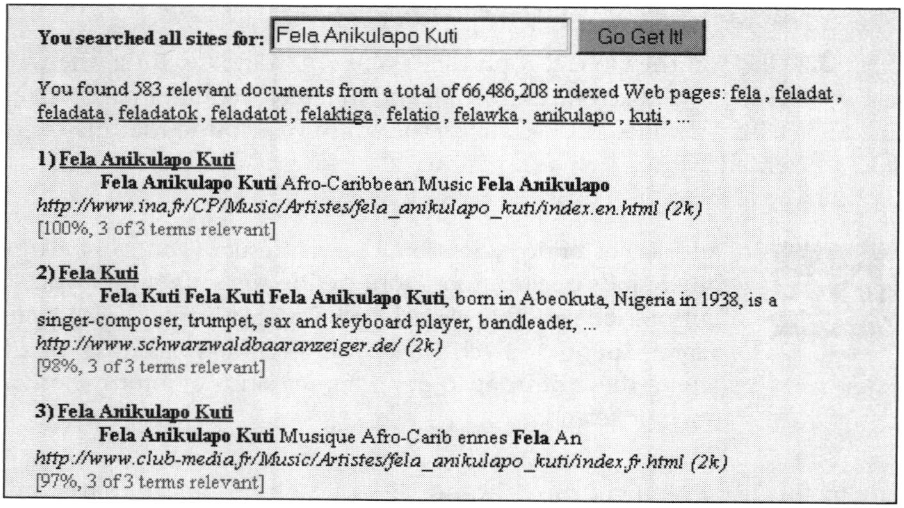

You searched all sites for: | Fela Anikulapo Kuti | | Go Get It! |

You found 583 relevant documents from a total of 66,486,208 indexed Web pages: <u>fela</u> , <u>feladat</u> , <u>feladata</u> , <u>feladatok</u> , <u>feladatot</u> , <u>felaktiga</u> , <u>felatio</u> , <u>felawka</u> , <u>anikulapo</u> , <u>kuti</u> , ...

1) <u>Fela Anikulapo Kuti</u>
    Fela Anikulapo Kuti Afro-Caribbean Music **Fela Anikulapo**
http://www.ina.fr/CP/Music/Artistes/fela_anikulapo_kuti/index.en.html (2k)
[100%, 3 of 3 terms relevant]

2) <u>Fela Kuti</u>
    Fela Kuti Fela Kuti Fela Anikulapo Kuti, born in Abeokuta, Nigeria in 1938, is a
singer-composer, trumpet, sax and keyboard player, bandleader, ...
http://www.schwarzwaldbaaranzeiger.de/ (2k)
[98%, 3 of 3 terms relevant]

3) <u>Fela Anikulapo Kuti</u>
    Fela Anikulapo Kuti Musique Afro-Carib ennes **Fela An**
http://www.club-media.fr/Music/Artistes/fela_anikulapo_kuti/index.fr.html (2k)
[97%, 3 of 3 terms relevant]

Figure 8.8: Lycos found a whole bunch of information on the Web about Fela Anikulapo Kuti, a popular but not entirely famous Nigerian musician.

◆ Searching with HotBot

HotBot is a zippy search tool developed by Wired Ventures using the Inktomi search engine. Inktomi, which debuted in late 1995 amidst great fanfare, was an experimental Web searching tool developed by Eric A. Brewer and Paul Gauthier at the University of California at Berkeley. They developed it as a sample application for *parallel computing*—which just means it runs on more than one computer at a time. This is good, because if one machine fails or slows down, another takes over and keeps the work going. (You may recall that this is the same principle on which the Internet was founded.) What started as the parallel computing experiment of a group of CS (Computer Science) students became a wonderfully useful—and *fast*—tool for finding information on the Web, a tool that was then developed into a slick, user-friendly search tool by the folks who bring you HotWired.

What's Out There

HotBot is there for all the world to work with, at http://www.hotbot.com/.

HotBot is very simple to use; in fact, it's pretty much the most user-friendly search tool going. Basically you just type in some text that describes what you want to find and click on the Search graphic. Let's go over the steps in detail, however:

1. Open the HotBot home page. In the text box, type a word or phrase that describes what you seek.

2. Choose whether you want to search the Web or Usenet.

3. Using the handy pull-down menu, you can specify whether to look for

   ◆ All of the words

   ◆ Any of the words

   ◆ The exact phrase

   ◆ The person

   ◆ Links to this URL

   ◆ The Boolean expression (lets you use terms such as AND and OR)

 If you have a home page of your own, and you want to know how many of the documents in HotBot's database include a link back to your page, you can find out who's linking to you by choosing the Links to This URL option.

4. Choose how many results you want to see on each page (the default is ten) and how much description you want to see on each page (full, brief, or URLs only).

5. Click on the Search button. The Netscape N icon will become animated as HotBot searches its database for matching documents, and in a few seconds a new page will appear listing the results.

The results will be shown in order of relevancy. In other words, if you type three words as your search criteria, the site that contains the largest number of references to all three of those words will appear first in the list of results.

HotBot typically displays only 10 documents at a time on its results page. If your search resulted in more than 10 matching documents, click on the red arrows to display the next set of matches. To revise your search, adjust the words displayed in the search box, or click on Revise Search.

Performing More Complicated Searches with HotBot

On the initial search page, HotBot includes some very easy-to-use features that let you control which documents it returns. The search options are in the form of buttons: You can click on a specific button to change certain options, or you can use the Open All button to change many options at once. This is where HotBot excels—the advanced search options are terrifically easy to use.

Here's how to perform more complex searches with HotBot:

1. On the HotBot search page, click on the Modify link to display advanced search options. A new HotBot page will appear, where you can focus your search.

HotBot offers even more advanced search options. To get to them, just click on the appropriate links below the search box on the HotBot home page. A bunch of pull-down lists and text boxes will appear, allowing you to search the Web based on a page's Modification Date, Media Type (HTML vs. Java for example), or Physical Location. You can open all of these at once by clicking on Open All.

2. Pull-down lists and text boxes appear in the page. Use them to specify whether you want pages that must, should, or must not contain the word, phrase, person, or URL you then type into a text box.

3. To accomplish the search, click on the Search button. The Netscape N icon will become animated, and in a few seconds the results of your search will appear.

HotBot is the newest of the big search tools. Keep an eye on how its features affect the capabilities of other search tools over time.

◆ Searching with Infoseek

Infoseek is yet another combination Web-crawler/database search engine. Infoseek (see Figure 8.9) has recently launched Ultraseek, which hides all the editorial pages and gives you just the search tool. You can jump to the other features at your leisure by using the menu that always appears on the left of the window.

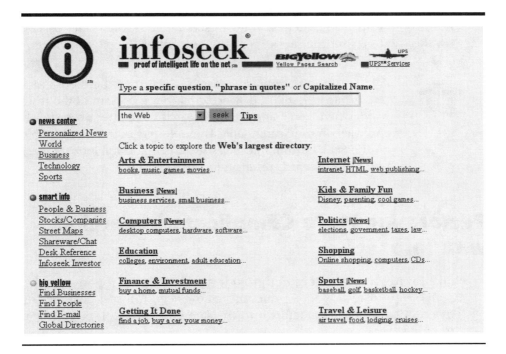

Figure 8.9: Infoseek offers you search tools, a directory, and a plethora of other handy gadgets.

Searching via Infoseek is a breeze. Simply follow these steps:

1. In the text box on the Infoseek home page, type a word or a phrase that describes what you seek.

2. Choose whether you want to search the Web, Usenet, newsgroups, news wires, premier news, e-mail addresses, company profiles, or Web FAQs.

What's Out There

Seek Infoseek, and ye shall find it at `http://www.infoseek.com/`.

3. Click on the Seek button. The Netscape N icon will become animated, and in a few seconds, the Infoseek Net Search Results page will appear, showing the results of your search.

Infoseek displays only 10 matches at first; if your search produced more than these initial 10 matches, you can see the additional ones by clicking on the <u>Next 10</u> link that appears at the bottom of the page.

If you want to narrow your search to less than the thousands of results Infoseek might deliver, scroll to the bottom of the results page, where you'll find another search box. Enter a word or two and click on the Search Only These Results button, and then click on the Seek button. Infoseek's search engine will look for the new terms in the search results it just brought up.

Performing More Complicated Searches with Infoseek

Like Excite, Infoseek does not provide a separate page for advanced searching—instead, you conduct more advanced Infoseek searches simply by entering special characters into the same text box you originally used to do a basic search in Infoseek.

To perform a more complicated search of Infoseek

1. In the text box where you enter the words that describe what you want to search for, you can add special characters before each word to control its meaning. Here are your options:

Use This	And That Will Mean
	Entering nothing special with a word means that the word may appear or may not appear in the document for the document to be considered a match.
+	Prefixing a word with a + means that the word must be in the document for the document to be considered a match.
-	Prefixing a word with a - means that the word must not appear in the document for the document to be considered a match.
" "	Surrounding words with quotation marks means that the words should appear next to each other in the document for the document to be considered a match.
-	Connecting words with a - has the same meaning as surrounding them with quotation marks. The specified words must appear next to each other in a document for the document to be considered a match.

As an example, to search for documents that are about Netscape Navigator, but not about version 2, you can type +**"Netscape Navigator"** –**"2.0"** in the search box. Or to find the phrase "seek and ye shall find," you could surround the phrase with quotation marks, or type in **seek-and-ye-shall-find**.

2. With the search criteria entered, click on the Seek button. The Netscape N icon will become animated, and in a few seconds the results of your search will appear.

Infoseek's search functions are case sensitive. This is actually handy when you're searching for proper names. If you search on a couple of words that start with uppercase letters, Infoseek assumes you are searching for someone (or thing) with a name. If, for example, you search for *Bill Gates*, Infoseek will seek the words *Bill* and *Gates* near each other, and will ignore all references to "paying your bills" and "gate crashing." You can find more handy Infoseek search tips by clicking on the <u>Tips</u> link on any Infoseek page.

♦ CNET: On the Air and Online

Is it a Web site, a TV show, or more? CNET is a unique venture that encompasses both television (in the form of a TV show about the online world) and the Web (in the form of a Web site that covers the same topic). Because this is a book about Communicator and not TV, we'll talk about the Web site, which is a good starting point for your general investigation of what's on the Internet. The CNET site offers constantly updated news (with a slant towards computers and the Internet), feature articles, reviews, and other special features. This (perhaps along with Wired's HotWired site) is the place to look for the latest news about the Web.

In addition to the primary CNET site, the folks who bring you CNET run a number of other Web sites, including <u>shareware.com</u> (a great place to find shareware) and <u>search.com</u> (a wonderful source for search tools—not just the biggies, but specialized ones that run the gamut from art to wines).

What's Out There

For Web news, reviews, and starting points, tune in to CNET at `http://www.cnet.com/`.

One-Stop Searching with search.com

For a starting point from which to launch a comprehensive search, try search.com (Figure 8.10), which was created by the folks at CNET. They composed this page by compiling what seems like every search gizmo around, ranging from the big whoppers such as AltaVista, Lycos, HotBot, and Infoseek, to smaller, more specialized search tools that cover specific topics. This wonderful resource provides you with the opportunity to go to a one-stop location and search a bunch of databases quickly and conveniently. Best yet, the folks at CNET describe each and every site included in their list of sites to search; their favorites are marked "*top pick.*"

Figure 8.10: For a place to start any kind of search, the extraordinarily comprehensive search.com can't be beat.

Once you have search.com's home page on screen, you are ready to search any one of many different search engines. On the search.com home page, you'll see text boxes and buttons for many of the popular search engines on the Web.

What's Out There

You can access search.com at `http://www.search.com/`.

 There are a bunch of specialized search tools listed by topic on the the search.com page. Click on a topic and the search.com page will display a list of search tools related to your chosen category. You can then select one and work with it as you like. To return to the search.com page, click on the search.com Home icon on the top of the search page you are using.

1. Open search.com's home page, and you'll see a search box. The Search the Web box uses any of several popular search tools as its engine. (The options you have in your search vary from one search tool to the next. We've talked about many of them in detail in other sections of this chapter, though, so you can find out more by turning to the appropriate section.) Type words describing what you are looking for in the search box.

2. Click on the Search button. In a few seconds, the search.com page will be replaced by your chosen search tool's listing of the sites that match your criteria.

CNET's search.com is a wonderful starting point for your Web travels no matter what your topic of interest, because it rounds up a lot of options and offers you convenient access to all of them. Be sure to add it to your Bookmark list; it may even be a good choice for a start-up home page.

What's Out There

William Cross created the "original" All-in-One Search page (`http://www .albany.net/allinone/`) by compiling every search gizmo of merit, ranging from the big whoppers to smaller, more specialized search tools. This wonderful resource provides you with an independent alternative to the big, bad search sites, and the opportunity to go to a one-stop location and search a bunch of databases quickly and conveniently.

Downloading Shareware, Helpers, and Plug-Ins

From CNET's shareware.com, you can easily search many repositories of shareware, freeware, and public domain software scattered throughout the Internet. Whatever you're looking for—from that handy little address book program to video players, you'll find it quickly via shareware.com. What's more, you'll find a short review of some software, a list of new and popular releases, and tips on downloading. And, of course, you'll be able to download the stuff that interests you.

Using shareware.com is a snap. All you have to do is

1. From Navigator's menu bar, select File ➤ Open Page. The Open Page dialog box will appear.

2. In the text box, type `http://www.shareware.com/` and press ↵. The Open Page dialog box will close and, in a few seconds, the shareware.com home page will appear, as shown in Figure 8.11.

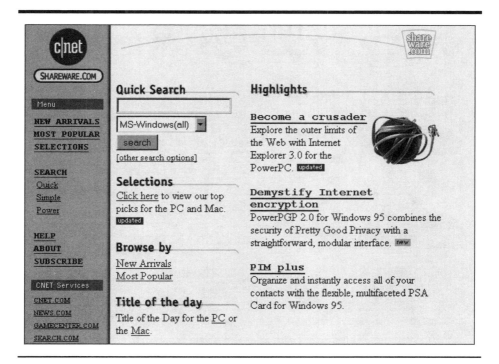

Figure 8.11: The shareware.com home page is your starting point for quickly finding and getting that shareware, freeware, or public domain file you've been seeking.

What's Out There

Your convenient source for shareware, freeware, and public domain software is shareware.com, at `http://www.shareware.com/`. Or try another CNET creation, download.com. Download.com, at `http://www.download.com/`, is a version of shareware.com that's customized for PC users—it operates the same way, but the only platform it's concerned with is Windows.

3. Enter what you are searching for in the text box along the top of the page and click on the Search button. (For example, to search for a program to play MPEG video files, type **MPEG** and click on the Search button. MPEG is a compressed video format commonly used on the Internet.) In a few seconds, the results of your search will appear (Figure 8.12), in a list with descriptions.

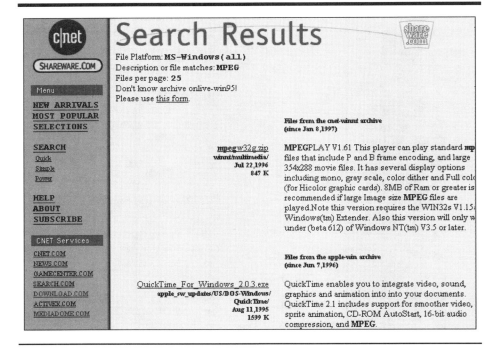

Figure 8.12:   We found a number of files related to MPEG video.

4. Look through the descriptions until you find something that appeals to you. Click on the link (the underlined filename) next to the description of interest. A page will appear listing links to the FTP sites that contain the file. You may have to scroll down the page a bit to find the list. The FTP sites will be listed based on reliability, with the most reliable at the top.

5. To download the file, click on the link at the top of the list. The Unknown File Type dialog box will appear:

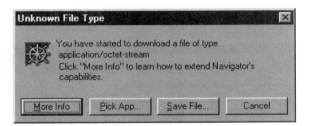

6. Click on Save File. The old familiar Save As dialog box will appear, allowing you to save the file to your local machine in the usual way. Just accept the filename as is, and click on Save. (This is when the file is actually downloaded.)

 The next time you download a file of the same type (ZIP or EXE, for example), you may not see the Unknown File Type dialog box. That's because that file type is no longer unknown to Navigator or to your computer, since you've already downloaded a file of the same name. Also, if you install a software decompression utility, this application may work with Communicator to launch automatically and streamline the downloading process. See "Dealing With Compressed Files," later in this chapter, for more information on WinZip and other decompression tools.

 If you don't experience success in downloading the file from the first site that appears in the list, try another site—search.com usually displays a dozen or so FTP sites that contain the file of interest, and one of them is bound to work.

That's about all there is to using shareware.com. As you can see, this is a gemlike way to get software for your computer quickly and conveniently.

Somebody releases some new plug-in or helper app that you can use with Communicator just about weekly. Each of these plug-ins or helper apps makes Communicator do something new or better than before, but keeping up with all the new stuff can become overwhelming. Luckily, those thoughtful people at Netscape maintain two pages about plug-ins and helper apps. *Plug-ins* are special programs written especially for Communicator. *Helper apps* are not written solely for Communicator—they are general Windows programs that Communicator can use to display some type of data it receives over the Net that's beyond its own capabilities.

What's Out There

Besides the glorious search.com and shareware.com, CNET operates several other sites that you might find useful. Gamecenter.com, at `http://www.gamecenter.com/`, is all about games for your PC, many of which you can download. To find the latest and greatest in ActiveX controls, pay a visit to ActiveX.com, at (what else?) `http://www.activex.com/`. And if you want to experience the highest-tech site yet, trot on over to Mediadome, a joint venture between CNET and Intel, at `http://www.mediadome.com/`. You can get to all this stuff with a single click from any CNET page.

Dealing with Compressed Files

Often you'll find that the software files you download from shareware.com (or from the Web in general) are *zipped*—they've been compressed with a utility such as PKZip or LHarc, which you'll know because the file extension is either .zip (for PKZip) or .lzh (for LHarc). Files are zipped (*compressed, shrunk,* or *compacted*) to make them smaller, so they can be transmitted more quickly. Compressed files can often be half the size of the original file; some files can be compressed to as little as 1/20 their original size. If a file has been compressed, you'll need a companion program to uncompress the file. PKZip/PKUnzip is available commercially; WinZip is downloadable shareware (which you must pay a fee for if you like it and want to keep using it); and LHarc is downloadable freeware (meaning you can use it without paying for it). Other compression/decompression programs are also available—some emulate or are compatible with their commercially available cousins (WinZip, for example, will compress and uncompress PKZip files). Of course, you can find all the compression utilities you need by using shareware.com.

What's Out There

WinZip is a very good Zip/Unzip program for Windows. You can find out all about it—and even download it—from `http://www.winzip.com/`.

◆ Search Tools for Your Every Need

As we've mentioned, there's more to online searching than the major search engines and directories. Many sites feature their own subject-specific guides and search gadgets, and there are oodles of them out there on more topics than you'd believe. We don't have the space to mention even a fraction of what's out there, but you can always find more at search.com or Netscape's own Net Search page. Here, we'll take a look at some of our perennial favorites.

Your Usenet Research Tool: Deja News

Over the years, thousands (if not millions) of articles have been posted to Usenet, a branch of the Internet that exists solely for that purpose. Deja News has archived every article posted since March 1995; chances are that any article posted there today will be archived by Deja News within minutes. What's great about Deja News is that you don't have to spend time sifting through newsgroups by hand to find a single article that's useful to you. Deja News lets you search the archives quickly and easily, and whether you're interested in Russian home-style cooking or artificial intelligence, there's a newsgroup out there that answers your questions.

So what the heck is Usenet, anyway? To find out more about Usenet news, just go read Chapter 5.

The Deja News home page offers several features:

◆ Quick Search, a fast and easy way to search the archives

◆ Power Search, which lets you fine-tune your search by date and topic

◆ A Newsgroup name search that helps you find out what news-groups cover the kind of information you're looking for

◆ Deja News Classifieds, which focuses attention on those news-groups that include wanted and for-sale ads

◆ Myriad help files that tell you all about Usenet, Deja News, and how to use them

Of course, the easiest way to search Deja News is the Quick Search box. Just like the search box featured on any other search engine, the Quick Search box lets you enter a few words, and when you click the Find but-ton, you'll get a list of Usenet articles related to your query. The articles are listed in reverse chronological order, so you'll get the most current articles first. You don't need a newsreader, or any knowledge of how Usenet works, to use Deja News. You can read these articles just by click-ing on their names in the search results list; the articles themselves will then appear in Netscape's viewing area.

If you want more searching power, just click on Power Search.

What's Out There

Read all the Usenet news you want without ever opening a newsreader. Just go to Deja News, at http://www.dejanews.com/.

Find Long Lost Friends: Four11

You know your old friend Sally from high school has an e-mail address, but you can't remember it, and you've lost her phone number, too. Or perhaps you want to know whether anyone from your college has taken the plunge and gotten online. Or maybe you have an odd name, like Kryniewski, and you want to know if there are any other Kryniewskis around. It used to be you had to guess at e-mail addresses if you didn't know them for sure, or just hope for a Christmas card to find out how to contact your old friends.

Four11 (see Figure 8.13), named after the telephone company's information service, lets you search their listings to find publicly available information about people. Mostly, Four11 is good for finding e-mail addresses, but some people's *profiles* (the search results) feature phone numbers, personal interests, company and alumni information, and even Internet Phone numbers.

Four11's home page features several text boxes, for things like first name, last name, city, state, and domain. (You might know that your cousin Bill is at berkeley.edu, but not know what to put in front of the @.) Fill in the text boxes you're sure of, and then click the search button to get a list of people who share those criteria. You can experiment with the fields you fill out; you may not find Roberta Kryniewski by searching for her whole name, but then, you might not know she's going by Bobbi these days.

Don't forget to try searching for your own name to see what comes up. If you're not listed, and you'd like to be, you can click on Add Me to fill out a profile for yourself. Creating a free membership this way also lets you use bonus features, such as Four11's free e-mail service, if you like.

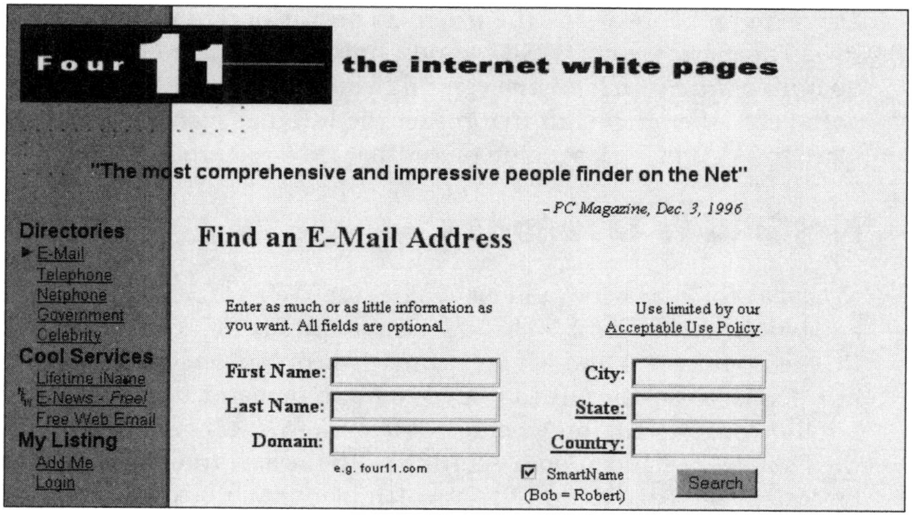

Figure 8.13: Find your old pals from college with Four11.

Four11 gets some of their listings from people who type them in, but it culls the others from the Internet at large. Usenet posts, public guestbooks, and some members-only Web sites are all fair game. If someone has sold your e-mail address to Four11 and you want it removed, or if the database includes inaccurate or obsolete data, write to them at support@Four11.com.

What's Out There

Find yourself (and other people) with Four11. Their address is easy to find: http://www.four11.com/.

You can search Four11 from Communicator's Address Book program. See Chapter 5 for more details.

Finding Non-Web Internet Stuff

As you're probably aware, the Internet consists of more than just Web sites. There are live chats, 3-D worlds, online games, and plenty more to do online. Any search engine can find you a Web site, but few offer pointers to the other stuff that makes the Internet such a happening place to be. Let's look at some places that show you the way.

NetGuide's Live Index

NetGuide, the magazine, and NetGuide, the Web site, both show you how and where to find great Web sites. Happenings is the section of NetGuide that tells you when and where to find live content such as chats, live broadcasts, and prerecorded live content on demand. Not only can you scroll through a lengthy schedule of live Internet events, you can search the listings for happenings occurring in the near future. Just scroll to the bottom of the page to find the now-familiar search boxes and pull-down menus that let you conduct your search. Don't miss the rest of NetGuide, either—it's quite a site!

What's Out There

NetGuide hangs out at http://www.netguide.com/. You can find the Net-Guide's Happenings page at http://www.netguide.com.server-java/NGPAGE/Happenings.

Visit Other Worlds with the Vertex

In Chapter 7, you read all about VRML and Live3D. The Vertex will help you find more worlds than a *Star Trek* expedition. You can search or browse through the Vertex, which is a paradise for both programmers and people who just want to have fun with VRML. Who knew there were so many VRML worlds about food or furniture? Most of the worlds featured at the Vertex are stored locally, rather than being a part of a larger site.

If you want to find more VRML worlds than the Vertex has, check out the VRML Review for news, reviews, and a slew of links. Or keep your eye on Proteinman's Top Ten VRML sites, a rotating list of the best VRML worlds available on the Web.

What's Out There

Step into the Vertex at http://www.thevertex.com/. Then, read the VRML Review at http://www.imaginative.com/VResources/vrml/, or see what Proteinman's got cooking at his Top Ten site, which we found at http://www.virtpark.com/theme/proteinman/.

Gamelan: All Java, All the Time

Drink too much coffee, and you'll be up all night. Spend too much time at Gamelan, and you'll be up all night downloading and playing with all the Java applets you'll find there. Gamelan is heaven for code geeks (a.k.a. programmers), but you'll find plenty to do there, as well. Any Java pro-grammer worth his salt has registered his Java applet with Gamelan, and you can browse through lists of Java applets by category (such as games and utilities) or search for something specific you're curious about.

What's Out There

Click yourself silly at Gamelan, whose home is `http://www.gamelan.com/index.shtml`.

Play Online Games Until Your Hands Fall Off

You've doubtless heard plenty about all the games you can play online, and you've probably wished for a rousing game of Scrabble a few times in the middle of work. Many of the biggest gaming sites on the Web focus on games you download or buy and then play on your PC. There are a few sites, however, that focus on games you play live, on the Web. Game Downer isn't searchable, but it has got links a-plenty to sites that let you play right away (or after a brief wait to download a Shockwave or Java toy). They also include links to some other gaming powerhouses.

What's Out There

Play away with Game Downer at `http://starcreations.com/gamedowner/`.

You've Got the Whole World on Your Desk: Travel and Geography Searches

Finding things on the Net may be easier sometimes than finding things in the physical world. Luckily, there are a battalion of sites available at your fingertips to help you find businesses, street addresses, zip codes, and information about travel and the world around you. Read on to find out how to make your PC into a combination atlas, phone book, and travel guide.

Look It Up in the BigBook

Out of quarters? Does your desk not have a phone book handy? Never fear, BigBook is here. It's a Yellow Pages for the whole United States, and it's fast and easy to use. BigBook's database includes Yellow Pages listings for towns great and small, and the search results include not only address and telephone information, but a link to a map of the area, in case you're visiting for the first time. You can also rate businesses and keep a personal address book at BigBook.

BigBook's home page features text boxes for business name, business category, city, state, and ZIP code. Fill in as much information as you know, then press the Look It Up button. In just a few seconds, you'll have more information than most phone books give you about the business of your choice. While many other sites, particularly the popular search engines, feature their own version of the Yellow Pages, we haven't found any that perform as well as BigBook.

What's Out There

Save yourself 50 cents and use BigBook, found at http://www.bigbook.com/.

 If you want to find a restaurant in Fresno, or an upholsterer in Boise, try looking up a business by category and city, leaving the name field blank. A list of categories is available on the BigBook site.

Travel the World with the Virtual Tourist and City.Net

The Virtual Tourist and City.Net help you locate two different kinds of information about the world around you. The Virtual Tourist directs you toward every Web server in the world, while the City.Net supplies you with travel and cultural information about the countries in question. You navigate both by clicking on maps of the world until you find what you're looking for.

City.Net is a great travel and tourism guide. You can look up information on nearly every city in the world, and when you get there, you'll find maps, links, and travel planning information. We use City.Net before we go on vacation.

What's Out There

Navigate through Web space with the Virtual Tourist, at http://www.vtourist .com/. To go directly to City.Net, visit http://www.city.net/.

Draw Yourself a Map with the Tiger Mapping Service

The Tiger Mapping Service is an accomplishment of the U.S. Census Bureau. Just enter a ZIP Code (a ZIP Code lookup is provided), the name of a town, or a latitude and longitude, and the Tiger Mapping Service will draw you a map. Better yet, these are *interactive* maps—you can place markers and locate highways on a map, zoom into it, and move the map over a few coordinates. Print it out and it's yours (see Figure 8.14).

To use the Tiger Mapping Service, just open its Web page and scroll to the bottom of the page to enter the name or ZIP Code of the place you want to look up. Click on Search to look up the data for that place. Each data page will have a link to a related map. To play with the map, click on the Map link; click on the buttons and boxes to mark up the map or zoom in and out, and then click on Redraw Map. It's fun *and* useful.

What's Out There

Thank the U.S. Government for the Tiger Mapping Service, found at http://tiger.census.gov/. Once you get there, click on the version number to open the actual mapping tools.

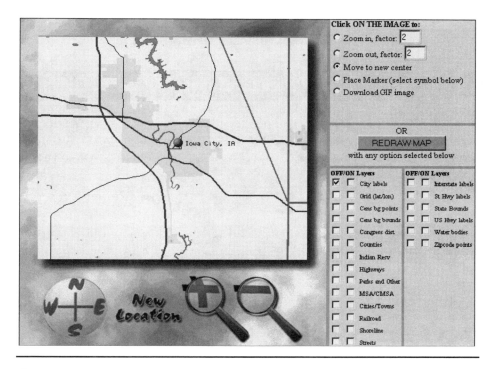

Figure 8.14: We drew it ourselves with the Tiger Mapping Service.

Stock Quotes, Get Your Stock Quotes Here

Don't worry about the price of your stocks until you're sure what the price is doing. There are several sites that will help you locate stock quotes and other valuable financial data:

◆ CheckFree lets you request up to five stock quotes at a time.

◆ NASDAQ features a search tool that lets you look up your favorite technology stock.

◆ Quote.com offers real-time stock quotes and SEC filings, as well as financial news.

◆ The international investor can look up currency exchange rates at Xenon Labs' Interactive Currency Table.

◆ For all-around great finance reporting, including several search options, visit the CNN Financial Network online.

What's Out There

CheckFree's Quote Server was found at `http://www.secapl.com/cgi-bin/qs`. The New York Stock Exchange and NASDAQ reside at `http://www.nyse.com/` and `http://www.nasdaq.com/`, respectively. Quote.com is at, well, `http://www.quote.com/`.

Look up the rates of Yen and Deutschmarks at `http://www.xe.net/currency/table.htm`.

Find your best bet for news at CNN Financial Network, whose URL is `http://cnnfn.com/`.

That's Entertainment (Searching)

Even entertainment sites are getting into the search tool act—and it's a good thing, too, because there's no better way to find something out than to ask the people who know about it. Keep clicking ahead to find out how to discover the best online entertainment pages available.

Visit Your Favorite Band (or At Least Their Home Page)

Someone, somewhere, has probably made a Web page all about your favorite band. If you want to find it, head right for the Ultimate Band List. Search or browse through listings for thousands of bands, and add a link to your own band's page, if you have one.

What's Out There

You'll find your favorite musicians in the Ultimate Band List, at `http://ubl.com/`.

Amazon.com: It's Not Just for Shopping Anymore

You may have heard that Amazon.com is the very best online bookstore there is. But you may not be aware that it's also a great research tool. Almost every book that's in print is listed in Amazon's extensive catalog. What that means for you is that looking up every title available by your favorite author, or browsing extensive bestseller and book award listings, is easier than ever before. Sure, Amazon wants you to buy books. And the Web site is so great, you may end up doing so.

What's Out There

As you might think, you'll find Amazon.com at http://www.amazon.com/.

Ultimate TV

Ultimate TV (the Web site formerly known as TV Net) has just about any TV-related information you could want. The reason Ultimate TV deserves mention here is its search functions: What's On Tonight, which lets you find out when your favorite shows are playing, and The Ultimate TV Show List, which guides you to still more Web sites about television. From one boob toob to another, Ultimate TV will help you find the shows you don't want to miss.

What's Out There

Turn on Ultimate TV at http://www.tvnet.com/.

IMDB: The Search Tool of the Stars

Trivia buffs and movie fans alike will revel in the Internet Movie Database. Started as a computer science project, the IMDB rapidly grew, as movie buffs from all over volunteered hours and hours to making the IMDB an unparalleled resource for film information. The IMDB consists mostly of filmographies—records of movies that list all major cast and crew members, as well as ratings information and other essential data. Most records for individual movies also include links to related sites on the Web, including sound and video clips.

What puts the IMDB in this chapter is its colossal search page. You can search dozens of different types of information, including actor's names, movie titles, Oscar winners, and Top 100 Movies (rated by the fans). To search the IMDB, just go there and click on <u>Search</u>. You'll win every movie trivia contest in town.

What's Out There

The Internet Movie Database resides at `http://www.imdb.com/`. Once you get there, click on the name of the country you're in to use the site physically closest to you.

Webster's Goes Digital

One might not think of *dictionary* and *search tool* in the same breath, but we think this clearly qualifies: The Hypertext Webster Interface online at Carnegie Mellon University lets you type the word of interest in a search box and then click on the Look Up Definition button to get a fully linked definition of the word of choice. (The interface actually searches several online "Webster's" dictionaries simultaneously to find what you seek.)

Another great online reference tool is Roget's Thesaurus—the original 1852 version (see Figure 8.15). Not only can you look up synonyms and antonyms, you can browse through the old outline of related words to see what Roget's logic was like. Roget's Thesaurus at thesaurus.com includes a great list of links to other online reference sites.

What's Out There

Search Webster's for your favorite words at `http://gs213.sp.cs.cmu.edu/prog/webster`, or visit Roget's Thesaurus online at `http://www.thesaurus.com/`.

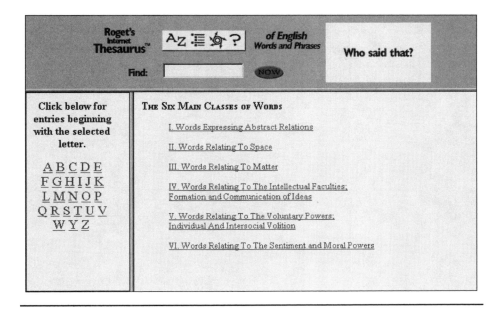

Figure 8.15: Roget's Thesaurus, at thesaurus.com, is colorful, useful, and amusing.

Now You Know

Having read this far, you now know everything you need to know to check out what's on the Web. Maybe at this point you'd like to find out how to publish your own Web pages, including how to make your own home page. In the next chapter, we'll look at Composer, Communicator's tool for Web publishing, and how to use it. We'll also explore including HTML in your e-mail messages, effectively making them into Web documents.

Composer: You Too Can Be a Web Publisher

By now, having used Navigator to roam the World Wide Web, you've seen the power of hypertext firsthand. You've seen that hypertext acts as both the Web's glue and its strands—binding it together yet hiding the complexities of Internet cruising. HTML (the HyperText Markup Language) is the standard (the agreed-upon system of marking up text to create pages and links) that makes the Web possible. Maybe you now want to get into the act. This chapter will tell you how to get started as a Web publisher using Netscape Composer, Communicator's Web page creation tool.

There are five basic steps to creating your own Web page:

◆ Organizing your concepts and materials

◆ Storyboarding (sketching out) the page(s) you intend to create

◆ Building a prototype

◆ Testing the prototype and making adjustments

◆ Putting your page on a server

This stuff isn't difficult—it helps to have a little experience, but, hey, everybody's got to start somewhere. Let's look at how HTML works and how you too can create HTML documents—without even using HTML!

 Don't expect to publish on the Net via your PC with a dial-up connection to the Internet. To actually publish a document for public viewing on the Web, you'll need access to an HTTP or FTP server. Most Internet service providers now provide access to an HTTP or FTP server at little or no additional cost. (We'll go over this in more detail at the end of this chapter.)

What's Out There

A great Beginner's Guide to HTML is available to all at `http://www.ncsa.uiuc.edu/General/Internet/WWW/HTMLPrimer.html`. The Composing Good HTML page is at `http://www.cs.cmu.edu/~tilt/cgh/`.

◆ About HTML: The HyperText Markup Language

There is plenty to know about HTML and creating and publishing Web documents. Sadly, we'll have to leave the finer points to the bigger books, but let's go over the basics: how to use formatting effects to make your page look attractive; how to make the heads in your documents appear in big, bold letters; how to link your documents to other documents; how to embed pictures in your documents; and how to make tables on your pages for organizing information.

The documents you see on the World Wide Web via Navigator look nice, but quite a bit of minor technological magic is going on. In actuality, the files for these documents are stored on a machine somewhere as plain ASCII text files—unlike word processing files, these ASCII text files include no formatting, and they employ no fancy fonts or attributes such as **bold** or *italics*.

They are plain as plain can be (see Figure 9.1). All the special effects that you see in a Web document—**bold**, *italic*, <u>links</u> to other documents—are represented in the ASCII text files with special codes that also are made up of plain text characters.

---

10 PM
by Brenda Kienan

How many women lie in darkness in Quakertown, Lansdale, Perkasie; considering their pasts, with the undusted rifle rack hanging over the bed and the green afghan heaped and dragging from the arm of a chair onto the carpet where the kids pulled it down and went on. Through the drawn shades the sound of a thousand crickets and wind sweeping between this trailer and the next. These are the elements of redemption: the wind rising,

```
10 PM
by Brenda Kienan

    How many women lie in darkness in Quakertown, Lansdale, Perkasie;
considering their pasts, with the undusted rifle rack hanging over the
bed and the green afghan heaped and dragging from the arm of a chair
onto the carpet where the kids pulled it down and went on. Through the
drawn shades the sound of a thousand crickets and wind sweeping between
```

Figure 9.1: The document shown on the top was created in a word-processing program; shown on the bottom is the same document in ASCII format. Notice that all the attributes (bold type) and all the formatting (different font sizes, for example) are lost in the translation.

This means, luckily, that you can use any word processor (Word for Windows 95, WordPerfect, whatever) or text editor (DOS Edit, Windows NotePad) to create your HTML documents. Of course, because you have Netscape Communicator, you can use Composer, the Web page creation tool, to compose your Web pages without even knowing HTML.

If you do decide to use a word processing program to edit HTML documents, make sure you save your files as plain ASCII text, or Navigator (or any other Web browser) won't be able to display them properly. Remember to turn off the smart quotes (or curly quotes) if you're using a word processor to create HTML; if you don't, those nifty curly quote marks will trip things up and your links and images won't work.

What's Out There

You'll find loads of resources for using just about any HTML trick at Sizzling HTML Jalfrezi—the URL is `http://www.woodhill.co.uk/html/html.htm`. Hotwired, that bastion of techno-gizmos, offers a site called Webmonkey that's all about designing and getting the most out of the Web. Visit Webmonkey at `http://www.webmonkey.com/`, or the beginner's guide, called Teaching Tool, at `http://www.webmonkey.com/webmonkey/teachingtool/`.

There are two basic kinds of HTML editors. One kind is like a fancy text editor that includes shortcuts and macros to help you insert HTML tags with little or no effort. The other kind of HTML editor is called a *WYSIWYG editor*—it includes the same shortcuts for creating effects on your Web pages, but you don't see the HTML tags while you're constructing the page itself. WYSIWYG stands for What You See Is What You Get, and that's the theory behind these editors. Instead of using code, you format the page using buttons and commands, making the document on the screen look exactly how you want your Web page to look. Microsoft Word, and other word processing programs, are another example of WYSIWYG programs—there's code involved in making words appear in special styles or different sizes, but you don't see the code, you just format the document. When you print out the word processing document, what you see on the printed page is what you saw on your screen.

Netscape Composer is an HTML editor of the WYSIWYG type. You use Composer just as you would a word processing program to add formatting to your page, and when you open the page with Navigator, it'll look pretty much the same as it did in Composer.

◆ The Elements of Web Page Design

Your Web home page will be accessed by anywhere from dozens to hundreds of thousands of people a day. You'll want it to convey clearly and concisely the message you intend to promote (whether that's your resume, your company's policy on hiring technical professionals, or an account of what's happening at the local soda pop machine). In this section, we'll cover some basic guidelines for successful Web page design, tossing out for your consideration all the big-hitting tips we've picked up in our Internet travels.

Get Organized

The best way to get started in the design of your home page is to organize your assets: the existing documents and images you want to work with, for example. Think about the message you want to convey and which types of images or text might be appropriate. (Is it fun and lighthearted or seriously corporate?)

Just What Is a Markup Language?

Traditionally, a markup language uses defined sequences of control characters or commands embedded within a document. These commands control what the document looks like when it is output to, say, a printer. When you print the document, the control character sequences or commands format the document, displaying such elements as bold headlines, subheads, bulleted items, and the like.

HTML is unlike typical markup languages in that it is not so much concerned with typefaces and character attributes, but rather with the internal document markup itself. In a traditional markup language, you use commands to indicate the typeface, font size, and style of text in a document. In HTML, the commands also indicate the headings, normal paragraphs, lists, and even links to other Web pages.

HTML is derived from the *Standard Generalized Markup Language* (SGML), which has come into increasingly common use in word processing and other programs for creating print documents. HTML follows the SGML paradigm in that it uses tags to do its formatting. Tags are little chunks of code that usually, but not always, come in pairs consisting of a start-tag and an end-tag marking off elements.

When you create HTML documents, bear in mind that not all Web browsers support all HTML extensions, or they may support other aspects of the HTML language differently. In fact, some of the HTML effects you can create with Composer are understood only by Netscape Navigator and Microsoft Internet Explorer. Be this as it may, the basic HTML structure presented in this chapter works well in most instances.

Create a Storyboard

With the stuff you want to work with in hand, sit down with paper and pencil (or some nifty drawing software) and plot the thing out. Storyboard (sketch) your home page and each page it will link to; include all the elements you're considering (text, images, buttons, hyperlinks). Don't be afraid to make adjustments; if your original concept doesn't flow nicely, can it and start again. You can't do too much advance planning.

Build a Prototype and Test It

When you've got your pages planned, go ahead and build a prototype. Then test it, test it, and test it again. Ask friends and colleagues to try it out and comment, and do all the fine-tuning you can. You want to make your *best* work public, not some funky work-in-progress.

 You can test your prototype without making it public. At the end of this chapter you'll find a section titled "Using Navigator to Check Your Web Page" that tells you how.

◆ A Quick Look at Successful Web Page Designs

The best way to get ideas and to explore creating a winning Web page is to study examples. We've been showing you Web pages throughout this book; here we're going to take a look at a few especially well-designed pages, pointing out what makes them so terrific. Most of the pages we've selected use fairly basic HTML to achieve stunning results. We've also included a few pages that use tables, frames, or forms to show you what you might one day aspire to—after you've learned the basics, you can move on to more complex and challenging effects as you see fit.

 If you want to see exactly what a Web designer did to create a specific page, launch Navigator, load the page of interest, and from the menu bar, select View ➤ Page Source. The HTML code for the page you're looking at will appear in a separate window, baring any "secret" techniques to you.

Top Tips for Pages That Eat Like a Meal

You have two seconds to grab your reader's attention. That's common knowledge in advertising and publishing circles. You can't go wrong if you follow these basic tips for designing an eye-catching page with links that work.

◆ Start with an idea, and watch your concept turn into content as you sketch out your ideas on a storyboard.

◆ Make the title short, catchy, descriptive, and accurate. And whatever you do, fulfill its promise. If you call your page "Thousands of Yummy Recipes," it had better be that.

◆ Provide clues about what you have to offer at the top of the page; don't *expect* anyone to scroll down.

◆ If your page is longer than three "screenfuls," break it up into more than one page.

◆ A sense of balance is key; don't let your page design get lopsided. But do balance white space, large and small images, and blocks of text to give your page interest and variety.

◆ It isn't "cool" to overload your page with extraneous doo-dads.

◆ Use text and link colors that complement rather than clash with the background.

◆ Be sure that anything that looks like a button behaves like one.

◆ Don't create two links with the same name that go two different places or two links with different names that go to one place.

◆ Make your links descriptive; avoid the generic. "Click Here!" isn't all that intriguing.

◆ Use well-compressed images that contain fewer than 50 colors.

◆ Use thumbnails as links to larger images.

◆ Remember that people will access your pages using different browsers that have different capabilities.

◆ Keep filenames short and make them consistent.

◆ Tell people the size of any downloadable files you include.

◆ Get permission to use text or images created by someone else.

◆ Make a link to the e-mail address of the Webmaster (that's you).

◆ Build a prototype and test it. Make sure you test every link on all of your pages before you announce your site to the world.

What's Out There

A great way to explore successful Web page design is to look at the sites of successful Web designers. You may find it useful to keep an eye on what's up with Organic at `http://www.organic.com`, Mann Consulting at `http://www.mann.com`, and Design/Systems of New York at `http://www.designsys.com`. Be sure to check out the pages of the clients, which are often given more attention than the designers' own home pages.

Another great way to get a grip on what works is to look at what not to do. Look as long as you're able at Clay Shirky's Worst Page on the World Wide Web at `http://www.panix.com/~clays/biff/`. For some more finger-pointing fun, check out Web Pages that Suck, at `http://www.webpagesthatsuck.com/`, or Yecch, a great parody of Yahoo, at `http://www.yeeeoww.com/yecch/yecchhome.html`.

Simple, Friendly, and Clear

Larry Rodrigues' U.S. Navy Airship Online Electronic Picture Book (Figure 9.2) documents his time spent around and aboard blimps while he was in the U.S. Navy in the 1950s. This picture book is an excellent example of how to combine pictures and text to make a page that's both easy to read and easy on the eye—even more so than many "real" photo albums that sit on coffee tables. The secret to this is that he kept things simple, using text wrapped around art in some of the site, and while he does use tables for attractive page headers, Larry created the main body of the picture book using simple HTML.

What's Out There

Fly by Larry Rodrigues' U.S. Navy Airship Online Electronic Picture Book at `http://www.GeoCities.com/CapeCanaveral/1022/`.

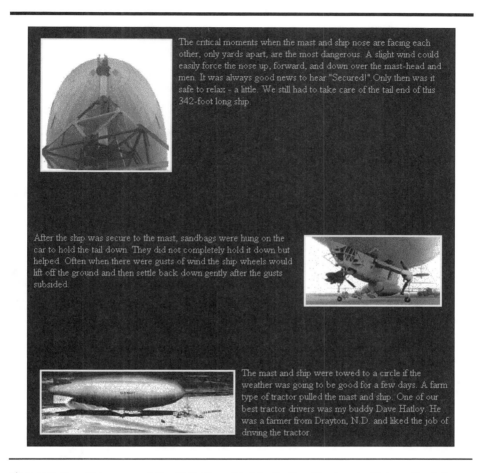

The critical moments when the mast and ship nose are facing each other, only yards apart, are the most dangerous. A slight wind could easily force the nose up, forward, and down over the mast-head and men. It was always good news to hear "Secured!". Only then was it safe to relax - a little. We still had to take care of the tail end of this 342-foot long ship.

After the ship was secure to the mast, sandbags were hung on the car to hold the tail down. They did not completely hold it down but helped. Often when there were gusts of wind the ship wheels would lift off the ground and then settle back down gently after the gusts subsided.

The mast and ship were towed to a circle if the weather was going to be good for a few days. A farm type of tractor pulled the mast and ship. One of our best tractor drivers was my buddy Dave Hatloy. He was a farmer from Drayton, N.D. and liked the job of driving the tractor.

Figure 9.2:   This page of the U.S. Navy Airship Online Electronic Picture Book is from the section called Refueling at Sea.

Terrifically Clickable

The Exploratorium's online exhibits are consistently well-designed—they're both beautiful to see and fun to navigate. The page shown in Figure 9.3 is from the section of the site called the Learning Studio. The red bar running down the left side of the page is a background GIF—this popular technique can be highly effective. The buttons also have plenty of eye appeal, and you can tell at a glance what lies behind them.

Figure 9.3: The Exploratorium's Learning Studio is fun, engaging, and no slouch when it comes to eye appeal.

What's Out There

Perhaps you've seen the Exploratorium's home page at http://www.exploratorium.edu. You should also check out the Learning Studio section of the site, located at http://www.exploratorium.edu/learning_studio/.

A Selective Color Palette

The Place of General Happiness (Figure 9.4) is not a run-of-the-mill personal home page, and Mark Thomas, its creator, doesn't use run-of-the-mill page design. Part electronic art exhibit, part creative writing journal, and part just plain weirdness, this site is a gem. Everything in these pages is kept simple, which is part of what makes the site look so good. A selective color palette helps pull together the visuals, and an icon at the bottom of every page to send you home helps pull together navigation.

Figure 9.4: The Place of General Happiness uses unconventional design for unconventional content.

What's Out There

Make your way to the Place of General Happiness at http://www.paranoia .com/~sorabji/. For a look at another unique navigation scheme, try the Hole, at http://www.paranoia.com/~sorabji/index2.html.

Clever Use of Fonts

Addicted to Stuff is a stylish, funny, and downright amazing home page produced by Linda Abrams. She doesn't do it for money, but it looks just as good as many big-budget commercial sites we know. Her front page

(Figure 9.5) is primarily made up of text, with different font types cleverly used to give the page visual interest. The columns are achieved through the use of tables with the borders turned off. Although most of this site is worth perusing, you might be particularly interested in her HTML tips for beginners, called Addicted to HTML or So You Want a Home Page.

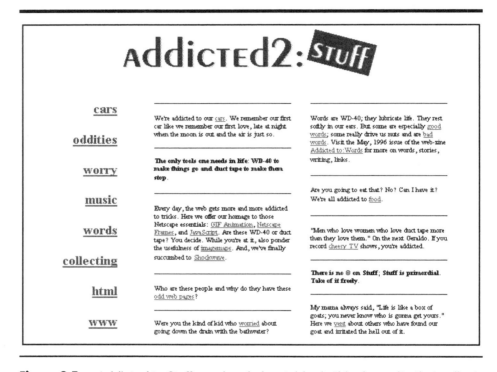

Figure 9.5: Addicted to Stuff uses borderless tables in this clever site that collects everything but dust.

What's Out There

Addicted to Stuff can be found at `http://www.morestuff.com/`. To jump right to Addicted to HTML, try `http://www.morestuff.com/htmlpage/a2html.htm`. For insight into using tables to create visual effects, scope out Netscape's guide to tables at `http://home.netscape.com/assist/net_sites/tables.html`.

Frames at Their Best

GroundZero (Figure 9.6) is a design firm that boasts clients ranging from ABC to CyberShop. Although the site is rife with borderless frames and JavaScript, you can take a few cues from their understated color scheme, their clever use of typography and images, and their clearly marked navigational tools.

Figure 9.6: The frames-driven home page at GroundZero uses buttons, colors, and of course, frames, wisely.

What's Out There

Visit GroundZero at http://www.groundzero.com/. When you're ready to tackle frames yourself, visit Netscape's guide at http://home.netscape.com/assist/net_sites/frames.html.

Button, Button, Who's Got the Button?

Using a button bar may well be one of the best ways to provide your site's users a clear navigation scheme. The one we show in Figure 9.7 is from the IRS's daily newsletter, a surprisingly non-stodgy piece of publishing from everybody's favorite government agency.

What's Out There

There's nothing taxing about the design at the IRS site (`http://www.irs.ustreas.gov/prod/cover.html`).

Figure 9.7: The button bar at the bottom of the IRS's pages is clearly clickable.

What's Out There

David Siegel is a master Web designer whose site is jam-packed with tips, solid information, examples, and links to other sites you may find helpful in your Web designing adventures. David Siegel has his own domain name, and his home page, at http://www.dsiegel.com/, is in itself an example of good design. Be sure to follow the Web Wonk and Typography links for great advice on Web page design, and go to the Nine Act Structure for wonderful information on structuring content. Siegel bestows the High Five Awards for excellence in Web design and presentation every week; take a look at http://www.highfive.com/ to see winners of this selective award. Other Siegel sites of interest include Killer Sites, at http://www.killersites.com/, which includes a heap of advice from his book by the same name; and Studio Verso, at http://www.verso.com/, the home of Siegel's design studio.

◆ Using HTML to Mark Up a Document

Now let's take a look at how all this is done. Marking up a document is a pretty simple matter of identifying what you want any given element to be and then literally marking it as that type of element (see Figure 9.8).

The markup, or tag, in HTML documents is surrounded by angle brackets, like this:

```
<title>
```

These tags usually come in pairs and affect everything between them. For example, surrounding a heading you'll see <h1> at the beginning, matching the </h1> at the end. This is called opening and closing an HTML tag, which Composer does automatically for all the tags that need it. More on this as we go along.

There are a few exceptions to the pairing of HTML tags, which we'll point out during the course of this chapter.

HTML tags can be written using upper- or lowercase letters—it doesn't matter.

```
<html>
<head>
<title>10 PM</title>
</head>
<body>
<h1>10 PM</h1>
<h2>by Brenda Kienan</h2>
<p>
        How many women lie in darkness in Quakertown, Lansdale, Perkasie;
considering their pasts, with the undusted rifle rack hanging over the bed and the
green afghan heaped and dragging from the arm of a chair onto the carpet where the
kids pulled it down and went on. Through the drawn shades the sounds of a thousand
crickets and wind sweeping between this trailer and the next. These are the elements
of redemption: the wind rising, rattling the corrugated plastic roof of the neighbor's
carport, the husband coughing over the droning tv news, the washer clicking and
getting louder as the clothes inside it spin out of balance. This is an ordering of events
that carries one day to the next.<p>
        How many women, each in her own separate darkness, surveying what might
have happened, while the rushing wind finds its way into heating ducts and whistles
through tin.<p>
        <i>Papa, it is vanishing.</i> The blue June evenings and the scent of dusty
pavement as a long-awaited rain falls. <i>I thought I'd still know, but I'm
drifting.</i> White tulips. Gold star confetti sprayed across starched tablecloths.
The priest's thick fingers holding a book.<p>
        How many women making a list, of the ways they might have gone, of the
friends they see in markets, marriages lost, pushing carts full of children, sugary
cereals, cheap meats. How many mornings of driving: her own child to another's care,
her husband (who's lost his license) to work, herds of teenagers in a yellow bus to
school. How many times the red-haired boy pushing his way to the seat behind her,
bringing her gifts of novelty pencils, a sandwich, cloisonn&eacute; earrings.<p>
        How many women wondering, each in her cool separate darkness, if the news
is yet over, if the wind will grow still.<p>
<h3>Copyright 1995 Brenda Kienan</h3>
</body>
</html>
```

10 PM

by Brenda Kienan

How many women lie in darkness in Quakertown, Lansdale, Perkasie; considering their pasts, with the undusted rifle rack hanging over the bed and the green afghan heaped and dragging from the arm of a chair onto the carpet where the kids pulled it down and went on. Through the drawn shades the sounds of a thousand crickets and wind sweeping between this trailer and the next. These are the elements of redemption: the wind rising, rattling the corrugated plastic roof of the neighbor's carport, the husband coughing over the droning tv news, the washer clicking and getting louder as the clothes inside it spin out of balance. This is an ordering of events that carries one day to the next.

How many women, each in her own separate darkness, surveying what might have happened, while the rushing wind finds its way into heating ducts and whistles through tin.

Papa, it is vanishing. The blue June evenings and the scent of dusty pavement as a long-awaited rain falls. *I thought I'd still know, but I'm drifting.* White tulips. Gold star confetti sprayed across starched tablecloths. The priest's thick fingers holding a book.

How many women making a list, of the ways they might have gone, of the friends they see in markets, marriages lost, pushing carts full of children, sugary cereals, cheap meats. How many mornings of driving: her own child to another's care, her husband (who's lost his license) to work, herds of teenagers in a yellow bus to school. How many times the red-haired boy pushing his way to the seat behind her, bringing her gifts of novelty pencils, a sandwich, cloisonné earrings.

How many women wondering, each in her cool separate darkness, if the news is yet over, if the wind will grow still.

Copyright 1995 Brenda Kienan

Figure 9.8: In an HTML-coded document (above) you see tags (within angle brackets) surrounding the element to which they refer. In the resulting Web document (below), you do not see the tags—you see only the effect they have on the document displayed.

In Figure 9.9 you can see all the elements of a basic HTML document. Take note of the following:

◆ The entire document enclosed between <html> and </html>

◆ The head of the document enclosed between <head> and </head>

◆ The title of the document enclosed between <title> and </title>

◆ The body of the document enclosed between <body> and </body>

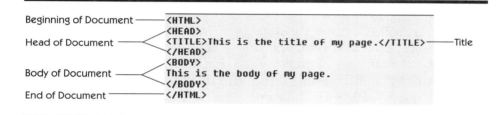

Figure 9.9: Here you can see the HTML coding for the basic elements of a Web document.

In the sections that follow, we'll look at the basic HTML tags you can use in your documents. Remember as we go along that, even though you don't see the code, Composer is putting it in there for you. The effects you create with Composer are still HTML codes, they're just hiding.

 If you're using a word processor to create an original document you intend for Web publication, you can, of course, simply write in the HTML coding as you go along; you don't have to write the document first and enter the tags afterward.

◆ Using Netscape Composer to Create a Web Page

It doesn't take a whole lot of technical know-how to get started and create a simple Web page using Netscape Composer. First, we need to open Composer. There are several ways you can do this:

◆ From the Windows 95 Start Menu, select Programs ➤ Netscape Communicator ➤ Netscape Composer.

◆ With Netscape Navigator open, use the menu bar to select File ➤ New ➤ Blank Page.

◆ From the Navigator menu bar, select Communicator ➤ Page Composer.

In any case, the Netscape Composer window will appear in all its glory. It looks like a cross between Navigator and a word processor, and that's because it basically is. The Composer icon features a pen and paper. If you use the Windows 95 Taskbar to shift between a Navigator window and a Composer window, you'll notice that the Composer icon is blue.

Let's take a quick look at the Composer window and what everything does (see Figure 9.10). Below the standard menu bar is the Composer toolbar, which includes a different selection of commands than does the Navigator toolbar. Below the toolbar is the style bar, which contains many of the same commands that similar style bars do in word processing programs. We'll review each button in turn.

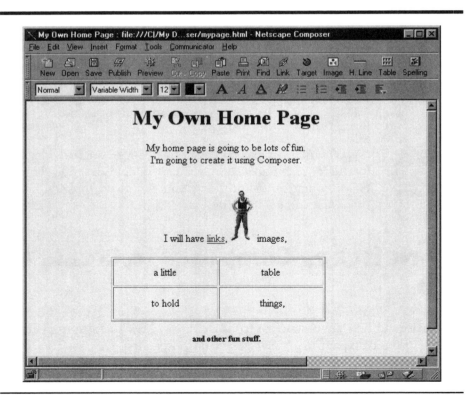

Figure 9.10:   Composer makes creating Web pages simple.

The Tool	Its Name	What It Does
New	New	Creates a new, blank HTML file
Open	Open	Opens a page from your hard drive
Save	Save	Saves the file you're working on
Publish	Publish	Uploads a file to a Web server
Preview	Preview	Loads the current page into a Navigator window
Cut	Cut	Cuts the selected text onto the Clipboard
Copy	Copy	Copies the selected text onto the Clipboard
Paste	Paste	Pastes the text from the Clipboard into the window
Print	Print	Prints the current document
Find	Find	Finds text on the current page
Link	Link	Creates a hypertext link
Target	Target	Marks a specific location you can link to
Image	Image	Inserts an image onto the page
H. Line	H. Line	Inserts a ruled line
Table	Table	Inserts a table
Spelling	Spelling	Checks the spelling of the current document

We'll find out exactly what these things do later in this chapter. Now let's look at the Composer style bar:

The Tool	Its Name	What You Do With It
Normal	Paragraph Style	Choose a formatting style for the selected text
Variable Width	Font	Choose a font face for selected text
12	Font Size	Choose a font size for selected text
	Font Color	Choose a font color for selected text
A	Bold	Make the selected text boldface
A	Italic	Make the selected text italicized
A	Underline	Make the selected text underlined
	Remove All Styles	Remove all font styles from the selected text
	Bulleted List	Make the selected text into a bulleted list
	Numbered List	Make the selected text into a numbered list
	Decrease Indent	Remove one indent level
	Increase Indent	Add one indent level
	Alignment	Align text to the left, center, or right

These buttons will make formatting text easy as cake, particularly if you've used a word processing program before.

There are two things you should know right off the bat when you're creating a page with Composer. One is how to save your files, and the other is how to preview them in the Navigator window.

Saving Web Pages on Your Hard Drive

As soon as you've created a new, blank file with Composer, you should save it. That way, you'll be able to use all of Composer's features, some of which require that your file be saved before they'll work.

1. From the Composer menu bar, select File ➤ Save. The familiar Save As dialog box will appear.

2. Choose a name for your file. Remember that although page.html will do for now, it'll be harder to keep track of which page is which should you go on to create several HTML documents.

 You can type a name such as **page** without specifying a file extension; Composer (and Windows 95) will automatically append .htm as the file extension. That might be okay with you right now, but Web conventions prefer that HTML files end in the extension .html. You can type in a name for your document such as **page.html** to automatically get in the habit of this Internet naming convention.

3. Click on Save to save your file and return to the Composer window.

Sometimes Composer disappears briefly while it's saving your file. Not to worry—if you can't see it, just use the Windows 95 Taskbar to get back to where you started from.

 Remember to save your work every time you make a major change. A quick shortcut for doing this is pressing Ctrl+S on the keyboard.

Checking Your Work with Navigator

As you follow along in this chapter, you can test out any or all of the Web page formatting techniques we talk about. If you want to see what your work-in-progress would look like online, you can preview your pages with Navigator. You can do this as often as you like to see how you're coming along. It's as easy as this single step:

1. On Composer's toolbar, click on the Preview button—that's the one that looks like the little Navigator icon. (If you haven't saved your most recent changes, you'll be prompted to do so.) A new Navigator window will open, displaying your creation.

That's all there is to that.

 If you make changes to your page and you want to view them, make sure you first save them in Composer. Then you can return to the Navigator window containing your Web project and click on the Reload button. The freshest version of your Web page will appear.

Every Document Must Have the "Required" Tags

Every HTML document must include certain tags, which essentially identify the document as an HTML document and, as such, show its beginning and end. Note that even these fundamental HTML tags come in pairs—the <html> at the beginning of the document matches the </html> at the end of the document. When you create a new page with Composer, it automatically inserts these tags for you, but you'll want to specify certain things, such as the title and author of the page.

You don't have to worry about the code for these essential tags, but it's easy to edit their content:

1. From the Composer menu bar, select Format ➤ Page Title. The Page Properties dialog box will appear, as seen in Figure 9.11

2. In the Title text box, type a title for your page. This is the title that will appear in the Navigator title bar. For example, on Netscape's home page, the page title is "Welcome to Netscape!"

3. If you like, type your name (or even a pseudonym) in the Author text box, and a description of your page in the Description text box.

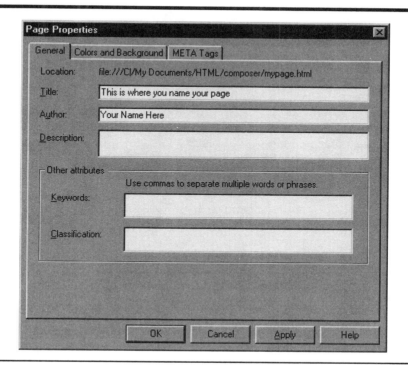

Figure 9.11: The Page Properties dialog box lets you name your page, among other things.

 Unlike the page title, the words you type in the Author and Description text boxes will not appear on your Web page, but they may be used by search engines in indexing your page once it's online.

4. When you're finished, click on OK to close the Page Properties dialog box and return to the Composer window. You'll see the title you chose in the title bar of the Composer window.

You now have all the basic elements of a Web page in place—except for content, that is. Once you give the page you created in Composer a title and save it, it is technically a fully sound document. But you don't want to show your friends how good you are at making blank Web pages. Let's move on to the meat of the page—the text.

Communicator's Edit Page Feature

Suppose you're surfing the Net, and you see a page you really like. Maybe you love the color scheme, or the way they did their tables, or the layout of the text and graphics. From Navigator's menu bar, just select File ➤ Edit Page. Navigator will download the page and all the images and open a Composer window, which allows you to change the Web page as you see fit. Be careful, however. You can't just change a couple words and then claim the page as your own; everything on the Web is copyrighted, unless it's declared to be in the public domain.

Another way you can use the Edit Page feature is to update your own pages. If you have a Web page up on a server somewhere and you want to change it, you can use the Edit Page feature to open your own pages in Composer. Then all you need to do is save the pages and upload them, without having to locate the most current version of the page on your hard drive first.

What's Out There

A U.S. copyright law page published by Cornell University is at http://www.law.cornell.edu/topics/copyright.html, and Terry Carroll's Copyright FAQ (frequently asked question) is at http://www.aimnet.com/~carroll/copyright/faq-home.html. For a quick overview of online copyright issues, check out Ten Big Myths about Copyright, found at http://www.clari.net/brad/copymyths.html.

Adding Text to Your Page

When you create a Web page with HTML, the entire visible page is surrounded by two tags: <HTML> and <Body>. Anything which is enclosed by these two tags, and not surrounded by any other tags, shows up in the viewing area of Navigator (and other Web browsers) as plain, vanilla text. The same goes for Composer. You can plunk your mouse down and start typing, and the text you type will appear on the Web page just as you typed it. In a little while, we'll get to how you can change the appearance of this text in several ways. Right now, let's put a header on your page.

 You don't have to type everything onto your Web page from scratch, you know. If you have text in another document that you want to put on your Web page, you can copy it to the Clipboard and paste it into the Composer window.

Marking Up Heads

Headers, headlines, or just plain heads, as they're called, are a familiar concept: big bold letters that tell the reader **This Is Important**. You can use heads on a Web page to announce the title of the page, to denote separate sections on a single page, or to catch the eye of the reader with really big text.

HTML supports six levels of heads. Each level of head will look different when it's displayed in a Web browser such as Navigator. The highest level (let's call this the "1" head) will be larger and more obvious; the lowest level (the "6" head) will be smallest and most discreet. All headers are generally displayed in bold, with a paragraph break following them automatically. The lowest level heads, such as the 6 head, may be smaller than the text of the page itself. In Figure 9.12 you can see what the various sizes of headings look like.

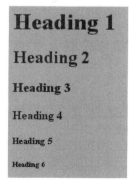

Figure 9.12:   Headings range in size from 1 (large) to 6 (tiny).

The actual way each head looks is different from one browser to the next. In other words, HTML allows you to say what text is a head, but not what the head will look like when User A accesses it with Navigator, User B with Spyglass Mosaic, and User C with Internet Explorer.

It is customary to start your document with a head of level 1, to indicate the important topic that comes first; you can use a head at the top of the document to reiterate the title of your page, which already appears in the title bar. You can follow a level 1 head with heads of lower levels; you can also place new level 1 heads farther down in your document, as you please. It's worth noting, however, that a lot of headlines for no apparent reason might look just plain silly.

Actually creating a head is simple:

1. In the Composer window, type some text that you'd like to make into a head.

2. From the Composer style bar, click on the Style text box and select Heading N, where N is the size of the head from 1 to 6.

3. The appearance of the selected text will change to reflect your choice; you can repeat steps 1 and 2 as often as you like until the text appears the way you want it to look.

Keep in mind that headings, as special kinds of text, aren't compatible with some other kinds of formatting (you can make a heading a link, for example, but you can't make it part of a list).

Using Paragraphs and Line Breaks

When you hit the carriage return in Composer, Composer adds code for either a line break or a paragraph break. A line break ends the current line and starts a new one; a paragraph break does the same thing, but it also adds an additional blank line between one block of text and the next. You might want to think of line breaks as single spacing and paragraph breaks as double spacing.

You can indicate a line break just by using the carriage return, and a paragraph break by pressing the carriage return twice.

 The way that Composer generates code, a double-carriage return actually inserts two <BR> tags, or break tags. In writing HTML by hand, a blank line, or paragraph break, is indicated by <P>. While it won't make a significant difference in how your page looks, you should be aware that the way Composer creates pages isn't the only way.

Changing the Alignment of Paragraphs

When you use the carriage return, what you'll get is the regular, left-justified paragraphs you're used to seeing most often in print. You can change the alignment of a paragraph—to make it either centered or right-justified—by highlighting the paragraph and using the alignment buttons on Composer's style bar.

To adjust the alignment of a paragraph, click the mouse so the cursor is anywhere in the paragraph you wish to center. From Composer's menu bar, select Format ➤ Align, and then choose between Left, Center, and Right.

Or you can use Composer's style bar. Click on the alignment button, and it will drop down to show the three alignment choices. The alignment you've chosen will appear as the "pushed" button.

You can change the alignment on any given paragraph easily by selecting the text you wish to change with the mouse and then using the alignment button to adjust the justification to your taste.

Using Indents to Justify Paragraphs

HTML makes no provisions for automatically indenting text with a new paragraph. Contrary to word processing conventions, paragraphs on Web pages are often indicated by using a blank line of space between each paragraph, rather than an indentation at the beginning of each paragraph.

Even more confounding: If you type five spaces in a row, most Web browsers (including Navigator) are only able to read one of them. Webmasters who do manage to give their paragraphs that indented-on-paper look usually resort to some sort of sorcery in order to do so; you can figure it out by viewing their source code, if you like.

There is a kind of space in HTML called a *nonbreaking space*; it's the kind of space Navigator inserts routinely instead of a plain old spacebar space. The code for this special character is < >. You *can* put a bunch of nonbreaking spaces in a row to create an indent effect, but it's an unwieldy solution.

So if you can't indent at the beginning of a paragraph, what's the purpose of this section? Well, you *can* indent entire paragraphs. The process of indenting paragraphs is similar to aligning them:

1. Select the paragraph you want to indent by highlighting it.

2. From the Composer menu bar, select Format ➤ Indent One Level.

    or

    On Composer's style bar, click on the Increase Indent button.

In either case, the entire paragraph you selected will indent one level. You can repeat this process as often as you like to indent your paragraph a little or a lot, although you should be aware that Composer adds some nonbreaking spaces in the process.

If you indent a paragraph and later decide you want to remove the indent, the process is quite similar:

1. Select the paragraph from which you want to remove the indent by clicking within it.

2. From the Composer menu bar, select Format ➤ Remove One Indent Level.

    or

    On Composer's style bar, click on the Decrease Indent button.

In either case, the entire paragraph you selected will un-indent one level.

 Indenting the text on your page may make it look more clean and polished than simply letting it hang out as left-justified text. You can justify the entire text of a page by using the blockquote function. Read on.

Using Blockquotes to Justify Paragraphs

If you want to justify (line up) both sides of the text in several paragraphs (or all the text on a page), you may want to use blockquotes. This is quite similar to indenting paragraphs, but if you select all the text on a page to be included in a blockquote, new paragraphs you add on the page will be indented automatically on both sides.

Creating a blockquote effect is easy:

1. Select a single paragraph by clicking within it, or several paragraphs by highlighting them with your mouse.

2. From the Composer menu bar, select Format ➤ Paragraph ➤ Block Quote. The paragraphs you selected will appear indented on both sides.

Inserting Ruled Lines

Rules, or ruled lines, are horizontal lines that you can use to separate parts of your document (see Figure 9.13). To place a rule in your document, use the Insert Horizontal Line button. This button inserts a shaded, engraved line that crosses your Web page (no matter what size the page appears to be on screen) from the left margin to the right. To insert a horizontal rule:

1. Click on the part of the page in the Composer window where you wish to insert the ruled line.

2. Click on the Horizontal Rule button on Composer's toolbar. A horizontal line will appear embedded in your page.

Send e-mail to webmaster@tarin.com for more information.

Thanks for visiting!

Figure 9.13: You can use ruled lines to divide sections of your Web page.

Composer also allows you to vary the look of ruled lines by applying formatting to them (just like you can align paragraphs). You can embed as many commands as you like to achieve the effect you want. For example, if you would like the ruled line to be exactly 250 pixels wide and to be centered on the page, you can use the following process:

1. Insert a horizontal rule, as just described.

2. Double-click on the horizontal rule, and the Horizontal Line Properties dialog box will appear, as seen in Figure 9.14.

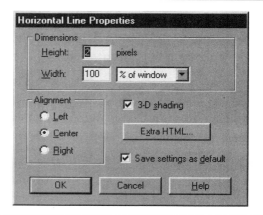

Figure 9.14: The Horizontal Line Properties dialog box lets you change the way your ruled lines look.

The Horizontal Line Properties dialog box allows you to adjust several properties of the line, including:

◆ The height of the line (in pixels)

◆ The width of the line (in pixels or in percentage of window space)

◆ The alignment of the line (left, right, or center)

◆ The use of 3-D shading for the line

3. To create a line 250 pixels wide, you would click in the Width text box and type **250**, and then click on the Width pull-down menu and select pixels.

4. To center this line, click on the radio button marked Center.

5. If you need to assign any other attributes to the horizontal rule, you can apply them by clicking on the Extra HTML button.

6. When you find a set of settings you like, you can make sure the Save Settings as Default box is checked. Close the Horizontal Line Properties dialog box when you're done by clicking on OK.

Go ahead and play around with all these options to see what kind of ruled lines are most effective in your document.

Creating Lists

You can have three types of lists in a Web document: numbered, bulleted, and definition. In HTML lingo, numbered lists are called *ordered lists*, and bulleted lists are called *unordered lists*.

Ordered Lists

Ordered (numbered) lists are lists in which each item is numbered; you don't need to number the items yourself, because the Web browser recognizes the list as such and numbers each item sequentially. Creating a numbered list with Composer is easy:

1. Type the items you want to appear in the list, *omitting the numbers*.

2. Select the list by highlighting it with your mouse.

3. From Composer's menu bar, select Format ➤ List ➤ Numbered. The items in your list will appear indented, with a # (pound sign) before each one.

    or

    Click on the Number List button on Composer's style bar.

For example, in the Composer window, a numbered list of types of fruit would look like this:

> # Apple
>
> # Orange
>
> # Cherry

A Web browser would display the list like this:

> 1. apple
> 2. orange
> 3. cherry

Unordered Lists

Unordered (bulleted) lists are quite similar to ordered lists, except, of course, the numbers are replaced by bullets. The process is quite similar to making a numbered list:

1. Type the items you want to appear in the list, and don't worry about the bullets.

2. Select the list by highlighting it with your mouse.

3. From Composer's menu bar, select Format ➤ List ➤ Bulleted. The items in your list will appear indented, with a • (bullet) before each one.

or

Click on the Bullet List button on Composer's style bar.

Bulleted lists you create in Composer will appear pretty much the same in the Composer window as they will in the Navigator window:

> • Apple
> • Orange
> • Cherry

Remember that the bullets will look different and will be different sizes in the various Web browsers.

You can make the items in your list links! Just follow the instructions under "Creating Links" next, and apply them to the items in your new list.

Creating Links

Now we get to the heart of things. As you know well by now, the beauty of the Web is the way documents are interrelated through being linked—that's what makes the Web so wonderfully webby. Let's take a look behind the scenes at the HTML underpinnings of a link.

In HTML lingo, a link is really what's called an *anchor*, the opening code for which is <a. What the anchor looks like when it appears as a link in a Web document will differ depending on the Web browser being used, but usually it'll show up as underlined text in a special color. When you click on the link, the anchor is activated, and the file with which it is associated (the other end of the link, if you will) is loaded and displayed on screen.

Here's an example of how this works in HTML: If you wanted the word *refrigerator* to appear in a document as a link, you'd code the word like this:

```
<a href="http://www.tarin.com/fridge.html">refrigerator</a>
```

Then, when the document is viewed with any Web browser, such as Navigator, the word <u>refrigerator</u> will appear as a link. When a user clicks on it, the file fridge.html will automatically be transferred from the HTTP server, and a page about a refrigerator will appear on screen.

Don't worry about trying to figure out the code or the file type. Composer helps you insert links easily and painlessly into your Web documents. There are a few things to keep in mind, however:

◆ A URL is simply a pathname; instead of showing the address for a file on your computer, however, it shows where a file is located somewhere on the Internet.

◆ URLs are case-sensitive, so capitalization counts (as do spelling and punctuation).

◆ Most URLs start with http:// or another protocol type; otherwise the file is assumed to be *local* (in the same directory as the file that includes the link).

Okay, Composer makes inserting links easy, so let's do it! Just follow this simple process:

1. In Composer's window, type the text you want to use as a link.

2. Highlight the word or words you want to make into a link by selecting them with your mouse.

3. From Composer's menu bar, select Insert ➤ Link. The Properties dialog box will appear, with the Link tab selected (see Figure 9.15).

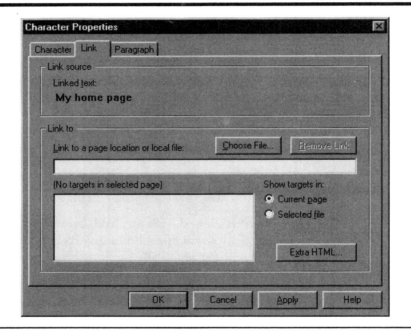

Figure 9.15: The Character Properties dialog box is where you make hypertext links.

Alternately, you can click on the Insert Link button on Composer's toolbar. That will also make the Properties dialog box appear.

4. In the Linked Text area of the dialog box, you should see the text that you just highlighted. If not, click on Cancel and highlight the proper text.

5. In the Link To area of the dialog box, type or paste in the full URL of the page to which you want your link to point.

6. Leave everything else alone for now. Click on OK, and the Properties dialog box will close, returning you to the Composer window.

Now the word you highlighted will appear underlined and in a different color from the text on the rest of the page. Wasn't that easy?

Probably the best way to include a link in your document is to locate it with Navigator. You can then click the right mouse button in the location bar and, from the pop-up menu that appears, select Copy. The URL will be copied to the Clipboard, and you can then paste it into the Composer Properties dialog box.

 If there is some text that's underlined in the Composer window, but you don't really want it to be linked text, just highlight the text that you want to de-link, and, from Composer's menu bar, select Edit ➤ Remove Links.

What's Behind That Sound, Graphic, or Video Link

In your Web roamings, you've probably found links that go not to HTML documents but instead to graphics, sounds, and videos. The URL in a link doesn't have to point to another HTML document; it can point to any type of file. For example, the anchor

```
<a href="http://www.iuma.com/IUMA/ftp/music/Madonna/
Secret.mpg">Madonna</a>
```

creates a link to the machine where a video clip from Madonna's Secret video is stored. When you click on the link, the video will be transferred to your computer, and a player for MEPG files will start up so you can see the video—the trigger for that action is in the HTML coding shown above. You can create links to any type of file in this manner—just include the full path to the file in the URL.

Inserting Addresses

Address is a special HTML element that was originally designed to hold the address of the author of the page (the snail-mail address, the e-mail address, or both). Most Web browsers display this element in an italic font, smaller than body text. You may want to include an address at the bottom of your Web pages so people can contact you; this can be a mailing address, an e-mail address, or both.

To create an address in your Web page:

1. Type the address the way you want it to appear.

2. Select the text of the address by highlighting it with your mouse.

3. From Composer's style bar, use the paragraph style menu to select Address. The text of the address will appear italicized.

Remember that different browsers will display address styles differently.

So why use the Address style rather than just italicizing your address? One convention of HTML is to include an address, enclosed between the <address> and </address> tags, near the end of the document. This, like many other HTML conventions, was intended to give HTML documents some consistency, especially for purposes of cataloguing. You may or may not want to include your address on every Web page, but it may be useful for a simple home page or an "About This Site" page.

Everyone in the world has potential access to the Internet. Although you may put up a Web page that only your mother would love, that doesn't mean that other, less friendly people won't see it. Before you put information on the Web such as your home address or telephone number, ask yourself whether you really want that information to be all that public. You may want to use a business address or a P.O. Box on your Web pages, rather than your home address.

Assigning Text Attributes

You are probably familiar with text attributes from word processors. Things such as bold, italic, and font color, which differentiate some text from the usual, are all known as *attributes* in a word processor. You can specify attributes such as these using Composer. These styles include:

◆ Bold

◆ Italic

◆ Underline

◆ Fixed Width (typewriter font)

◆ Superscript

◆ Subscript

◆ Strikethrough

◆ Blink (the text blinks on-screen)

When you're choosing a text style for your documents, make sure to consider your audience, as well as the readability of your page on the screen. For example, if too much of your text is bold, nothing in particular will stand out. If you use underlining for words that are not links, you may confuse your readers. And if you use blinking text, keep in mind that seasoned Web surfers consider blinking cheesy.

Changing the style of your text is incredibly easy (and intuitive, if you've used Microsoft Word or another word processor). Let's use **bold** as an example. It works like this:

1. In the Composer window, highlight the word you want to appear in boldface by selecting it with your mouse.

2. From Composer's menu bar, select Format ➤ Style ➤ Bold.

or

On Composer's style bar, click on the Bold button.

In either case, the word you selected will now appear in boldface type. Underlined and italic text also have buttons on Composer's style bar; the rest of the text style options available to you can be found on the Format ➤ Style menu.

 You can use these text styles in any combination. To make a word both bold and italic, for example, you would follow steps 1 and 2 above for bold, and then, leaving the word highlighted, repeat step 2 for italic text. To clear all text formatting, highlight the text you want to make into plain text and, from Composer's menu bar, select Format ➤ Clear All Styles.

Changing Font Size

Netscape allows you to change the size of the font in your document. You can use this feature to vary text size, down to the letter. Changing the font size allows you to use effects such as large initial capital letters (an elegant way to display important text).

The font size in an HTML document has a base value of 3 (this doesn't mean 3 point sizes; it's an arbitrary number set by Netscape). Font sizes are then expressed as being larger or smaller than this value of 3. There is a possible range of 7 point sizes in most HTML documents. You can think of the smallest as -2, and the largest as +4. The plus and minus signs indicate that the font will be larger or smaller than the default (normal) font size used on the rest of the page. In Composer, however, the interface design-ers decided to represent these text sizes in familiar point sizes, ranging from 8 (really small) to 36 (really big).You can see the various sizes here:

Size 8
Size 10
Size 12
Size 14
Size 18
Size 24
Size 36

Changing the font size is quite similar to changing the text style of a word. You can change the size of a single letter, an entire word, or an entire paragraph. Unlike heads, font sizes are not automatically bold, and they do not automatically include a paragraph break, so you can use different font sizes within a single paragraph, if you choose. This is how we do it:

1. Highlight the text whose size you want to adjust.

2. From Composer's style bar, click on the Font Size menu box and choose a size between 8 and 36. The size of the text will change to reflect your choice.

One nifty thing you can do with font sizes is create initial-capped words, which can be a classy effect you can use for section titles (as opposed to using headings). Just resize the first letter of your word, as described above. You'll get an effect something like the text shown here.

Changing the Default Font Size

Composer prefers that you use relative sizes rather than absolute sizes. What this means is that the font will appear larger than normal, or smaller than normal, which means that your page is likely to appear similar to the way you want it to appear, rather than using the exact size you intend.

You can, however, set a different *basefont* size using a simple piece of code. What this means is that the size of the basefont, whose value is always 3, will be larger or smaller than the default size. To set a larger basefont value, we're going to insert an HTML tag at the beginning of the document. Follow these steps:

1. Insert your cursor at the beginning of the document, before any text that's already on the page.

2. From Composer's menu bar, select Insert ➤ HTML Tag. The HTML Tag dialog box will appear.

3. In the text box, type the following code:

```
<BASEFONT SIZE=n>
```

where *n* is a number between 1 and 7. Remember that using 3 would be silly, since that's the default.

4. When you're finished typing, click on OK, and the HTML Tag dialog box will disappear. Where you inserted the tag, you'll see the Special Tag symbol in the Composer window.

You won't notice any difference in the Composer window, but Web browsers, such as Navigator, will display the text using a different default size. When you're done with your document, repeat the above steps near the end of the document, substituting </BASEFONT> for the code in step 3. That's called closing the tags.

 Are you saving the changes to your page that you make as you go along?

Changing Fonts and Backgrounds

Not only can you vary text size, you can specify colors for any text in an HTML document, as well as for the background. You're probably aware that links generally appear in different colors from the regular text, but you can also specify a color for regular text, and you have several other options for text colors as well. First we'll look at setting the default colors for a Web page; then we'll see how you can change the font colors within a document.

Setting the Default Colors of Your Page

You have several choices when you're thinking about adjusting the colors of your Web page; you can change all, none, or some of these colors to change the look of your Web page. Your choices are

◆ Background

◆ Regular Text

◆ Link Text

◆ Visited Link Text (hyperlinks that have already been visited)

◆ Active Link Text (links that can change colors while you're clicking on them)

If you don't specify any colors to be used as the default for a Web page, every person who views your page will see the default colors they have set in their own copy of Netscape Communicator. If they haven't changed the colors that Navigator (or another browser) uses as the "factory default," then they'll generally see a grey background with black text, blue links, purple visited links, and no particular color for active links. You may want to give your page a different look and feel than the "generic Web page" look, and that's easy to do with colors.

As for the colors themselves, Netscape recognizes the hexadecimal color system. This system uses a six-digit code to specify the red, green, and blue balance of the color. This may seem like a bit of esoteric information, but you can use it to create beautiful effects on your page. You don't particularly have to be aware of the code used to make a color, but if you see a font or background color you particularly like while you're surfing, you can view the source for that page and find the code for that color: from the Navigator menu bar, select View ➤ Page Source.

Not all browsers "understand" the use of custom colors in an HTML document. Even those of your readers who are using Netscape Navigator may have monitors with limited or no color capability. Keep these caveats in mind when using color in your Web pages.

What's Out There

You don't have to memorize hex codes to be able to add color to your Web page. InfiNet's Color page lists about 100 colors you can choose from, along with their hexadecimal equivalents. Visit http://colors.infi.net/colorindex.html to open this big box of color. If you know what color you want, try using the interactive color picker called ColorServe Pro, at http://www.biola.edu/cgi-bin/colorpro/.

Once you've got a feeling for what colors you want on your page, setting them is easy. Let's choose a text color:

1. Open the page containing the colors you like in the Composer window, and select Format ➤ Page Colors and Properties. The Page Properties dialog box will appear.

2. If the Colors and Background tab is not selected, click on it, and the Page Properties dialog box will change to reflect your choice (see Figure 9.16).

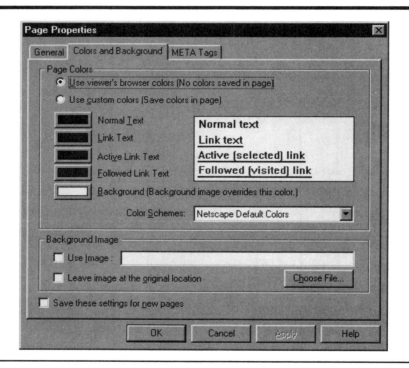

Figure 9.16: Use the Colors and Background tab of the Page Properties dialog box to create the color scheme for your page.

3. Within this dialog box, you'll see buttons for Normal Text, Link Text, Active Link Text, Followed Link Text, and Background. To the right of these buttons is a small preview window that shows you what the colors look like on the background. Click on the button for the color property that you wish to adjust; in our example, it's the text color, called Normal Text. The Color dialog box will appear.

4. The Color dialog box includes 48 basic colors from which you can choose, as well as spaces for 16 custom colors. To choose a basic color, click on the box containing it. You're done for now; click on OK.

or

To define a brand new color, click on Define Custom Colors. The Colors dialog box will expand, showing two rainbow-like arrays of color. From here, you move on to step 5.

5. The left-hand (larger) box indicates the *hue*, or basic color. Click around in this box, and the colors in the right-hand, or *shade*, box will change. When you like the range of colors in the shade box, click within the shade box until you find the right level of lightness or darkness. The color you choose will be shown in the box marked Color/Solid.

6. When you've played around with the colors and found one that you like, click on the Add to Custom Colors button. The color you just made will appear in the Colors dialog box under Custom Colors. To use this color as your text color, click on the box containing that color, and then click on OK. The Colors dialog box will close, and your choice will be reflected in the preview area of the Page Properties dialog box.

You can repeat this step for each of the five choices, if you like.

 Because the text color commands are embedded in the <body> tag, they can be set only once for each Web page. You cannot change link color halfway through your document, for example.

Changing Colors within a Document

Although you can only set link colors once, you can change the font color of a particular (non-linked) word, or even a whole paragraph. For example, you might want to make the word plum appear in purple, the word strawberry in red, and the word orange in orange. Or you may want to attract attention to a particular paragraph by making the text slightly lighter or darker than the rest of the text on the page.

Changing a font color is easy:

1. In the Composer window, highlight the text whose color you want to change with your mouse.

2. On Composer's style bar, click on the Font Color menu box to choose one of Netscape's default colors.

or

To choose a custom color from Composer's menu bar, select Format ➤ Color. The Choose Text Color Dialog box will appear.

3. To choose one of the default colors, click on that color and click on OK. For custom colors, click on More Colors and follow steps 4 and 5 in the previous list.

In any case, the text you selected will appear in a new color.

Don't go too crazy when you're choosing colors, or no one will be able to read your page! The color or image you choose for your background should harmonize with the color(s) of your text. We've seen quite a few examples of enthusiastic Web authors who pick flamboyant colors for their documents, only to render them unreadable.

Using an Image for Your Background

Another way to spice up your document is to use an image for its background. You can use any GIF or JPG graphic file as your background image (any browser that recognizes custom backgrounds can also display JPG images). For example, many companies like to use dimmed versions of their logos as background graphics—kind of like a watermark in expensive stationery (see Figure 9.17).

Not all Web browsers can display custom colors or images as backgrounds. For this reason, be sure your document depends on the overall design of text and graphics—not on the background— to look good.

Figure 9.17: Microsoft uses its logo here as a background graphic.

 Netscape *tiles* the graphic you specify as a background to make it fill up the entire window. That is, it will repeat the graphic in its original size until it covers the page's viewing area.

Specifying a GIF or JPG file as your background image is just as easy as setting the background color. Your page can't have *both* a background image *and* a background color—if you choose a background image, that will override any background color you chose previously. Just try this:

1. With the page open in the Composer window, use Composer's menu bar to select Format ➤ Page Properties. The Properties dialog box will appear, with the Colors/Background tab selected.

2. Near the bottom of the dialog box is the Background Image option. To choose a background image, click on Choose File. The Select Image File dialog box will appear, which is quite similar to the familiar Open dialog box. Choose an image file (GIF, JPG, or JPEG format) to use as the background for your page, and then click on OK.

3. The name of the image should appear in the Use Image text box, and the checkbox marked Use Image should be selected. If everything's hunky dory, click on Open.

You may not see the image in the Composer window, although Navigator will likely display it.

 More and more Web browsers recognize Netscape-specific design features, such as nifty background colors, but some older or less capable browsers can't interpret the bgcolor command. When a page that uses this command is accessed by a browser that doesn't recognize background color, the browser will just ignore the command and use whatever its default background color is—probably gray or white. No harm done.

What's Out There

Asha Dornfest, an author and Webmaster, maintains a solid site full of resources for designers, at http://www.dnai.com/webpub/. Check out her HTML page, Software Library page, and the Image Maps Made Easy article especially.

Embedding Images

Images that appear as part of a Web page are called *inline images*. Although it is possible to place many, many inline images in your document, remember that including them will greatly increase the time required to load and view the document.

 It's best in some circumstances to place thumbnails of images in your page—thumbnails load a lot faster than larger images—and link the thumbnail to the larger image, allowing users to download the bigger image if they want to and have time to wait for it. See "Using Pictures As Links" later in this chapter.

Any image that you want to include as an inline image in a Web document must be in one of two graphics file formats: GIF or JPG. Let's look more closely at the ever-popular GIF format in this section.

Some Web browsers (including Navigator) can display inline images in JPG format. JPG files are much smaller in size than other image files, so they appear on screen much more quickly—a real advantage. The drawback for the publisher, however, is that not all Web browsers can display them. If you use JPG and a user tries viewing your document with a browser that can't handle JPG, all he or she will see is a little error message where the image should be. Additionally, the JPG format is optimal for digitized photographs, but for illustrations and text, you'll lose some quality if you use JPG instead of GIF.

Placing an Image on Your Web Page

Inserting an image is quite similar to inserting a link. Let's see how:

1. In the Composer window, place the cursor where you want your image to appear by clicking your mouse pointer there.

2. On Composer's toolbar, click on the Image button. The Properties dialog box will appear, with the Image tab selected (see Figure 9.18).

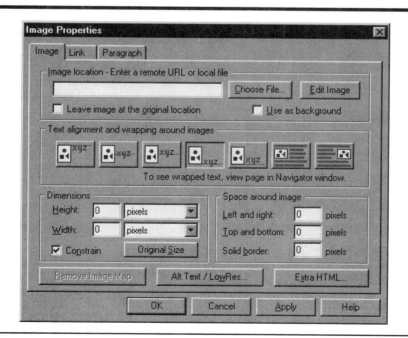

Figure 9.18: The Images Properties dialog box is what you use to place your images.

The first thing you need to do is locate the image you want to display. This can be an image somewhere on the Internet, or an image on your local machine.

3. If your image already has an Internet address, type or paste its location into the Image Location text box. Otherwise, click on Choose File, and the Select Image File dialog box will appear (see Figure 9.19). This dialog box is quite similar to the familiar Open dialog box. Browse through your hard drive and select the image you want. When you're finished, click on Open, and the Select Image File dialog box will close, returning you to the Properties dialog box.

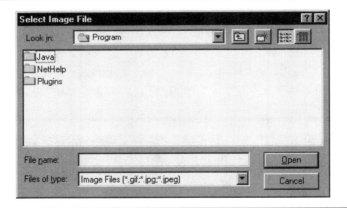

Figure 9.19: Use the Select Image File dialog box to locate an image on your hard drive.

That's really all you need to do to place an image, but let's go over a few other options you have available when putting images on your Web pages.

4. If you want text near or wrapped around your image, Composer offers several ready-made options. In the Text Alignment or Wrap-ping around Images area of the Properties dialog box, click on the option you like. (We'll go over how to change this in a minute).

5. You can choose a size for your image, too. To have your image appear actual size, click on Original Size. To adjust the size of the image, enter the Height and Width you want the image to appear in the appropriate text boxes.

If you want to know the pixel size of your original image, Navigator can tell you. From Navigator's menu bar, select File ➤ Open Page. From the Open Page dialog box, click on Browse, and the Open dialog box will appear. Use the Open dialog box to choose the image you want to examine. Click on Open, and then Open again, and Navigator will display your image. Look at the title bar—those crazy numbers are the pixel height and width of your image. Use those numbers to figure out half size, double size, or some other grand proportion for the image size.

6. If you want some space around your image, you can "pad" it with blank space. In the Space around Image area of the Properties dialog box, choose an amount of space (in pixels) around the Left and Right or Top and Bottom of the image.

7. To place a solid border around your image, choose a number (in pixels) and enter it in the Solid Border text box.

8. Proper HTML dictates that you give your image an ALT tag; that is, a little text description of the image that people will see if they're surfing the Web without image loading enabled. To give your image an ALT tag, click on Alt Text/Low Res. The Alternate Image Properties dialog box will appear.

9. In the Alternate Text text box, type a word or phrase that describes your image. Click on OK to return to the Properties dialog box.

10. We're done. Click on OK to close the Properties dialog box and return to the Composer window.

Your image will show up in Composer's window right away, just the way you told it to.

What's Out There

Get loads of tips and examples of creative image use from the experts at Adobe, by visiting http://www.adobe.com/studio/main.html. A helpful guide to Creating Web Graphics is at http://www.widearea.co.uk/designer/. Transparent GIFs are GIFs in which one of the colors is invisible. (You might want to do this if you'd like the background color of the page to be one of the colors in the image.) To find out how you can make your GIFs transparent, look into the URL http://members.aol.com/htmlguru/transparent_images.html. Or try your hand at animated GIFs—read (and watch) http://members.aol.com/royalef/gifanim.htm.

Adjusting Your Image Once You've Placed It

So what happens if you go through all that rigamarole to put an image on your page, but it looks yucky when you get done? Is there any way to fix it? Yes, dear reader. Just right-click on the image in question and, from the pop-up menu that appears, select Image Properties. The Properties dialog box will resurface, and from there, you can change any image property you want—including which image you chose.

 You may want to tinker with your images, particularly the text wrapping, sizing, and spacing aspects, until it feels right to you. You can adjust your image as many times as you want until you're satisfied.

Using Pictures As Links

You can make an image act as a link to another document (isn't that exciting?). It's really quite simple.

1. Once you've placed an image in your document with Composer as described previously, just click on the image to highlight it. A black border will appear around the image to indicate a highlight.

2. Now that the image is highlighted, right-click on it. From the pop-up menu that appears, select Create Link Using Selected. The Image Properties dialog box will appear, with the Link tab selected. The rest of this process is just like making a piece of text into a link. In the Link Source area of the dialog box, you'll see the name of the image.

3. In the Link To area of the dialog box, type or paste a URL.

4. Click on OK to close the Properties dialog box and return to the Composer window.

Your image won't *look* any different, but when visitors to your page drag their mouse over the image, their cursor will become a pointing hand. When these teeming masses click on the image, they'll get sent to the place you pointed them. Neato!

Java: The Hot Ticket to Live Action

If you've been out Websurfing of late, you've probably come across sites that include "live action." These are often examples of Netscape's support for Java, a programming language developed by Sun Microsystems that enables a vast new frontier of interactivity. Using Java, developers can create little applications, called applets, which, when they're embedded in HTML documents, create dazzling effects, such as animation that might be used in games or for illustrations; ticker tape feeds for news, sports, and stock data; real-time interactivity that can be used for anything from crossword puzzles to the sharing of medical data; and handy gadgets such as mouse pointers that change shape when you drag them over something. Creating Java applets requires a fairly high level of programming knowledge and, as such, is beyond the scope of this book. Still, you should know that it is an option should you decide to become a Web-publishing guru. You can find out more about Java in Chapter 7.

Using Tables for Creative Design

Tables are one of the best ways to create attractive pages that combine text and images. Tables in Web pages are also useful for the same things as tables in books and other documents—displaying information neatly arrayed in rows and columns. Composer makes inserting and editing tables deliciously easy. Let's find out how.

Adding a Table to Your Page

Tables are made up of *cells* that hold information—text, pictures, whatever. These cells are arranged into rows and columns (vertical rows) into which you can put information. The easiest way to make a table using Composer is to create the table first, and then put the content into the cells. Putting a table on your page is fairly straightforward:

1. Get Composer running, and open the page on which you'd like to put a table. Click your cursor where you want the table to appear and, from Composer's menu bar, select Insert ➤ Table ➤ Table. The New Table Properties dialog box will appear, as seen in Figure 9.20.

2. Decide how many columns and rows you want to start with. Type the appropriate figures in the Number of Rows and Number of Columns text boxes.

3. You can choose to display a border around the cells in your table. The default border size is 1 pixel wide; 50 pixels is probably as wide as you want to get. Choose a border size from 0 (no border) to 50 (a really huge border), and type that number in the Border Line Width text box.

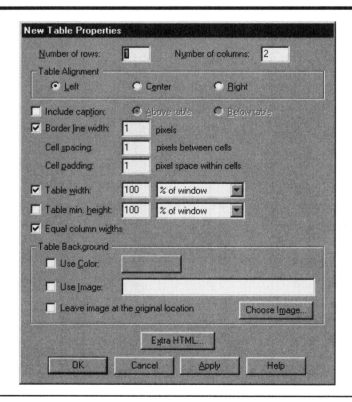

Figure 9.20:   Create a table for your Web page with the New Table Properties dialog box.

Even if you decide not to use a border on your table, tables are often easier to work with if you start out using a border and turn it off later.

4. *Cell spacing* is the amount of space around each cell. The default size for cell spacing is 1; the higher the number you choose, the more space there will be around each cell and around the table as a whole. You can leave this number set at 1, or you can increase the cell spacing of your table by typing a different number in the Cell Spacing text box.

5. *Cell padding* is the amount of white space between the items you put in the table and the walls of the cell. The default size for cell padding is 1; increasing this number adds breathing room to the stuff in your table. You can leave this number set at 1, or you can increase the cell padding of your table by typing a different number in the Cell Padding text box.

6. Tables are generally auto-sized by Composer, depending on how big the stuff is that you put in them. You can adjust the width of your table, however, using either percentage of screen space or number of pixels as your unit of measure. To adjust the width of your table, place a checkmark in the Table Width box. Then choose a number between 1 and 100 (for percent of window) or a number between 1 and 750 (for pixels).

A table 750 pixels wide will fit in the window of a Windows user with Navigator maximized and a 15-inch monitor with a resolution setting of 800x600. A table 400 pixels wide will fit in the default Navigator window of a Macintosh user. You can make your tables as large as you want, but keep in mind that different users have different screen real estate, and that many people are annoyed when they must use horizontal scrolling.

7. You can choose a minimum height for your table as well. For example, to make your table the height of the viewer's window, check the box marked Table Min. Height. Then type **100** in the text box and choose % of Window from the pull-down menu to the right of the text box. (You can do the same for any table height, using either percent of window or pixels as your unit of measure.)

8. Your tables don't have to be the same color as the background. To choose a color for your table that differs from the background color, place a checkmark in the box marked Use Color, and click on the Choose Color button. The Color dialog box will appear, allowing you

to choose a color for your table. (For more on using the Color dialog box, see the section called "Changing Fonts and Backgrounds," earlier in this chapter.)

9. You can place a caption, or heading, above or below the table. To leave room for a caption cell, place a checkmark in the Include Caption box, and choose either Above Table or Below Table by clicking on the appropriate radio button.

10. Your table can reside to the left of your page, in the center, or on the right. To adjust the table alignment, click on one of the radio buttons marked Left, Center, or Right.

11. When you're finished making choices, click on OK to close the New Table Properties dialog box and return to the Composer window.

There you are—you've just made a table. In particular, if you have a border on your table, you'll see it in the Composer window.

Putting Stuff in a Table

Within your table, you have the freedom to put text, images, or both into each and every cell. You can type or paste text or insert an image into any cell you like simply by clicking from cell to cell with your mouse and using the cursor to place your text or image.

 You can move from table cell to table cell in Composer by using the Tab key on your keyboard.

You can use any other feature of Composer within the table. For example, you can put a bold, bulleted list in one cell, an image in another, a hyper-linked head in another cell, and an address in another. That would look pretty silly, but now you have some idea of the flexibility of tables—you can treat each cell like its own mini-page, or you can design the entire table consistently (which will probably look better in the long run). You can also put stuff on your page above or below the table.

Changing the Way Your Table Looks

Now that you have a table, how do you change it? Once you put text, links, images, and other fun stuff into your table, it may look different than you thought it would. You may decide to change the color, the cell spacing, the cell padding, and the borders. You may want to add columns or rows to your table. Or you may decide that you want to choose a height and width for your table after it's full.

You can easily edit a table in Composer. One way to do this is by using the mouse. Drag the mouse pointer over the table in question, and when the big arrow turns into a little double arrow, you can click with the left mouse button and drag the border of the table to be wider or narrower than before.

The other, more all-encompassing way to change a table is with the Table Properties dialog box. To open this dialog box, right-click on the table, and from the pop-up menu that appears, choose Table Properties. The Table Properties dialog box is just like the dialog box you used to create the table in the first place. You can also click on the Row or Cell tabs to tinker with one part of the table at a time. You can adjust as many properties as you want, as often as you want, until you're satisfied with the way it looks.

To change the number of columns and rows in your table, just right-click on the table. From the pop-up menu that appears, select Insert ➤ Row, Column, or Cell, and a dialog box will appear tht will let you add items to the table.

There's plenty more you can do with tables, but the finer points are beyond the scope of this book. Play around with the Table Properties dialog box and have fun with it.

◆ Creating a Quick and Dirty Home Page

If you've been following along, you may have already created a Web page (or half a dozen of them) by now. Let's quickly go over the very basic things you need to do to make a Web page.

To follow along, start up Composer with a new, empty document window. (Or, from Composer's menu bar, select File ➤ New ➤ Blank Page.) This is going to be a whirlwind course in creating the barest of all bare bones Web pages, so don't worry if you can't remember everything at once (you can look it up in the appropriate section of this chapter).

Just because we're making a Web page doesn't mean that the page you make will be on the Web. If you want to put your pages online, contact your Internet service provider to find out how.

1. With Composer open, and a new, blank window staring you in the face, select Format ➤ Page Title from the menu bar. The Page Properties dialog box will appear.

2. Now, in the Title text box, type **Herkimer Uglyface's Home Page**. (You can replace Herkimer Uglyface with your own name, which is probably more attractive anyway.) This will make the title of your home page appear in the title bar when your page is viewed by a user. You can also type your own name in the Author text box. When you're finished, click on OK to close the Page Properties dialog box and return to the Composer window.

3. Now type **Herkimer Uglyface's Home Page** and press ↵. Highlight the text you just typed, and from the Paragraph Style box on Composer's style bar, select Heading 1. This will make the title of your home page appear at the top of your home page. (Although it's customary to use the same text for the title and the first head, you can actually enter whatever you want in place of "Herkimer Uglyface's Home Page" here.)

4. Now we are ready to enter some body text, so type away.

5. This would be the part where you'd make a table, add some images and links, and change all the colors, if you were making a real Web page.

6. If you want people viewing your page to reach you by e-mail, you can add a link to your e-mail address. Type your name, the word **Webmaster**, or your e-mail address, whatever you want people to click on to send a mail message. Highlight the text you just typed, and from Composer's menu bar, select Insert Link. The Characters Properties dialog box will appear with the Link tab selected. In the Link To text box, type `mailto:` followed immediately by your e-mail address (with no space after).

7. Click on OK to return to the Composer window.

Now it's time to save the document.

1. From the Composer menu bar, select File ➤ Save As. The Save As dialog box will appear.

2. In the Save As dialog box, type a path and a filename for the file in the File Name text box. If you're saving the file to your hard disk and placing it in your Netscape directory, the path will probably be C:\Program Files\Netscape. Our hero, Herkimer Uglyface, named his file herkpage.html—you can name yours what you like, but you'll have to end the file with the extension .html, because this is an HTML file you are saving.

3. Click on the Save button to save the file. When Composer is finished saving the file, the Save As dialog box will close automatically.

Good work. We're ready to look at the file with Navigator to see how it turned out.

◆ Using Navigator to Check Your Web Page

You've created an HTML document and saved it as a text file on your hard disk. Before you make your page public, you'll want to test it. You can use Navigator to see what your finely crafted page will look like when it's viewed with a Web browser. To load a file from your hard disk into Navigator, follow these steps:

1. Start Navigator and select File ➤ Open Page from the menu bar. The Open Page dialog box will appear.

2. Click on Choose File. The Open dialog box will appear.

3. In the Open dialog box, highlight the filename you gave your page. (The Open dialog box works here just as it does in any Windows application.)

4. Click on the Open button. The dialog box will close, and in a few seconds your home page will appear on-screen, in the form of a beautiful Web document!

This is the right time to check all your links, even if you think they work. Have a friend proofread your page for you, and make sure you check easily overlooked things, like the name of the page in the title bar.

 If an old version of your HTML document appears by some chance, select View ➤ Reload from the menu bar to load the latest version of your HTML document into memory.

What's Out There

For help in checking your page for typos, errors in grammar, and consistency in style and usage, stop by The Slot (formerly known as the Crusty Old Slot Man's Copy-Editing Peeve Page) at http://www.theslot.com/. Look into the archive for some real gems of wisdom.

 You won't be able to fix typos or other errors or add things to your HTML document while you are viewing it with Navigator. If you want to make changes, open the file in Composer and make the changes there. Then, you can save the modified file, and click on Reload in Navigator to see the changes you just made.

After Your Page Is Rich and Famous

You say your page is up and running? Great, but...you're not finished yet! You need to maintain the thing. Here's how to make sure your Web page is as good in a month as it is now:

◆ Check your links. Make sure they haven't eroded over time. If you rename a file, you have to rename all the links to it. If you're linked to the outside world, make sure those links are live.

◆ Respond to feedback. If someone e-mails you about a problem with your page, they are not criticizing you as a person, only the parts of your page that don't work. Thank your helpful fan for caring enough to point out what concerns him or her, and make a decision on your own about what to do with the feedback.

◆ Keep your content fresh. If you promise to add more content, people will hold you to it. Telling visitors that you'll post a new joke every day and then following up once a month instead is bad form.

◆ Making Your HTML Document Available to the World

Having created a wonderful HTML document on your own computer, you'll want to make it available to the world. As a Web publisher, you can, if you have a big pile of money, buy a machine and set it up as a Web server. This is simply not practical for most people, so we're going to skip it. You can also, if you have access to a Web server at a university or elsewhere, sneak your page onto that server (but don't say we said so). A third option, more practical for a lot of people, might be to publish your page with the help of your Internet service provider.

Many Internet service providers (and even some commercial online services) offer you the option of publishing your Web page on their server as a perk for your use of their service. Unfortunately, however, this is sometimes not free—check with your service provider about costs, and if there is an unreasonable charge, switch providers.

The technical specifics of making your Web pages available to the world vary from one Internet service provider to another, so we cannot go into great detail in this book. Contact your service provider to see how it recommends you make your documents available to the Internet public.

There are a few rules of thumb to keep in mind, however. When you load your page onto the server, make sure you load all the images, too. Recheck all your links, particularly if you've made more than one page, and you link from one of your pages to another of your pages.

What's Out There

There are a few places that offer free Web page services. You make the page, and they host it for free. One of the most flexible places to have a page is Geocities, located at `http://www.geocities.com/`. You may also want to try Angelfire, at `http://www.angelfire.com/`.

Yahoo! maintains a list of places that offer free home pages. Some of these sites offer pages to people or organizations who meet certain criteria, and others include "kits" to help you make your page. That listing was found at `http://www.yahoo.com/Business_and_Economy/Companies/Internet_Services/Web_Presence_Providers/Free_Web_Pages/`.

◆ When Your Page Is Ready, Publicize It

If there are no links to your page, you will get no hits. This is a law of physics on the Web. You want many entry points to your site, and lots for people to do and see once they get there. You want backlinks (links from other sites to yours), and listings in directories and search engine databases. You want to get your site the attention it deserves.

 The best way to get publicity for your site is to make it such a whiz-bang piece of genius that no one can ignore it. Make sure your site includes outstandingly well-developed content presented in an appropriate style, with great design, easy navigation, a dash of wit, and a pinch of originality. That will make it easier for visitors to your site to recommend it to friends and colleagues, and will make your site appealing to those in the know who see so many and recommend so few. That's your best bet.

Get Listed with Directories and Search Engines   You can get your page listed in many big directories such as Yahoo! or Excite quite easily by submitting your URL via a handy form that you'll find at the directory's site. Or you can go to a central location (like Pointers to Pointers or Submit It!) that lists a lot of these places, select as many or as few directories as you'd like your site to appear in, click on an oh-so-easy-to-use Submit button, and—wham-o!—an announcement of your site's birth is blasted off to all the appropriate places in cyberspace in no time flat.

What's Out There

Pointers to Pointers is at `http://www.homecom.com/global/pointers.html`; Submit It! is at `http://www.submit-it.com/`. To check out other places to promote your page, visit Yahoo!'s list of Announcement Services at `http://www.yahoo.com/Computers_and_Internet/Internet/World_Wide_Web/Announcement_Services`.

If your site is a personal home page, go to `http://www.yahoo.com/Entertainment/People/` and click on the Add URL icon. If it is commercial, try the LinkStar commercial directory, at `http://www.linkstar.com`.

Get Webmasters to Backlink to You   Surely you're not the only person on the planet who collects lunchboxes, goes spelunking, or conducts genetic programming experiments with marmosets. Find like-minded Webmasters and trade links.

Get Listed with "What's New"   Your page is new—and some special pages post links to other pages that have just launched. The criteria for acceptance varies; some are choosy, like Netscape's What's New, while others, like What's New Too, list anybody who's new.

Exchange Ads with Other Webmasters   One way to get hits is to run ads on other people's pages—not necessarily a costly prospect. Sites such as the Internet Link Exchange run networks in which your ad is run on other members' sites in exchange for the ad you place on your own Web page. The Commonwealth Network is similar, and you may even make some money by running their ads. If your site is connected to a business, this is one way to find out if the advertising model is worth the time and space required.

What's Out There

Anything goes at Internet Magazine's What's New page (`http://www.emap.com/whatsnew/`). What's New Too is at `http://newtoo.manifest.com/WhatsNewToo/`. You can investigate free or cheap advertising options at the Internet Link Exchange (`http://www.linkexchange.com/`) or the Commonwealth Network (`http://commonwealth.riddler.com/`).

Pay for Premium Listings   If you've got a big-ticket budget for promoting your page, you may want to invest in premium listings. You can spend upwards of $1,000 to have your site appear in Yahoo!'s Web Launch or Lycos' New2Net for one week. Getting listed on Netscape's What's Cool page may be even more pricey.

What's Out There

Yahoo!'s Web Launch (`http://www.yahoo.com/docs/pr/launchform.html`), Lycos' New2Net (`http://www.lycos.com/new2net.html`), and commercial announcement services like WebPromote (`http://www.webpromote.com/`) or PostMaster (`http://www.netcreations.com/postmaster/`) are not for low-budget amateurs.

Announce Your Site in Selected Newsgroups   You can announce your site in various newsgroups and mailing lists via announcement services; just be sure to choose appropriate venues based on whether their topics are related to the topic of your page. Be discreet—no one wants to get junk mail in newsgroups any more than in "real" life. Make sure your announcement is timely, relevant, to the point, and respectful of a particular newsgroup's culture.

Take Advantage of E-Mail Publicity   Place your site address in a very brief signature file that appears at the conclusion of all your e-mail messages. This will get the word out to those with whom you correspond on any topic. Also, create an e-mail mailing list so you can send out announcements to interested parties when you launch or update your page. You can embed your URL into an e-mail message and send that out (see the next section "HTML in Netscape's Electrifying E-Mail").

Don't send e-mail to every e-mail address you see. It's important to avoid the very rude practice known as *spamming*—the unnecessary junking up of newsgroups or people's e-mail inboxes with messages of no interest to them.

You can also announce your page via Internet mailing lists such as Net-Happenings. NetHappenings, by the way, is a wonderful way to stay current on what's happening on the Internet. To subscribe to NetHappenings, send e-mail to `majordomo@lists.internic.net`; in the body of your message, type **subscribe <net-happenings>**.

Use Print Media Print your site's URL on your business card (if that's appropriate), your stationery, or in ads (if yours is a commercial venture). Some magazines list the addresses of Web sites, sometimes for a small fee.

◆ HTML in Netscape's Electrifying E-Mail

You can embed hyperlinks, inline images, and other HTML tags right into the body of your e-mail messages, effectively transforming them into working HTML documents. This is remarkably easy. Figure 9.21 shows an e-mail message with an image embedded in it.

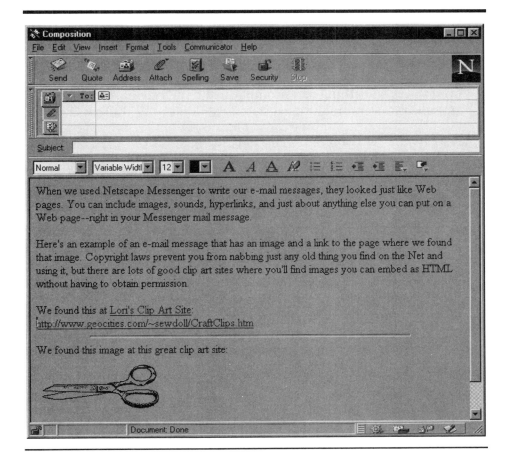

Figure 9.21: You can embed links, images, and other HTML right into your e-mail message.

 Make sure that anyone to whom you send HTML marked-up e-mail is using Netscape Mail. Remember that if you embed HTML into your e-mail message and send it to a friend who is not using Netscape Mail, all that lucky person will see is a bunch of gibberish-like HTML coding.

With this handy integrated e-mail capability, readers of your e-mail messages can, for example, jump directly to a Web page without a second thought. No more cutting and pasting URLs from your e-mail into the Open Page dialog box; it's as if your e-mail messages were mini Web pages in and of themselves!

 You can incorporate links to Web pages in your e-mail most easily by typing URLs directly into regular e-mail messages. (Whenever a URL appears in a Netscape Mail or Netscape News message, the URL automatically becomes an actual link to the page it specifies.)

You might want to delve into using HTML itself in an e-mail message if you've got something more complicated than a couple of URLs you want to send off. Here are the details:

1. From the Windows 95 Start Menu, open the Netscape Message Center by selecting Programs ➤ Netscape Communicator ➤ Netscape Messenger.

2. Click on the New Msg button. A blank e-mail message will appear.

3. Each outgoing message has a menu bar and a style bar which are quite similar to those featured in Composer. You can use these buttons and commands to jazz up your message.

4. Follow the steps and guidelines throughout earlier sections in this chapter to enhance your message with any of the HTML trappings you want. You can use any of the features we discuss in this chapter in Netscape e-mail. As an example, to insert an image into your message, select Insert ➤ Image and use the Image Properties text box as described earlier in this chapter. Click on OK to return to your e-mail message, which will then have an image visible in its text area.

5. Now send off your HTML file, just as you would any other e-mail message, by clicking on the Message Composition window's Send button. The HTML Mail Question dialog box will appear.

This dialog box will ask you to confirm that you want to send an HTML mail message to the recipients indicated. Click on Send to send your message and return to Messenger.

When your message arrives, the HTML file you created will look just like any other e-mail message, but it will contain whatever HTML functionality you built into it.

That's all there is to using HTML in your e-mail. You can experiment with using the different HTML options discussed in this chapter in your e-mail messages. Try sending yourself a zinged-up HTML e-mail to see how it looks.

What's Next?

Well. Now you know all you need to know to browse the Web, search for what you find intriguing or useful, create your own home page, and include HTML in your Netscape e-mail messages. In Chapters 10 and 11, we're going to cover the nitty-gritty technical details: how to get connected and install Netscape.

Part Three:

Getting Started with Communicator

Laying the Groundwork
for Installing Communicator

Roll up your sleeves—this is the part where we get down and dirty and put things together. In this chapter, we're going to get you on the Net, set up your Internet connection, and go get Communicator from the Internet itself.

Before you can start using Communicator—or even download the program to your computer—you have to have your Internet connection ready to go. Connecting to the Internet is no sweat, really, because Windows 95 or Windows NT includes the software you need to access the Internet via any Internet service provider (you don't need separate, special SLIP/PPP software any more, though you do need a SLIP/PPP account). Also, many commercial online services (such as America Online and CompuServe) now offer Internet access to their subscribers as part of their services.

Internet Service Providers and Commercial Online Services: The Big Difference

Believe it or not, commercial online services such as America Online and CompuServe are not part of the Internet. They do provide Internet access these days, but in actuality, commercial online services are separate, distinct entities—what's the difference? Well, a *commercial online service* provides content, such as consumer reports, reference material, forums in which people discuss their interests, and online access to celebrities—whatever is deemed commercially viable and of interest—to subscribers who pay a (usually monthly) fee for that service. As part of all this, the commercial online services provide access to the Internet as well. An *Internet service provider* gives you access to the Internet for a (usually monthly) fee, but does not usually provide any content whatsoever—all the content, in this case, comes from the Internet itself. Commercial online services often charge extra for some "premium" aspect of their services; they may also charge for receipt of e-mail. Internet service providers generally charge only for access time, not for any kind of premium stuff…. Now you know.

In this chapter we'll cover the major ways to get connected and get Netscape:

◆ Using Windows 95 or NT Dial-Up Networking to access the Internet via any of a lot of Internet service providers

◆ Using Netcom's Netcomplete software to access the Internet

◆ Using software provided by some of the major commercial online services—America Online, CompuServe, or Microsoft Network—to access the Internet

If you're just getting started using the Internet, you may want to read this entire chapter before you decide which method of connecting is best for you. If you already have an account with an Internet service provider, turn to the sections titled "Installing Windows Dial-Up Networking" and "Connecting via Windows NT Dial-Up Networking;" if you have an account with Netcom's Netcomplete, turn to the section titled "Connecting via Netcom's

Netcomplete;" if you have an account with America Online, turn to the section titled "Connecting via America Online"; if you have an account with CompuServe, turn to the section titled "Connecting via CompuServe WinCIM"; and if you have an account with the Microsoft Network, turn to the section titled "Connecting via the Microsoft Network."

Depending on the type of Internet connection you use (Windows Dial-Up Networking, AOL, Netcomplete, WinCIM, and so on) you'll get and use either the 32-bit or 16-bit version of Netscape. Turn to "A Tale of Two Versions" in Chapter 11 for a description of these two versions.

◆ Getting Connected via Windows 95 and Windows NT Dial-Up Networking

When it comes to using an Internet service provider and your Windows PC to access the Internet, there are two eras: before Windows 95, and after Windows 95. Before Windows 95, setting up your Netscape connection with an Internet service provider was a big drag. You had to install several separate pieces of software (including special SLIP/PPP software that "introduced" your Internet service provider to Netscape at the beginning of every session). Then you had to configure your machine and all this software to work neatly together—it might have taken a whole day!

You still need an account with an Internet service provider, but you're saved from all that other hassle, because Windows 95 and Windows NT include all the software you need to get connected to the Internet. You do still need a SLIP/PPP account, but you don't need special SLIP/PPP software. You can use Windows Dial-Up Networking with just about any Internet service provider that offers SLIP or PPP, and these days, they pretty much all do.

What's Out There

You can get the latest news about Dial-Up Networking on Windows95.com's TCP/IP set-up page at http://www.windows95.com/connect/tcp.html.

What You Need

To run Netscape on your Windows PC using an Internet service provider, you need:

◆ An account with an Internet service provider

◆ Netscape Communicator itself, which you can download once you are connected to the Internet

◆ Windows Dial-Up Networking Software (which comes with Windows 95 or Windows NT)

Setting up an account with an Internet service provider is up to you. Suffice it to say, the most important considerations in selecting an Internet service provider are

◆ Whether it provides a local access phone number so you can avoid long distance charges

◆ Whether it offers SLIP/PPP accounts (most do, but verify anyway)

You also need a Windows PC with at least 8MB of RAM (12MB is the *minimum* you'll need to run Windows NT), 20MB of available hard disk space, and a fast modem (at the very least 9600bps, although 14,400bps, 28,800bps, or 33,600bps is much better). Except for the modem, this is the same stuff you need to run most Windows programs, so you're probably set.

Just How Minimum Are Those Requirements?

If you've had experience with minimum requirements, you know they get you minimum results. Yes, you can run Communicator with the minimum setup, but the performance you get may make you wonder why people think the Internet is so great. Up to a certain point, the more you can add to your system's capacity, the better the performance will be. If you're thinking of making additions to your system, start with a faster modem—28.8Kbps or better will provide a comfortable browsing speed. Then add memory—16MB will do but try for 32MB. If you can, get yourself more hard disk space, too. Try to keep 25 to 50MB of free space on your hard disk to allow room for creating temp files and for downloading.

In the section that follows this one, we'll talk a bit more about choosing an appropriate Internet service provider. We've included a list of some reputable Internet service providers you can contact if you like; but first read on so you'll know what you need.

By the way, getting Netscape Communicator is usually a matter of going out on the Internet and downloading an evaluation copy of the software; we'll go over that in an upcoming section of this chapter. You can also get Communicator in a box from any of many retail outlets, but we're going to leave it to the documentation in that box to tell you how to install Communicator if you go that route. The thing to remember is that, no matter how you got your copy of Communicator and how you connect to the Internet, the software itself runs the same.

Okey dokey, let's get cracking. Before we do, however, a few words of caution: This section is going to deal with material that's a little more technically demanding than what we've done so far in this book. Setting up Windows 95 and Windows NT Dial-Up Networking involves a lot of making little "pieces" work together. Don't let this discourage you—take your time, have patience, read carefully, and ask your Internet service provider for help if you get stuck.

Take into consideration the willingness of an Internet service provider to help you get your Windows Dial-Up Networking working when you choose whether to set up an account with that service provider—it's an indication of that company's overall attitude toward customer service.

In the end, you'll have Communicator running, and it'll be well worth your effort.

Selecting an Internet Service Provider

You need to think about some things as you select an Internet service provider to work with Communicator. Let's go over the important points.

Whether you're using Windows 95 or Windows NT, you will want to go over the next three sections because they apply to both environments. When you get to the installation process in Chapter 11, you'll find that the instructions for installing Communicator for Windows 95 and for Windows NT are identical. (There are some differences between the two in getting connected; we'll cover those in this chapter.)

Ask about SLIP/PPP

If you're going to run Communicator on a home computer equipped with a modem (that's what we're here for, isn't it?), you're going to need a SLIP account or a PPP account. Most Internet service providers offer SLIP/PPP now as their primary service, and commercial online service accounts such as America Online and CompuServe include it, too.

SLIP stands for *Serial Line Internet Protocol*, and PPP stands for *Point-to-Point Protocol*. Some Internet service providers offer one, some offer the other, some offer both. For your purposes at home, they are equivalent; either kind of account will allow you to run Communicator just fine (that's why we talk about them as a unit, using "SLIP/PPP" for shorthand).

In telecommunications jargon, SLIP/PPP allows you to send TCP/IP packets (see Chapters 1 and 2) over a serial communications device—a modem. Remember, while you are logged on to your SLIP/PPP account, your machine at home is actually part of the Internet. Your machine becomes part of the network of millions of computers that make up the Internet, and you can communicate with any one of them by sending and receiving e-mail, files, or whatever.

Consider the Costs

A major consideration in selecting a service provider is cost. Essentially two costs are involved: a monthly or hourly fee you pay the service provider for access, and the fee you pay (or do not pay if you are clever and find a service provider with local access) to the phone company for long distance charges. Shop around for a good deal, and when you ask about the deal, remember to ask about a local access number.

Ask about technical support too. Is it available by telephone seven days a week or only through e-mail? Is the provider's technical support group fully staffed? Are people available at the time you'll call? If you have pals you can consult, ask them about the quality of support and the provider's reputation for reliability.

Perhaps you already have a corporate account that allows you online access, but for lots of reasons, you may want to establish a separate personal account with an Internet service provider (ISP). You may want to receive personal e-mail (unrelated to your job) at home, or you may have a personal business project you'd like to distinguish from your 9-to-5 job. Also, you may find that one e-mail account is better than another at handling files received from a wide range of e-mail systems. You sure don't want to be stuck with getting e-mail that arrives as a bunch of garbled happy-face characters.

In any case, Table 10.1 lists some Internet service providers you can check out in the English-speaking world. This list is by no means comprehensive; we've stuck to the biggies with lots of POPs (points of presence, or local access phone numbers). But it'll get you started.

 For international calls from the United States, enter 011 (the international access code), then enter the country code, the city code, and the local telephone number. Look in the front of your local phone book for further directions.

Table 10.1:   Internet Service Providers

ISPs in the United States		
Company	**Coverage**	**Phone Number**
Netcom Online Communications Services	330 POPs nationwide	800 353-6600
Mindspring Enterprises	235 POPs nationwide	800 719-4332
UUNet Technologies	240 POPs nationwide	703 206-5600
AT&T World Net	200 POPs nationwide	800 967-5363

ISPs in Canada		
Company	**Coverage**	**Phone Number**
Power Windows	Ontario	905 508-7013
Internet Direct	Ontario	416 233-7150

ISPs in the United Kingdom and Ireland		
Company	**Coverage**	**Phone Number**
PSINet UK Ltd.	All over United Kingdom	44 223 577577
U-NET Limited	Local access for anywhere in the United Kingdom	01 925 484444
Charis Internet Services Ltd.	Complete United Kingdom	01 21 4466100
Ireland On-line	POPs throughout most of Ireland	353 1 8551739

Table 10.1:   Internet Service Providers (continued)

ISPs in Australia and New Zealand		
Company	**Coverage**	**Phone Number**
OzEmail	POPs throughout Australia	1800 805874
Access One	Access throughout Australia	1800 672395
Voyager Network	Local access everywhere in New Zealand	0800 8692437

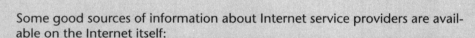

Some good sources of information about Internet service providers are available on the Internet itself:

◆ The List is a comprehensive directory of Internet service providers worldwide, searchable by country, area code, and name. You'll find The List at http://thelist.iworld.com/.

◆ Yahoo's list of Internet service providers is also extensive and easy to use. It's at http://www.yahoo.com/Business_and_Economy/Companies/ Internet_Services/Internet_Access_Providers/.

◆ CNET also has a page that's worth your attention—you can find reviews of many ISPs at http://www.CNET.com/Content/Reviews/Compare/ISP/.

Make Note of Some Technical Details

Once you choose a provider, you can usually set up your account over the telephone. It should take only a few days (if that) for your service provider to get you going.

But let's back up a minute. While you've got them on the line, find out some of the technical information you'll need to set up Windows 95 and Windows NT Dial-Up Networking for use with Communicator. Make note of

ISDN and Cable Modem Options

In this chapter, we concentrate on using Dial-Up Networking with a modem to attach to the Internet over a standard telephone line. You can also use Dial-Up Networking, or other similar pieces of communication software, to connect to the Internet at much faster speeds with new technologies. Some of these technologies include ISDN and cable modems, which promise connection speeds from four to over 350 times as fast as the fastest modem.

Two good sources of information about cable modems are @Home (a company that is building the physical network on which they'll work) at `http://www` `.home.net` and the Cable Modem Resources on the Web page at `http://rpcp` `.mit.edu/~gingold/cable/`. For a good list of ISDN resources, load up Yahoo's Computers and Internet: Communications and Networking: ISDN page at `http://www.yahoo.com/Computers_and_Internet/Communications_and` `_Networking/ISDN/`.

the answers as you go—we'll use this information later in this chapter. Specifically, ask for the following information:

◆ The IP Address assigned to your machine at home (unless your provider "dynamically assigns" an IP address)

◆ The IP Address of the provider's primary domain-name server

◆ The IP Address of the provider's secondary domain-name server, if any

If you're already familiar with addresses in the `domain.names.separated` `.by.periods` format, you'll know that `violet.berkeley.edu` is a machine at the University of California, Berkeley. This is not what you want here, however. In our discussion in Chapters 1 and 2, we described how an address such as `violet.berkeley.edu` is the easier-to-remember version of what's really a numeric address. You want the IP address in a numeric format—numbers separated by periods—such as `126.54.32.1`.

Ask for the four-number address the provider is assigning to your computer. Every computer on the Internet has such an address, called an *IP* (Internet Protocol) address. Note that some providers assign your machine a permanent IP address; others assign an IP address "dynamically," meaning that each time you log on to your SLIP/PPP account, the provider's server auto-matically assigns your computer an address for use in that session only.

If your provider assigns your machine a permanent IP address, write it here:

_____._____._____._____

If your provider assigns an IP address dynamically, just leave these blanks empty.

Last, you will need to know the IP address of your service provider's primary and, if it has one, secondary domain-name servers. Write these addresses here:

_____._____._____._____

_____._____._____._____

In addition to the IP addresses above, you also need the names of a few servers that your Internet service provider maintains:

◆ News (also known as NNTP) server.

◆ Mail (also known as the POP3 and SMTP or IMAP) servers. This may be a single server, or it may be two different servers.

Write the name of the news server here:

_____

> **NOTE** You'll use these server names in the next chapter when you get Communicator running. You don't need the numeric IP addresses here. Simply entering the servers' names, such as news.abc.com, is fine.

Now write down the name of the POP3 and SMTP servers here (if the same server is used for both, simply write down the name twice):

_____

_____

There is one teensy caveat here: If you want to connect via a SLIP account (rather than PPP), you'll need the CD-ROM version of Windows 95. The

CD-ROM version includes both SLIP and PPP capability; the diskette version does not include the Windows 95 SLIP driver. PPP is more commonly offered than SLIP, however, and PPP has some performance advantages over SLIP. So unless you have some special reason to want SLIP, the PPP driver that comes with Windows 95 will probably fit your needs.

Connecting via Windows 95 Dial-Up Networking

The process of installing Dial-Up Networking for Windows 95 and NT are similar. If you are running Windows 95 on your computer, read on. If you have Windows NT installed, skip ahead to the section titled *"Installing Windows NT Dial-Up Networking."*

Installing Windows 95 Dial-Up Networking

Now that you have an account with an Internet service provider, you are ready to install and set up Dial-Up Networking. (Actually, you can go ahead and install Dial-Up Networking before you have your Internet service provider account; you just can't finish installing and using it until you get the account information from your provider.) You must (obviously) install Dial-Up Networking before you can use it to connect to your Internet service provider. If, during your installation of Windows 95, you indicated that you wanted Dial-Up Networking installed, it'll be there, but the Windows 95 installation process does not automatically assume that you want Dial-Up Networking. You can install Dial-Up Networking now if you need to, using the Add/Remove Software Component Control Panel. To do so, follow these steps:

1. From the Start menu, select Settings ➤ Control Panel. The Control Panel window will appear.

2. In the Control Panel window, double-click on the Add/Remove Programs icon.

Add/Remove
Programs

The Add/Remove Programs Properties dialog box will appear (see Figure 10.1).

Click here to
display installed
Windows 95
components.

Click here to display
Communications
components.

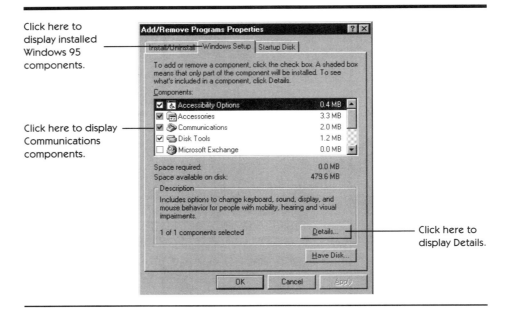

Click here to
display Details.

Figure 10.1: You can use the Add/Remove Programs Properties dialog box to add Windows 95 Dial-Up Networking components to your computer if you don't have this gem installed already.

3. Along the top of the dialog box, you'll see a number of tabs. Click on the Windows Setup tab, and the window's contents will change to show which portions of Windows 95 have been installed on your computer.

4. Because Dial-Up Networking is all about communicating, it is grouped with other communications options in Windows 95. Click on the Communications entry in the Components list along the left side of the dialog box, and then click on the Details button. The Communications dialog box will appear, showing the Windows 95 communications options you can install.

5. In the Communications dialog box, click on the checkbox next to the Dial-Up Networking entry. (This indicates that you want to install Dial-Up Networking on your computer.) Now, click on the OK button to continue. The Add/Remove Programs Properties dialog box will reappear.

6. In the Add/Remove Programs Properties dialog box, click on the OK button to start installing Dial-Up Networking. Windows will ask you to insert either the Windows 95 diskettes or the CD-ROM as files are copied from them to your computer. Insert the diskettes or CD-ROM as requested.

7. When Dial-Up Networking is installed, a dialog box will appear telling you that you must restart your machine before Dial-Up Networking will actually work.

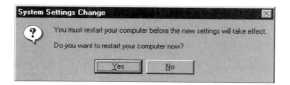

Click on the Yes button to finish. Your computer will restart, and Windows 95 will start running again.

When your machine restarts, Dial-Up Networking is installed. You will not see any obvious changes as a result of the installation (except that you will have a new icon in your My Computer window called Dial-Up Networking). Even though you now have the software required to access your Internet service provider, you still need to create a new connection for your ISP and enter relevant information. Once you complete these two steps, you'll be ready to start using the Internet.

Introducing Dial-Up Networking to Your Internet Service Provider

Now you're going to set up Dial-Up Networking to work with your Internet service provider. In particular, you'll create the connection that tells Dial-Up Networking the telephone number to dial for your ISP. You will also configure the connection so that Dial-Up Networking knows how to access the Internet via your ISP.

If your PC is on a LAN (a Local Area Network), you must contact your network administrator before you configure Dial-Up Networking—otherwise you can make a real mess of things and cause that person a lot of grief.

To start creating the connection you'll use to hook up with your Internet service provider:

1. From the Start menu, select Settings ➤ Control Panel. The Control Panel window will appear.

2. In the window, double-click on the Network icon.

Network

The Network dialog box will appear.

3. In the Network dialog box, click on the Add button. The Select Network Component Type dialog box will appear (see Figure 10.2).

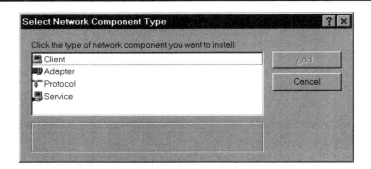

Figure 10.2: The Select Network Component Type dialog box

4. Now, in the Select Network Component Type dialog box's list box, double-click on the word Protocol. The Select Network Protocol dialog box will appear (see Figure 10.3).

5. Along the left side of the Select Network Protocol dialog box, you will see a list box labeled Manufacturers. In the list, highlight Microsoft, and you will see a list of network protocols—the software that Windows uses to communicate over a network such as the Internet.

6. In the list of network protocols (which you can see in Figure 10.3), click on the entry titled TCP/IP (remember, TCP/IP is the Internet protocol we discussed in Chapter 2).

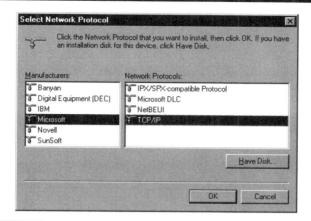

Figure 10.3: The Select Network Protocol dialog box with Microsoft and TCP/IP highlighted

7. With the TCP/IP entry highlighted, click on the OK button. The Network dialog box will reappear, with TCP/IP now listed in the Network Components list as shown in Figure 10.4.

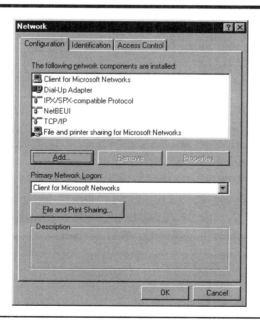

Figure 10.4: TCP/IP is now listed under Network Components.

8. When you installed Dial-Up Networking, Windows set it up to access a bunch of networks, such as Microsoft NT and Novell Netware, in addition to the Internet. In this step, we'll remove the pieces that are used to access these other networks, just leaving what is required to access the Internet. In the Network dialog box's Network Components list, highlight IPX/SPX-Compatible Protocol, and click on the Remove button, and then highlight NetBEUI, and click again on the Remove button. Finally, highlight File and Printer Sharing for Microsoft Networks and click once more on the Remove button.

If your machine is on a LAN, messing around too much with this list can really wreak havoc. Please, please talk to your network administrator first.

9. At this point, only Client for Microsoft Networks, Dial-Up Adapter, and TCP/IP should appear in the Network Components list. If this is so, click on the OK button to continue. The Network dialog box will close, leaving you with your familiar Desktop.

You've established all the network settings required to access the Internet using Dial-Up Networking. Now you have to create the actual Dial-Up Networking connection, which means in essence that you must provide Windows with detailed information about your Internet service provider.

Creating a New Dial-Up Networking Connection   To actually use Dial-Up Networking, you create something called a *connection*. According to Microsoft, a connection holds information about your Internet service provider—for example, its telephone number. Once you have created the connection, you can use Dial-Up Networking by double-clicking on the Connections icon on the Desktop.

You must have a modem installed in your computer and configured for Windows 95 in order to use Dial-Up Networking. If you don't, you'll be prompted to rectify matters during this set-up procedure.

To create a connection, follow these steps:

1. When you installed Dial-Up Networking, Windows created a new icon in the My Computer window called Dial-Up Networking. Open the

My Computer window by double-clicking on the My Computer icon on the Desktop. Now double-click on the Dial-Up Networking icon.

Dial-Up
Networking

The Dial-Up Networking window will appear. As you create Dial-Up Networking connections, they will appear in the Dial-Up Networking window as icons.

2. In the Dial-Up Networking window, double-click on the Make New Connection icon. You double-click on this icon whenever you want to create a new connection for Dial-Up Networking. The Make New Connection dialog box will appear, as shown in Figure 10.5.

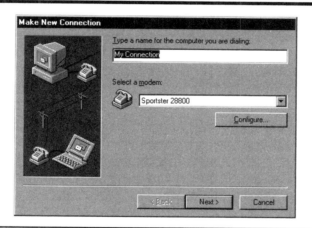

Figure 10.5: In the Make New Connection dialog box, you'll provide detailed information about your Internet service provider.

3. In the Make New Connection dialog box, type a name for the connection—the name of your Internet service provider is a logical choice—in the Type a Name for the Computer You Are Dialing text box. Don't press the ↵ key after you enter the name; we still need to enter some additional information in this dialog box before moving along.

4. In the Select a Modem pull-down list, select the modem you plan to use. Odds are that you have only a single modem installed on your computer, so this should be simple—you probably won't have to make any changes to this item.

5. Now click on the Next button to move to the next Make New Connection dialog box (don't get confused—all the dialog boxes used to create the connection have the same title). In this dialog box, enter the phone number you will use to dial up your Internet service provider.

6. First, type the area code in the Area Code text box, and then type the telephone number in the Telephone Number text box.

 Do not enter a 1 or any other special access numbers before the area code. Windows treats all those special access digits specially— you specify them when you set up your modem.

7. Now, in the Country Code pull-down list, select the country where your Internet access provider is located. (Odds are this already indicates the correct country, unless you are calling internationally for your Internet access.) Click on the Next button to continue. The last Make New Connection dialog box will appear.

8. The last Make New Connection dialog box informs you that you have successfully created the connection. Click on the Finish button to finish creating the connection, or if you see a boo-bette, click on the Back button to return to the previous Make New Connection dialog box so you can fix it. (You can travel back and forth through the Make New Connection dialog boxes by clicking on the Next and Back buttons. When you're done making corrections, simply click on the Next button until you get to the last Make New Connection dialog box, and then click on the Finish button.) The Dial-Up Networking window will appear on the Desktop (as shown in Figure 10.6) listing the new connection that you just created.

Now it's time to actually introduce your Internet service provider to your machine and to Windows.

Configuring Your Dial-Up Networking Connection   You've created the connection for your Internet service provider, and in the process of that you specified your Internet service provider's name and telephone number. Now you must specify all that other information you got from your Internet service provider when you set up your account (remember that from the earlier section?). That's all part of configuring (setting up) your connection.

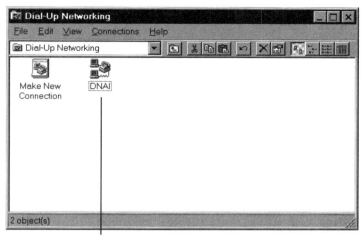

Here is the connection you just created.

Figure 10.6: The new connection you just made appears in the Dial-Up Networking window.

Follow these steps:

1. In the Dial-Up Networking window, which should still appear on your Desktop, right-click on the icon for the connection you just created.

DNAI

A menu will appear.

 Note that the name of the icon will depend on the name you entered in the first Make New Connection dialog box in the last section. It is probably the same name as your Internet service provider. In the menu, select Properties. The Properties dialog box will appear, as shown in Figure 10.7.

2. In the Properties dialog box (again, see Figure 10.7), click on the Server Type button. The Server Types dialog box will appear (see Figure 10.8).

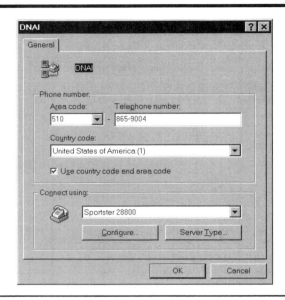

Figure 10.7: Here is the Properties dialog box. The name of your Internet service provider will appear in the title bar.

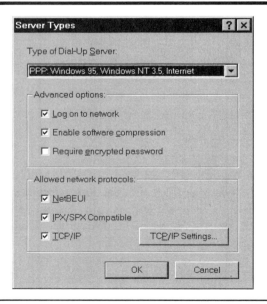

Figure 10.8: In the Server Types dialog box, you'll verify that PPP is selected as the service type.

3. In the Server Types dialog box, you'll specify a number of things about your Internet service provider. In the Type of Dial-Up Server drop-down list, the phrase *PPP: Windows 95, Windows NT 3.5, Internet* should appear. If you don't see this phrase, pull down the Type of Dial-Up Server list and select the entry *PPP: Windows 95, Windows NT 3.5, Internet*.

You can also use Dial-Up Networking to make a SLIP connection, though we're just describing the more common PPP connection here. To use SLIP to connect to the Internet, you need to install the SLIP driver that comes only on the Windows 95 CD-ROM (not on the diskettes). Refer to the Windows 95 Resource Kit, also on the Windows 95 CD-ROM, for details.

4. Now, in the Server Types dialog box, click on the TCP/IP Settings button, and the TCP/IP Settings dialog box will appear (see Figure 10.9).

5. In the TCP/IP Settings dialog box's Specify an IP Address text box, enter the IP address assigned to you by your Internet service provider. If your provider uses dynamic IP—in other words, if it gives you a new IP address each time you connect—simply select the Server Assigned IP Address button.

6. In the Primary DNS (Domain Name Server) box, enter the IP address of your Internet service provider's primary domain-name server. Again, if your Internet service provider assigns you a DNS server every time you connect, select the Server Assigned Name Server Addresses button.

7. If your Internet service provider gave you the IP address of a secondary domain-name server, enter its address in the Secondary DNS text box. A secondary domain-name server is not required, however; so if you don't happen to know it, leave this field blank.

8. You're finished with this bit, so click on the OK button. The Server Types dialog box will reappear.

9. In the Server Types dialog box, click on the OK button, and the Properties dialog box will reappear.

10. Finally, in the Properties dialog box, click on the OK button to save the information you just entered. The Dial-Up Networking window will appear on the Desktop again.

Click here if a new IP address is assigned each time you call.

Enter your IP address here.

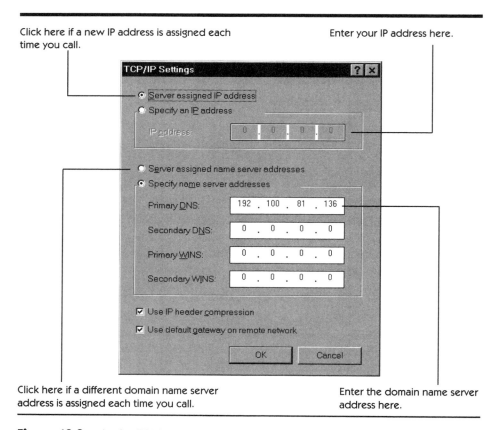

Click here if a different domain name server address is assigned each time you call.

Enter the domain name server address here.

Figure 10.9: In the TCP/IP Settings dialog box, you'll enter all that pertinent information you got from your Internet service provider.

You have entered all the information necessary to access the Internet via your Internet service provider and Dial-Up Networking. You are now ready to connect to the Internet.

Actually Connecting! Now that you've created and configured your connection, you are ready to actually connect to the Internet. Remember, you must start up the connection before you use Netscape. This connection is what allows Netscape or any other Internet application on your computer to talk to the world. To connect, follow these steps:

1. The Dial-Up Networking window should still be displayed on your screen. In the Dial-Up Networking window, double-click on the icon for the connection you created. The Connect To dialog box will appear.

2. In the Connect To dialog box, enter your user and password into the appropriate text boxes. Then, click on the Connect button. Windows dials the phone number you specified and then waits for your Internet service provider to answer.

3. You'll hear your modem dialing your Internet service provider. When you're actually connected, a small dialog box will appear showing how long you've been connected.

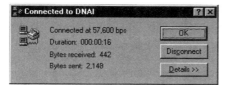

This dialog box remains in view until you disconnect from the Internet. You can minimize this dialog box by clicking on its Minimize button in the upper-right corner of your screen. That will get it out of your way.

Now that you are connected to the Internet, it is time to download Netscape Communicator. Turn to the section titled "Getting Communicator from the Internet via Dial-Up Networking" to do so.

Connecting via Windows NT Dial-Up Networking

Microsoft Windows NT 4 is a true 32-bit operating system—what many expected Windows 95 to be. What's the diff? Well, while Windows 95 does offer the ability to run 32-bit applications, it's still technically tied to the 16-bit heritage of MS-DOS and Windows 3.1; so in reality, Windows 95 is just a shell running on top of DOS like Windows 3.1. This had to be so because millions of Microsoft users who had 16-bit applications that ran on Windows 3.1 wanted those applications to work when they upgraded to Windows 95. Windows NT is less happy with 16-bit applications than Windows 95, which if you have upgraded to NT already, you already know.

The software and hardware restrictions imposed by NT may seem severe, but there are big-time payoffs as well. NT 4's slick interface (actually just the Windows 95 interface) is combined with the stability of a true 32-bit operating system.

If you've made the big jump already and are living in a 32-bit world, you'll find the process of setting up Dial-Up Networking for Windows NT requires the same sort of information as for Windows 95. Once you've set up an account with an Internet service provider and you are ready to set up a connection, follow the instructions in the section titled "Introducing Dial-Up Networking to Your Internet Service Provider" earlier in this chapter; then you can proceed to the section following this one.

Installing Windows NT Dial-Up Networking

Once you set up an account with an Internet service provider, you're all set to install and set up Dial-Up Networking. (You can actually go ahead and install Dial-Up Networking even before your Internet service provider account is in place; you just can't finish installing it and start using it until you get the account information from your provider.) Note that you do have to install Dial-Up Networking before you can use it to connect to your Internet service provider. If, during your installation of Windows NT, you chose the option *This computer will participate on a network*, with the TCP/IP protocol and Dial-Up Networking, all you'll have to do is create a connection to your Internet service provider. If you haven't set up Dial-Up Networking, follow these steps:

1. From the Start menu, select Settings, then click on Control Panel. The Control Panel window will appear.

2. In the Control Panel window, double-click on the Network icon.

Network

The Network dialog box will appear (see Figure 10.10).

3. Along the top of the dialog box, you'll see a number of tabs. Click on the Protocols tab, and the window's contents change to show which protocols have been installed on your computer.

4. If TCP/IP is already installed, it will appear in the Network Protocols list. If TCP/IP is not installed, click on Add. Select TCP/IP Protocol in the Network Protocol list and click on OK.

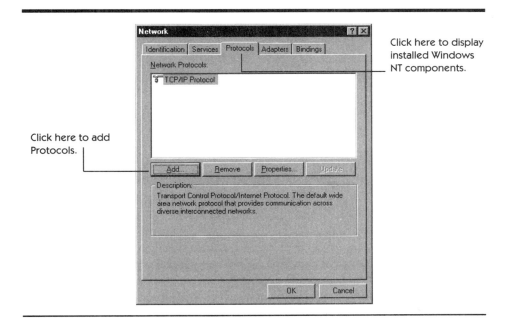

Figure 10.10: You can use the Network dialog box to add the TCP/IP Protocol to your computer if you don't have it installed already.

5. You'll be prompted to specify Yes to use *DHCP* (Dynamic Host Configuration Protocol—a method by which Windows NT servers can allocate temporary IP addresses to the client computers on the network for the length of the network session), or No to assign an IP address manually.

6. Then you'll be prompted to enter the location of the TCP/IP source files. If it is not already loaded, insert the Windows NT CD, and enter the location of the CD ROM drive (that would be D: if you have one hard drive). Windows NT will copy the files and prompt you to shut down and restart the computer before the changes take effect. The installation of TCP/IP is completed.

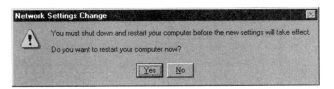

When you Click on the Yes button, your computer will restart and Windows NT will start running again. When your machine restarts, Dial-Up Networking is installed. You will not see any obvious changes as a result of the installation (except that you will have a new icon in your My Computer window called Dial-Up Networking).

If you chose No in step 5 and need to configure TCP/IP manually, be sure to enter your static IP address which has been assigned to you by your provider, as described in the section titled "Configuring the Network Protocol Settings" later in this chapter.

You now have the software required to access your Internet service provider, but you still have to create a new connection for your ISP and enter relevant information. Once you complete these few steps, you'll be all set to cruise the Internet.

Introducing Dial-Up Networking to Your ISP

Now you're going to set up Dial-Up Networking to work with your Internet service provider. In particular, you'll create the connection that tells Dial-Up Networking the telephone number to dial for your ISP. You'll also configure the connection so that Dial-Up Networking knows how to access the Internet via your ISP.

Here's what you do to set up a Dial-Up Networking connection:

1. On the task bar at the bottom of your screen, click on the Start button. From the menu that appears, choose Programs ➤ Accessories ➤ Dial-Up Networking. The Dial-Up Networking dialog box will appear.

2. Click on the New button. The New Phonebook Entry Wizard will appear, as shown in Figure 10.11.

3. In the text box labeled *MyDialUpServer*, type the name of your Internet service provider as the dial-up server. That way, if you create entries to several ISPs—one to Compuserve or AOL, another to a local Internet service provider, and yet another to your corporate network—each will be easily identifiable. Click on the Next button. The Server dialog box will appear.

4. Because we are setting up an Internet connection here, click on the box next to *I am calling the Internet*.

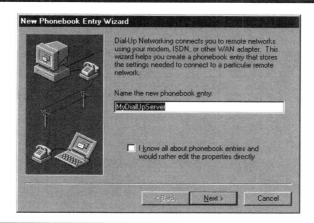

Figure 10.11: The New Phonebook Entry Wizard will guide you through the process of setting up a connection with your ISP.

5. Find out from your Internet service provider whether to enter your password only when you log on or to enter your password a second time in a *terminal window* (a text window that has a black screen and asks you for your login id and password) that comes up after connecting. Then, in the Server dialog box, click on the checkbox indicating the appropriate choice according to your ISP's requirements.

6. Click on the Next button. The Phone Number dialog box will appear.

7. In the Phone Number text box, enter the phone number of your ISP. If you have more than one local access number, you can enter the alternate numbers so you can switch to another if the first one is busy. Click on the Next button. The final New Phonebook Entry Wizard dialog box will appear, telling you the process is complete.

8. Click on Finish, and you're done. The Network dialog box will close, leaving you with your familiar Desktop.

When you next open the Dial-Up Networking window (by double-clicking on the Dial-Up Networking icon found in your My Computer window), the connection you just set up will appear there, as shown in Figure 10.12.

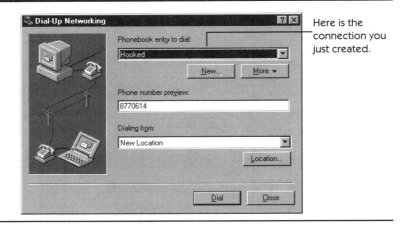

Here is the connection you just created.

Figure 10.12: The new connection you just made appears in the Dial-Up Networking window.

Configuring the Network Protocol Settings   Before you use the connection you have just set up using the Phonebook Wizard, you must check the network protocol settings. To start this procedure:

1. On the Desktop, double-click on the My Computer icon. In the My Computer window that opens, double-click on the Dial-Up Networking icon. You will see the Dial-Up Networking window open, as shown in Figure 10.13.

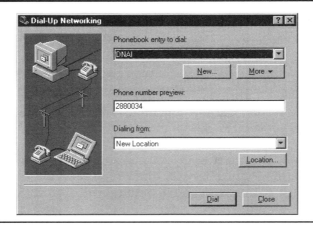

Figure 10.13: The Dial-Up Networking window shows the last connection you have used in the Phonebook Entry to Dial text box.

2. Click on the More button. A drop-down menu will appear. Select Edit Entry and Modem Properties and the Edit Phonebook Entry dialog box will open, as shown in Figure 10.14.

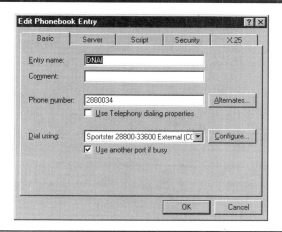

Figure 10.14: The Edit Phonebook Entry dialog box is where you can change your Dial-Up Network settings.

3. The Basic tab allows you to change the entry name, enter the phone number for connecting, and configure your modem. Check your entries here to see that they're all correct.

Click on the Alternates button to enter other phone numbers to dial if your Internet service provider's primary number is busy.

4. Click on the Server tab and the dialog box will change to look like Figure 10.15. In the Dial-Up Server Type text box, select the connection type you have—you can select from the available choices by clicking on the button at the right end of the text box.

5. In the Network Protocols area, click on the checkbox next to TCP/IP. If you have selected PPP or SLIP, you will see a dialog box that corresponds to Figure 10.16.

6. In the IP Address window, leave the IP address blank (if you are assigned a dynamic address), or enter your IP address (if you have a static address). In the Specify Name Server Addresses box, enter the

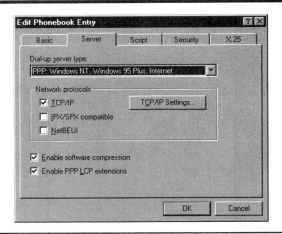

Figure 10.15:   Here's where you enter the information you got from your Internet service provider about your network connection.

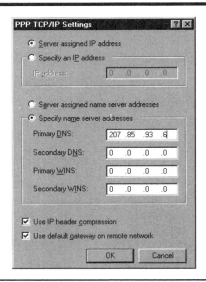

Figure 10.16:   Enter the network configuration information from your ISP or network administrator here.

IP address of your Internet server in the Primary DNS (Domain Name Server) box—if you have a Secondary DNS address, enter that in the Secondary DNS box; or if you dial into a Windows NT WINS

(Windows Internet Name Service) server, enter the IP address in the Primary WINS server box—if you have a Secondary WINS address, enter that in the Secondary WINS box.

7. When you've entered the information that you collected from your ISP, click on OK. The Edit Phonebook Entry dialog box will appear. Click on the Server tab if it's not already showing.

8. At the bottom of the Server tab are two checkboxes: Enable Software Compression and Enable PPP LCP Extensions. Your ISP will advise you about whether to check off these options.

9. If your ISP has instructed you to use a Login script, click on the Script tab and indicate its location in the Login Script window, or have a terminal window.

10. Click on the Security tab and select the option as directed by your ISP. The levels of security increase as you move down the list.

11. Unless you have an X.25 provider, you can ignore the X.25 tab. When you have entered all the information that pertains to your network connection, click on OK and you will be returned to the Dial-Up Networking window.

You're all set to connect—the hard stuff is done.

Don't hesitate to call up your ISP for advice about how to fill out this information. They can help you get set up correctly.

Actually Connecting!

Now that you've created and configured your connection, you are ready to actually connect to the Internet. Remember, you must start up the connection before you use Communicator. This connection is what allows Communicator or any other Internet application on your computer to talk to the world. To connect, follow these steps:

1. From the Windows Desktop, double-click on the My Computer icon. The My Computer window will appear.

2. In the window, double-click on the Dial-Up Networking icon to open the Dial-Up Networking window (see Figure 10.13). A text box labeled Phonebook Entry to Dial appears at the top of the window. If several entries appear there, locate the one you want to connect to and click on the Dial button at the bottom of the window. The Connect to Your Choice dialog box will appear.

3. In the Connect to Your Choice dialog box, enter your User Name and Password.

If you check the Save Password box, your User Name and Password will be saved and you will not see this screen again when you click on OK to begin dialing.

4. Click on OK; Windows will dial the phone number you specified and wait for your ISP to answer. You'll hear your modem dialing your Internet service provider, and the Connection Complete dialog box will appear, as shown in Figure 10.17.

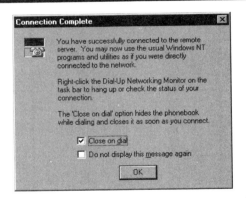

Figure 10.17: The Connection Complete dialog box appears after you have successfully logged in to your ISP.

5. There are two checkboxes (Close on Dial, and Do Not Display This Message Again) appearing at the bottom of the Connection Complete dialog box. Use these to configure some cosmetic options if you like.

6. Click on OK, and the Dial-Up Networking monitor will appear as a button on the task bar.

7. After you have connected, you can right-click on the DUN monitor and a pop-up menu will appear with options for opening the monitor to check the status, dialing another connection if your session is interrupted, or hanging up when you're done.

When you want to see information about the status of your connection, how long you've been connected, and your connection device, click on Open on the DUN Monitor menu. A dialog box like the one shown in Figure 10.18 will appear.

That's all there is to setting up Dial-Up Networking. Turn to the next section. The procedure for downloading Communicator is the same for either Windows 95 or NT Dial Up Networking.

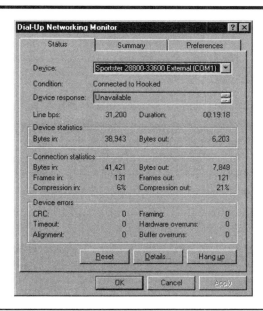

Figure 10.18:   Open Dial-Up Networking Monitor to review the status of your connection.

Getting Communicator via Dial-Up Networking

Now we can move on to our bigger purpose—getting a copy of Communicator so you can install and use it. As mentioned earlier, you can get Communicator from the Internet itself or, more specifically, from the Netscape FTP site. An FTP site is essentially a public archive of files that are accessible to anyone with an FTP program (like the one you have in Dial-Up Networking).

The FTP program that comes with Windows 95 is character-based, meaning it does not offer the nifty graphical interface Windows programs have; you'll be typing text-based commands to make it work.

To get Communicator, follow these steps:

1. If you aren't still connected to the Internet, connect now, using the instructions in the section that came before this one.

2. From the Start menu, select Run. The Run dialog box will appear.

3. In the dialog box's Open text box, type **ftp ftp.netscape.com**. Press the ↵ key. An FTP window will appear.

Way too many people try to use Netscape's FTP server at once. For best results, you might try at odd hours (like 2 a.m.), or you may have to make several attempts before you connect successfully. The worst time to try is noon. Everybody on the Net seems to get on at lunchtime, so forget doing your FTPing over a turkey on rye.

4. Near the top of the FTP window, a line that says *User* will appear, followed by the name of a computer on the Internet. Netscape has things set up so that when you access **ftp.netscape.com**, you are actually accessing any of a number of identical FTP servers. Don't worry—each server contains the same set of files. The Netscape folks do it this way so that the thousands of simultaneous FTP connections they get when they release a new version of the software won't bring the house down. We are using anonymous FTP to get Communicator; so at the User prompt mentioned earlier in this step, type **anonymous** and press ↵. A request for a password will appear.

5. It's customary to enter your e-mail address as a password when you use anonymous FTP. This gives the people who run the FTP site some information about who is using their site. Go ahead and type your e-mail address and press the ↵ key. A welcome message will appear.

Steps 4 and 5 describe the standard conventions for using anonymous FTP.

6. Communicator is in the directory /Pub/Communicator/4.0/Windows on Netscape's FTP server. Type **cd/pub/communicator/4.0/ windows/** and press ⏎ to change to the directory that holds Communicator for Windows. (Note that those are forward slashes instead of the familiar backslashes used by DOS.) A message describing Communicator and its licensing terms will appear.

7. Now type **bin** and press the ⏎ key. The bin command tells FTP that you are transferring binary files instead of ASCII text files.

8. You must now specify where on your local computer the file you transfer should be stored. Type **lcd c:** and press the ⏎ key. This tells FTP to store files that you transfer in the root directory of your C: drive.

9. Now type **ls** and press the ⏎ key. A list of files like those shown in Figure 10.19 will appear. In the list of files, locate the one called c32e40.exe. This is the one that contains the 32-bit version of Netscape Communicator for Windows 95.

Figure 10.19: In this list of files you'll see one called c32e40.exe. That's the one you want.

10. Type **get c32e40.exe** and press the ⏎ key to start the transfer. This file is more than 9MB in size; it may take 45 minutes or so to arrive. The FTP prompt will appear on screen once again when the transfer is finished.

Make a note of the size of the file before you actually begin downloading; then check that number against the size of the file you finally receive. If your file transfer ends before the complete file arrives (which you'll know has happened when you check the size of the file), you'll have to repeat the process until you successfully receive the whole file.

11. When the transfer is finished and the files are on your machine, type **quit** and press the ↵ key to quit FTP. The Windows 95 Desktop will appear again.

Now Communicator is on your machine; let's disconnect from the Internet, just for practice. This is something you'll have to do pretty much every time you shut down Communicator; it's the technique for closing down your Dial-Up Networking Internet connection.

1. Earlier, you minimized the Connected To dialog box to get it out of your way. Now you need to see it again. Click on the Connect To button on the task bar, and the dialog box will reappear.

2. In the Connected To dialog box, click on the Disconnect button. The Connected To dialog box will close, and your connection to the Internet will be snapped.

You made it! You've got a copy of Netscape, just waiting to be installed and configured on your machine. So, when you're ready, turn to Chapter 11 and let's install it already.

◆ Connecting via Netcom's Netcomplete

Netcomplete is a popular all-in-one Internet access package from Netcom that provides not only Internet access but also a really nifty point-and-click interface that's great for beginners and powerful enough to grow into once you've got some experience under your belt. Netcomplete is like Netcom's former service, NetCruiser, except that it's updated and includes some content, too. Like a commercial online service such as WinCIM, Netcomplete software works only with Netcom's Internet service, not with other ISPs. Netcomplete includes access to all the popular features of the Internet—including the World Wide Web—but its Web browser is notoriously weak, lacking many of the more advanced features found in Netscape and loved by millions. Because of this combination of factors, many people enjoy running Communicator on top of Netcomplete, which is in many ways the best of both worlds.

 Netcom's new Netcomplete package is similar to their old NetCruiser access software. You can follow all the directions we give here for getting going with Netcomplete and Communicator if you are using NetCruiser. The one exception is that you should download and install the 16-bit version of Netscape Communicator to use with NetCruiser instead of the 32-bit version. (You can and should use the 32-bit version with Netcomplete.) See "A Tale of Two Versions" in Chapter 11 for more on the two versions of Communicator.

What's Out There

You can find out more about Netcom and Netcomplete from Netcom's home page at http://www.netcom.com.

What You Need

To run Netcomplete, you need a Windows 95 PC with 8MB of memory, VGA graphics capability, a color monitor, and about 12MB of free disk space. A 9600bps modem is the bare minimum; a 14,400 or preferably even 28,800bps is better. You also need Netcomplete itself. You can often pick up the disk for free at trade shows, in computer periodicals, or computer stores, but it will come without documentation. Perhaps the best way to get Netcomplete is along with a terrific book, *Access the Internet!*, written by David Peal and Jennifer Kirby, and published by Sybex, that will tell you all about using Netcomplete.

 Netcomplete and NetCruiser are included among the connectivity options on the CD that comes with this book.

Installing Netcomplete is an incredibly simple matter that is described in a phrase on the disk and in detail in the book. Here, we're going to focus on getting Communicator by using Netcomplete, and then on making a Communicator connection via your Netcomplete account.

Getting Ready to Run Communicator with Netcomplete

You don't really have to do anything to get ready to run Communicator along with your Netcomplete software. Netcomplete is ready to run Communicator—as well as any other Internet application you wish to run—without any fussing.

Getting Communicator via Netcomplete

Although you have Netcomplete and it is ready to run Communicator, you're still missing one crucial piece of stuff: Communicator. In this section, you'll learn to download Communicator to your computer using Netcomplete. In the next chapter, you will learn how to install Communicator. To get Communicator, follow these steps:

1. Start up Netcomplete and connect as you usually do.

2. From the Netcomplete menu bar, select Internet ➤ FTP Download. The FTP To: dialog box will appear, as shown in Figure 10.20.

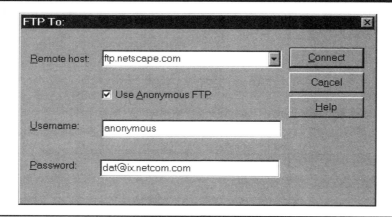

Figure 10.20: The FTP To: dialog box after we entered the address of Netscape's FTP server

3. In the Remote host text box, type **ftp.netscape.com**. Then click on the Use Anonymous FTP checkbox to select it.

4. Now click on the Connect button to accept the default entries. The NETCOMplete - ftp.netscape.com:/:4 window will appear.

5. This window is split into two sections—the left part of the window contains directory names, and the right part of the window contains filenames. Scroll the list until you see the Pub directory, and then double-click on it. The contents of the right part of the window will change to show the filenames in the Pub directory.

6. Now double-click, in order, on the Communicator, 4.0, Current, and Windows directories in the left part of the window. The right part of the ftp.netscape.com window will change to list the files located in the /Pub/Communicator/4.0/Windows directory.

7. Locate the file named c32e40.exe in the lower part of the window, and double-click on it. This is the file that contains the 32-bit version of Communicator for Windows 95. The Save As dialog box will appear.

8. In the File Name field of the Save As dialog box, type **c:\c32e40.exe** and press ↵. Netscape will transfer the file you need to your local computer. You can see the progress of the file transfer in the status bar along the bottom of the FTP To: dialog box.

9. When the transfer is finished, close the ftp.netscape.com window by clicking on its close box in the upper-right corner.

You now have a copy of Netscape Communicator on your computer, and you're ready to install it. Turn to Chapter 11 to find out how.

◆ Connecting via America Online

AOL is at the moment America's most popular commercial online service; its Web browser, however, is very disappointing compared to Netscape. So—what's a Net surfer to do? Happily, you can use Communicator with AOL.

Getting and installing the America Online software is plenty easy, because the America Online software is often bundled with magazines and new modems, as well as sent in the mail, and the installation process is simple as pie. Most of the time when you sign up, you can get a trial membership (with all of the privileges of a fully paid membership) that allows you a certain number of hours online for the first month. If you're not sure you want to commit yourself after your first trial period has expired, don't hesitate to try another service. You may just find out that the first one better suits your needs and end up signing up with them after all.

 AOL software is also included on the CD that comes with this book.

What You Need

To get and use Communicator with America Online, all you need is version 3 of the America Online software for Windows, along with a 14,400bps or preferably 28,800bps modem, and enough memory to run these two programs simultaneously. While you can get by with 8MB of RAM, you'll be much happier with your performance by increasing to 16MB of RAM.

Getting Ready to Run Communicator with America Online

That's all there is to making your copy of America Online Communicator-savvy. You're all set to move along to downloading and installing Communicator.

Upgrading to the Current Version of AOL Software

If you are running a version of AOL software older than 3, you should upgrade to the newest version. To upgrade do this: Connect to AOL, click on the keyword icon, type in **upgrade**, and click on Go. Then just follow the instructions that appear for downloading and installing the software. If you're using Windows 95, you'll want to download the 32-bit version of AOL software; if you are using Windows 3.1, you'll want to get the 16-bit version. This has bearing on which version of Communicator you can run. See "A Tale of Two Versions" in Chapter 11.

Getting Communicator via America Online

You have two options for getting Communicator via America Online. You can use America Online's FTP tool to download it straight from Netscape's site, or you can download it from America Online's own area. We're going to show you how to download it straight from the Netscape site because the Netscape site always has the most up-to-date version of Communicator available. (And you wouldn't want to be using an old version of Communicator, would you?)

1. Start up an AOL session. Then, from AOL's menu bar, select Go To ➤ Keyword or click on the Keyword icon. The Keyword dialog box will appear.

2. In the Keyword dialog box, type **FTP**. The File Transfer Protocol dialog box will appear, as shown in Figure 10.21.

3. In the File Transfer Protocol dialog box, click on the Go to FTP button. The Anonymous FTP dialog box will appear.

4. In the Anonymous FTP dialog box, click on the Other Site button. The Other Site dialog box will appear.

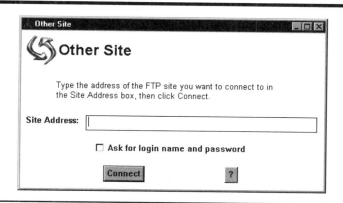

Figure 10.21: The File Transfer Protocol dialog box, titled Other Site, is your doorway into FTP sites on the Internet.

5. In the Other Site dialog box's Site Address text box, type `ftp.netscape.com` and click on the Connect button. The Connected dialog box will appear, as shown in Figure 10.22.

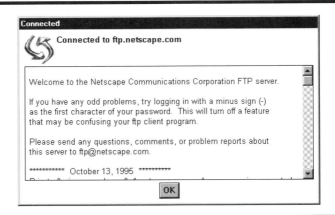

Figure 10.22: The Connected dialog box contains relevant information about using the Netscape FTP server.

6. The Connected dialog box contains some information about the Netscape FTP server. It's not a bad idea to read this stuff. Click on the OK button to continue. The ftp.netscape.com dialog box will appear, as shown in Figure 10.23.

Figure 10.23: You can use America Online's ftp.netscape.com dialog box to download software from Netscape's FTP server.

7. Now we need to go to the directory on Netscape's server that holds Communicator. In the list of directories, in turn, double-click on

Pub, Communicator, 4.0, Current, and Windows. A list of files will appear, including the file c32e40.exe, the 32-bit version of Netscape.

8. Double-click on c32e40.exe. The ftp.netscape.com dialog box, shown in Figure 10.23, will appear.

9. In the dialog box, click on the Download Now button to start downloading Netscape. The Download Manager dialog box will appear.

10. The Download Manager dialog box is actually a standard Windows Save As dialog box. Select C:\ as the directory into which you want to save the file you are downloading. Click on the OK button. The Download Manager dialog box will close and a dialog box showing the status of your download will appear.

11. Once downloading is completed, a dialog box will appear saying that the file has been downloaded. Click on the OK button to close that dialog box.

When the download is done, you'll have Communicator on your computer and be ready to install it. Turn to Chapter 11 for the full scoop on that.

Online Support from America Online

America Online offers online support services that will provide you with quick answers to your AOL or Internet questions. In AOL's menu bar, click on Help, and from the drop-down menu that appears, select Online Support. The Welcome to Member Services dialog box will appear; in it, click on the Contact Us button. Now the Contact Us dialog box will appear; in this one, double-click on the Member Help Interactive button. The Member Help Interactive dialog box will now appear, and here you can choose General Help or Technical Support. Type in your questions for a fast response from an AOL support representative.

◆ Connecting via CompuServe's WinCIM

CompuServe offers the usual range of commercial online service content, but it is known widely as a more business- and tech-oriented service. CompuServe includes quite credible Internet access right from within WinCIM version 2 or later. (Version 3 is the more recent one as of this writing.) WinCIM comes with a Web browser, but many people prefer running Netscape Communicator's Navigator browser instead because of Navigator's many state-of-the-art features and popularity.

What You Need

To run CompuServe's WinCIM, you need a Windows PC with 8MB of memory and about 8MB of free disk space. A 9600bps modem is the bare minimum; a 14,400 or preferably even 28,800bps is better. You also need a CompuServe account. Disks that will get you going are frequently bundled with magazines and modems for free and are also often available at trade shows or in computer stores.

Upgrading to the Current Version of WinCIM software

If you are running a version of WinCIM software older than 3, you may want to upgrade to the newest version. Keep these considerations in mind, however:

◆ If you have Windows 3.1, you *must* use the 16-bit version of WinCIM, because Windows 3.1 is a 16-bit operating system—trying to use 32-bit Communicator in a 16-bit environment doesn't work.

◆ If you don't have enough RAM to meet the increased needs of WinCIM 3.1, you might want to try WinCIM 2.5. You need a computer with only 4MB of RAM and a 386 processor to run this one successfully.

◆ If you are using Windows 95, you'll probably want to take advantage of the increased performance using 32-bit software offers, but if for some reason you want to go another way, the 16-bit version of WinCIM will still work with Windows 95.

(continued on the next page)

For more information on 16-bit vs. 32-bit environments, see "A Tale of Two Versions" in Chapter 11.

To upgrade to the latest version of WinCIM:

1. Start a CompuServe session. In the menu bar, click on Access, and from the drop-down menu that appears, click on Go. (Or simply click on the Go button on the toolbar.) The Go dialog box will appear.

2. In the Go dialog box, type **cissoft** and click on OK. A forum containing CompuServe Software will appear.

3. The first time you enter a forum, you will be asked if you want to join—click on the Join button to enjoy the full benefits of the forum—it won't cost you any extra unless you are informed otherwise.

4. Select the Download Now or Order Now option available for the version of WinCIM that's suited to your system, and proceed according to instructions that follow.

Installing WinCIM and setting up a CompuServe account is very easy; you'll be walked through that process on screen when you pop the disk into your machine. Here, we'll focus on getting Communicator by using CompuServe's WinCIM.

Online Support from Compuserve

To get interactive help from Compuserve staff members, click on the Go button and type **cslive**, which will bring up Member Services, where you can enter live discussions with staff members who offer immediate answers to your questions.

Getting Ready to Run Communicator with WinCIM

WinCIM 3 comes ready to run Internet applications like Communicator. You're all set to move along to downloading and installing Communicator.

Getting Communicator via WinCIM

To download Communicator, follow these steps:

1. Start WinCIM as you usually do.

2. From the WinCIM menu bar, select Services ➤ Internet. The CompuServe Internet window, shown in Figure 10.24, will appear.

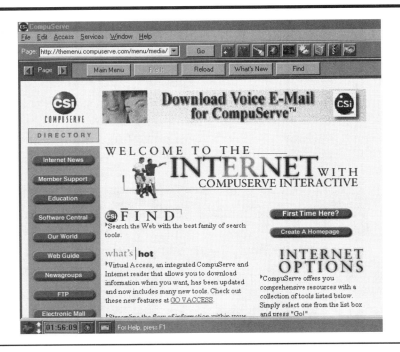

Figure 10.24: Selecting Internet from the Services drop-down menu will bring up the Internet Conferences window.

3. From the Internet Conferences window, click on the FTP button. An FTP dialog box will appear, with a warning that you are responsible for any files you download.

4. Click on Proceed. Another window will open; in it, click on the Access a Specific Site button. The Access a Specific Site dialog box will appear, as shown in Figure 10.25.

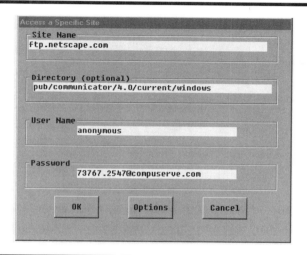

Figure 10.25:   In this dialog box, you can enter the site name and directory you want to access.

5. Now, in the Site Name text box, enter **ftp.netscape.com**. In the Directory text box, type **pub/communicator/4.0/windows**. Click on OK. The contents of the directory on Netscape's FTP server will appear, as shown in Figure 10.26.

Netscape's FTP servers are so popular that they're often overworked, and sometimes they just plain don't respond to anonymous FTP requests. The worst time to do something like this is lunchtime, when everybody seems to be on the Net and many procedures slow to a crawl—and it gets *really* bad the week after Netscape announces the availability of new software. You may have to try several times or at odd hours (like at 2 a.m.) before you can connect successfully.

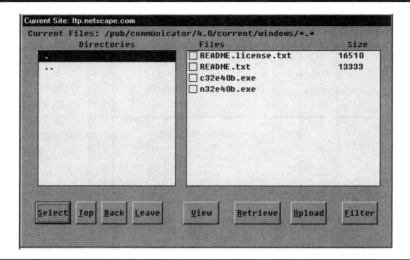

Figure 10.26: The contents of Netscape's FTP server as displayed by CompuServe's Web browser

6. You'll have to indicate which of the listed files you want to download; click on the link c32e40.exe. That's the one for the 32-bit, Windows 95 or NT version of Communicator. For the 16-bit version for Windows 3.1, select c16e40.exe. Click on Retrieve, and a dialog box will appear asking if you want to save the file to disk.

7. Click on the Yes button. The Save As dialog box will appear.

8. In the Save As dialog box, the name of the file you just selected will appear in the File Name text box—that's fine. Press the ↵ key. The Save As dialog box will close as the file transfer begins.

9. As the file is transferred from Netscape's FTP server to your computer, a Retrieve in Progress dialog box will appear to show the procedure's progress. When the status bar has moved all the way to the right side, the file transfer is complete. The dialog box will close automatically.

It's time now to install Communicator. Turn to Chapter 11 for detailed directions.

◆ Connecting via the Microsoft Network

The Microsoft Network is Microsoft's very own online service, designed to work in tandem with Windows 95. Starting with version 1.05 of the Microsoft Network software, you have full access to the Internet from your computer—you won't even need Windows 95 Dial-Up Networking. If you have an earlier version of Microsoft Network, however (which you very well may, because early copies of Windows 95, of course, included earlier versions of Microsoft Network), you'll have to download an update from the Microsoft Network's Internet Center. (You'll also find directions and support for doing this at the Internet Center.)

What You Need

You can run Microsoft Network on any computer that runs Windows 95 and is equipped with a modem. For best performance, you should have at least 8MB of RAM. The Microsoft Network software takes up an additional 10MB of disk space. You also need a 9600bps or faster modem—14,400 or even 28,800bps is much better.

Getting Ready to Run Communicator with Microsoft Network

There isn't much to this; the Windows 95 installation process installs the Microsoft Network. If you have Windows 95 installed on your machine, you're set.

Getting Communicator via Microsoft Network

Microsoft Network comes with Microsoft Internet Explorer—a Web browser similar to Navigator, but perhaps not as popular. We're going to use Internet Explorer to download Netscape Communicator to your computer. To do this, follow these steps:

1. In the Windows 95 Desktop, double-click on The Internet icon:

Internet Explorer will start.

2 From the Internet Explorer menu bar, select File ➤ Open. The Open dialog box will appear, giving you a chance to enter an Internet Address.

3. In the Open dialog box's text box, type **ftp://ftp.netscape.com/ pub/communicator/4.0/windows**. Press the ↵ key. In a few seconds, the contents of Netscape's FTP server will appear, as shown in Figure 10.27.

4. Click on the link c32e40.exe. This is the link for the 32-bit version of Communicator (for Windows 95). The Confirm File Open dialog box will appear.

5. In the dialog box, click on the Save As button. The Save As dialog box will appear.

6. In the Save As dialog box's File Name text box, type **c:\c32e40.exe**. Press the ↵ key. The file will transfer from Netscape's FTP server to your machine. You can monitor the transfer progress by watching the bar that appears as part of the status bar at the bottom of the Internet Explorer window.

7. When the transfer is done, quit Internet Explorer by selecting File ➤ Exit. The now familiar Windows 95 Desktop will reappear.

You now have a copy of Communicator on your machine, and you're ready to install it. Turn to Chapter 11 to find out how.

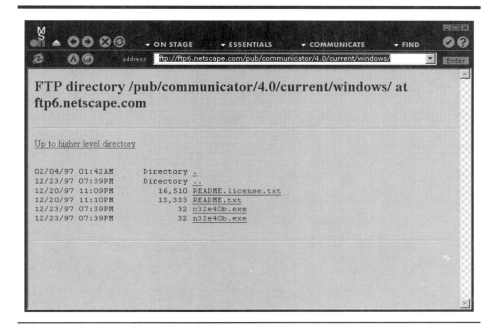

Figure 10.27:   The Netscape FTP server as seen from the Microsoft Internet Explorer.

Forging Ahead

Whether your preferred connectivity option is Windows 95 or NT Dial-Up Networking, Netcom's Netcomplete or NetCruiser, America Online, Compu-Serve, or the Microsoft Network, you now have a connection to the Internet going and a copy of Communicator sitting on your hard drive. In the next chapter, you'll actually install it, which is a simple enough process. Then, with Communicator installed, you'll be fully equipped to start cruising and using the very wonderful World Wide Web.

Getting Communicator Going

In Chapter 10, we walked you through actually getting Communicator by downloading the appropriate version from the Internet. In this chapter, we're going to make the software work. First, we'll install it (a simple, largely automatic process), then we'll make it run, and finally we'll show you how to make some minor changes to enhance operations.

◆ Installing Netscape Communicator

Installation varies slightly between the 32- and 16-bit versions of the program. If you are using Windows 95 or Windows NT Dial-Up Networking, the Microsoft Network, or a 32-bit version of the software from one of the other online services to connect to the Internet, you downloaded the 32-bit version of Communicator and should follow the directions in the "Installing the 32-Bit Version" section. If you are using Windows 3.1 or 3.11, follow the directions in the "Installing the 16-Bit Version" section later in this chapter.

A Tale of Two Versions

There are two versions of Netscape Communicator. One, the 32-bit version, works with Windows 95 or Windows NT Dial-Up Networking and the 32-bit versions of the software from the online services. It offers faster and more reliable response than the 16-bit version. The 16-bit version works with 16-bit versions of Compu-Serve WinCIM, America Online, and with many other types of Internet access software. The real difference between these versions is that the 32-bit version only works with 32-bit operating systems—Windows 95 or Windows NT, in other words. If you're still using Windows 3.1 or Internet access software that's designed for Windows 3.1, you need the 16-bit version of Netscape Communicator.

Thus, the file you downloaded in Chapter 10 would have been one of two versions, depending on whether you needed the 32-bit version or the 16-bit version. If you are using Windows 95 or Windows NT as your operating system, you downloaded cc32e40.exe—the 32-bit version. If you are connecting with Windows 3.1 or 3.11 using a 16-bit version of CompuServe WinCIM or America Online, you downloaded c16e40.exe—the 16-bit version.

Installing the 32-Bit Version for Windows 95 or NT

The 32-bit version of Netscape Communicator works with 32-bit Internet connection software, such as Dial-Up Networking for Windows 95 or Windows NT.

Here's how to install it (instructions are the same for Windows 95 and Windows NT):

Before you start the install process, close any files that you have open; otherwise, you will have to stop in the middle of the installation procedure and close them.

1. Click on the Windows Start button to display the Start menu, and select Run. The Run dialog box will appear.

2. In the Run dialog box's Open field, type **c:\c32e40** and press ↵. The Run dialog box will close, and the InstallShield Self-Extracting Exe dialog box will appear. The InstallShield dialog box asks if you wish to install Netscape Communicator.

If you get an error message telling you the file is damaged when you try to run it, go ahead and delete the file, because you'll have to download it again. Don't worry, you didn't do anything wrong, this is just an occasional by-product of the process of downloading a file this large.

3. Click on Yes to continue. A status bar will appear in the InstallShield dialog box as shown in Figure 11.1. After a few minutes, the Install-Shield dialog box will close and the Netscape Communicator 4.0 Setup dialog box will appear. The Netscape Communicator 4.0 Setup dialog box includes a warning about closing any running applications.

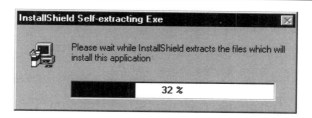

Figure 11.1: This dialog box shows the progress of the self-extraction of the Communicator installation files.

4. Since you've already exited all of the other applications running (in case you haven't, do it now), click on the Next button to continue. The dialog box will be replaced with the Software License Agreement dialog box.

5. Read the software license and click on Yes to continue (that is, if you agree with it; if you don't, click No and you'll be returned to the Windows Desktop). The Setup Type dialog box appears. In the Setup Type dialog box you elect whether you want to install all of the components that make up Communicator, or just selected components.

6. You'll want to install all of the components, so select the Typical radio button. Leave the contents of the Destination Directory text box unchanged—so Communicator will be installed to its default location of c:\program files\netscape\communicator. Click on the Next button to continue. The dialog box will close and the Select Program Folder dialog box will appear. In the Select Program Folder dialog box, you'll specify the name of the folder into which the Communicator icons will appear.

 Later you can run the setup program again and use Custom Setup to selectively install or reinstall Communicator components.

7. The default name of the folder is Netscape Communicator, and unless you have a good reason to call it something else, just leave the name alone. Click on Next to continue. The dialog box will close and the Start Copying dialog box will appear, listing all of the options you've selected.

 If you find yourself short of space, make sure you've cleaned up any files with a .tmp extension, and if you have a browser already, empty the disk cache. Also, remember that you will want from 10 to 25MB of free disk space after Communicator is installed for it to use as cache (temporary work) space.

8. As with any of the preceding steps, you can click on the Back button to return to an earlier step and change one of your choices. Once you are happy with your selections, click on the Install button. (Of course, the Cancel button will stop the whole process in its tracks and return you to the Windows Desktop). The dialog box will close and, in a few seconds, a new Setup dialog box will appear.

9. As files are installed, progress will be shown in the Setup dialog box. After all of the copying is completed successfully, a Question dialog box will appear asking if you would like to view the Readme file containing information about the version of Communicator you just installed. Click on Yes to open the file in Notepad or No to continue. If you open the text file to read it, close it by selecting File ➤ Exit from Notepad's menu bar when you're done.

10. Next, an Information dialog will box appear, informing you that setup is complete and that you must restart the computer before you run Communicator. Click on OK to restart your computer.

You're all finished with installation. You will find a Netscape Communicator icon on your Desktop and a new entry in your Start menu containing all of the icons for Communicator's programs.

 The Netscape program archive c32e40.exe is still in your C:\ folder (or wherever you put it). It's always a good idea to have backups in case something unfortunate happens, so move c32e40.exe to another folder on your hard disk, or make a backup of it just in case—providing you've got the space on your drive for a 13.3MB file.

You've got Communicator installed on your machine now, but you still have to do a thing or two (or three or four) to set everything up to work properly. Skip to the section titled "Making a Netscape Communicator Connection" to find out about configuring Communicator to work on your machine.

Installing the 16-Bit Version

If you have Windows 3.1 or 3.11 as your operating system or are using online service software designed for Windows 3.1 or 3.11, you'll need to use the 16-bit version of Netscape Communicator. It'll work just fine, and the 16-bit version of the program will do just about everything that the 32-bit version will do.

 The art in this book shows the 32-bit version of Communicator, which was designed for use with Windows 95 and Windows NT, but the 16-bit version behaves pretty much identically. You can use this book as a guide to either version.

Next, let's perform the installation procedure for the 16-bit Netscape Communicator. In this uncomplicated procedure, you'll actually install the software.

Installing the Program

Here's what you do to install that downloaded Netscape Communicator program:

1. From the Program Manager menu bar, select File ➤ Run. The Run dialog box will appear.

2. In the Run dialog box's text box, type **c:\c16e40** and press ↵. The InstallShield Self-Extracting Exe dialog box will appear. The Install-Shield dialog box asks if you wish to install Netscape Communicator.

3. Click on Yes to continue. A status bar will appear in the Shield dialog box. After a few minutes, the InstallShield dialog box will close and the Netscape Communicator 4.0 Setup dialog box will appear. The Netscape Communicator 4.0 Setup dialog box includes a warning about closing any running applications.

4. Because you've already done this (in case you haven't, do it now), click on the Next button to continue. The dialog box will be replaced with the Software License Agreement dialog box.

5. Read the software license agreement and click on Yes to continue (that is, if you agree with it; if you don't, click No and you'll be returned to the Windows Desktop). The Setup Type dialog box will appear. In the Setup Type dialog box you'll elect whether you want to install all of the components that make up Communicator, or just selected components.

6. You'll want to install all of the components, so select the Typical radio button. Leave the contents of the Destination Directory text box unchanged—so Communicator will be installed to its default location of c:\netscape\comm. Click on the Next button to continue. The dialog box will close and the Select Program Folder dialog box will appear.

7. In the Select Program Folder dialog box, you can specify the name of the folder into which the Communicator icons will appear. The default name of the folder is Netscape Communicator, and unless you have a good reason to call it something else, just leave the name alone. Click on Next to continue. The dialog box will close and the Start Copying dialog box will appear. In the Start Copying dialog box you can see a summary of all of the options you selected.

8. As with any of the preceding steps, you can click on the Back button to return to an earlier step and change one of your choices. Once you are happy with your selections, click on the Install button. (Of course, the Cancel button will stop the whole process in it's tracks and return you to the Windows Desktop). The dialog box will close and, in a few seconds, a new Setup dialog box will appear.

9. As files are installed, progress will be shown in the Setup dialog box. After all of the copying is completed successfully, a Question dialog box will appear asking if you would like to view the Readme file containing information about the version of Communicator you just installed.

10. Click on Yes to open the file in Notepad or No to continue. If you open the text file to read it, close it by selecting File ➤ Exit from Notepad's menu bar when you're done.

11. Next, an Information dialog box will appear, informing you that setup is complete and that you must restart the computer before you run Communicator. Click on OK to restart your computer.

After your computer has restarted, you're all finished with installation. If you are running Windows 95, you will find a Netscape Communicator icon on your Desktop and a new entry in your Start menu. Likewise, if you're running Windows 3.1, you'll find a new group in the Program Manager titled Communicator. Either way, you'll see entries for all of Communicator's programs.

Communicator is installed on your machine, just as we promised, but you still have to set up everything to work together properly. The next section, "Making a Netscape Communicator Connection," shows you how to configure Netscape to work on your machine.

 The Netscape program archive c16e40.exe and all its component files are still in your Temp folder (or wherever you put them). It's always a good idea to have backups, so copy c16e40.exe to a different directory on your hard disk, just in case. Having done this, you can delete all the files in Temp and the folder itself.

◆ Making a Netscape Communicator Connection

Because Netscape Communicator is a suite of Internet programs, you need to start up your Internet connection before you can actually use Communicator to access the Internet. But most of what we're going to do now doesn't require you to be connected to the Internet. First, we're going to start Communicator.

When you use Communicator to access the Internet, you have to engage in a two-step process that involves first starting up your Internet connection and *then* starting Communicator. In the procedure that follows, we're starting Communicator without first getting connected.

Starting Netscape Communicator

You can start a Netscape Communicator component in any of several ways:

◆ Double-click on the Netscape Communicator icon on your Desktop—this will start up a session of Netscape Communicator.

◆ From the Windows Start menu, select Programs ➤ Netscape Communicator. From the menu that appears, select the Netscape component (such as Netscape Navigator) you wish to run.

◆ Double-click on any Internet shortcut. Once Communicator is installed on your computer, Internet shortcuts may appear as Netscape icons on the Desktop, in other folders, in e-mail messages, or even in other applications' files. You can find out more about Internet shortcuts in Chapter 4.

Remember—to get connected and use Netscape Communicator to surf the Net, you have to start your Internet connection software and then start Communicator. But getting connected is not necessary in order to configure the software, as we're about to do...

Setting Up Communicator

If you have never installed an earlier version of Communicator, your initial launch of Communicator will bring up the Profile Setup Wizard. You will be guided through a set of dialog boxes that will help you set up your User Profile, which contains information like your name, your e-mail address, and other information about your Internet connection.

1. Start Communicator. Because this is the first time you've used the program, the New Profile Setup dialog box will appear.

2. Click on Next. The contents of the dialog box will change.

3. In the dialog box, shown in Figure 11.2, enter your name—your normal, everyday name—and your e-mail address. (If you don't know your e-mail address, you should contact your Internet Service provider.) Click on Next. The contents of the dialog box will change again.

4. Now you need to name your profile. By default, the first part of your e-mail address will be suggested. For instance, if your e-mail address is vox@company.com, it might be *vox*. This name will also be used as the default name for a directory that is created to hold your profile information. When you have made any changes you wish in this dialog box, click on the Next button. The dialog box will close and the Mail and Discussion Groups Setup dialog box will appear.

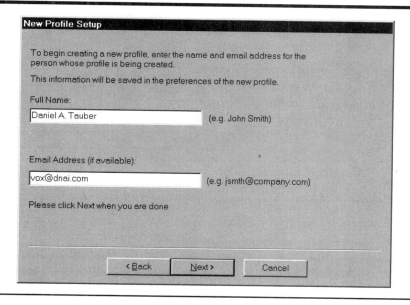

Figure 11.2: You can enter a nickname or pseudonym in the Full Name text box, but the e-mail address must be your true address.

5. Next you'll provide information about the mail and news servers run by your ISP. In the text box labeled Outgoing Mail (see Figure 11.3), enter the name of your outgoing mail server (Table 11.1 lists this for some common ISPs). The name should look something like mail .server.com. Click on the Next button to continue. The contents of the dialog box will change.

You can change the default name or the default directory here, but unless you have a good reason to, it's not recommended.

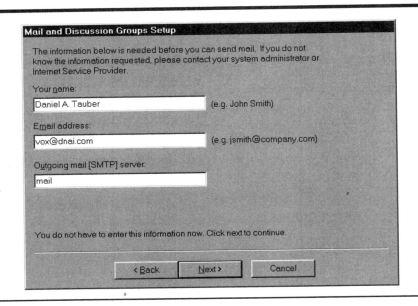

Figure 11.3: The information you provide here will facilitate e-mail and news-group connections.

Table 11.1: Server Names for Some Common Connections

Connection	Outgoing Mail (SMTP) Server	Incoming Mail (POP) Server	News (NNTP) Server
CompuServe	mail.compuserve.com	mail.compuserve.com	news.compuserve.com
NETCOMplete or NetCruiser	smtp.ix.netcom.com	popd.ix.netcom.com	nntp.ix.netcom.com
Microsoft Network	mail.msn.com	mail.msn.com	news.msn.com

6. Next (see Figure 11.4), you'll enter your POP (Post Office Protocol) or your IMAP (Internet Message Access Protocol) server name (again, Table 11.1 lists this for some common ISPs). These are the servers through which incoming mail will be received. Often they have the same name as your SMTP server. Once you have entered this information, click on the Next button to continue. The dialog box will be replaced with the final New Profile Setup dialog box.

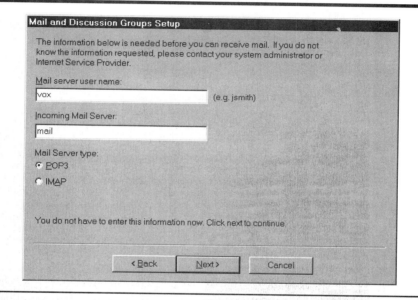

Figure 11.4:   The user name required here is the user name that appears in your e-mail address, not your regular name.

7. Finally, you must provide information about your news server. This is the server through which you'll access news (or discussion) groups. You should get this information from your ISP or system administrator (Table 11.1 lists the values for some common ISPs). Click on the Finish button to complete the process.

You can set up individual profiles for different users of the same computer by opening the User Profile Manager. Just click on the Start button, and select Programs ➤ Netscape Communicator ➤ Setup New User Profile. The User Profile Manager dialog box will appear. Follow steps 2–7 above.

When you open up Netscape Communicator for the first time, you can expect to see something like Figure 11.5.

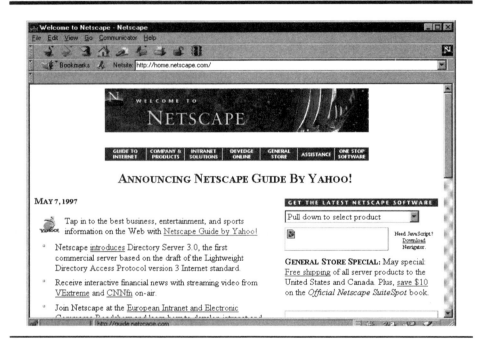

Figure 11.5: The Welcome to Netscape home page

You'll probably want to change your default home page to a location at your service provider, your place of employment, or something of more immediate significance to you. Chapter 8 tells you how to do this.

Enhancing the Program's Look and Performance

Okay, we told you in the preceding sections that all you had to do was unpack the files and start up Communicator, and that's true. This is not to say you can't or don't have to configure Communicator; it's just that Communicator can start up and do some useful things before it is configured. You can configure Communicator (if you like) to make it work the way you want it to work.

Configuring Communicator is quick and easy. We've already done a little configuring earlier in the book, but we didn't make a big deal of it. In Chapter 3, we told you how to change the base font to make Communicator display text in a size and color that you like, and then we told you how to get Navigator to load inline images only on demand, speeding up Communicator's performance noticeably.

Making the Viewing Area Bigger

Controlling the look of the program is not just a matter of cosmetics; it can be a matter of making the viewing area larger and easier to work with. Above the document-viewing window and below the menu bar, you'll usually see a row of icons representing tools and features, a box showing the URL of the page you are currently viewing, and a row of directory buttons that take you to various pages.

These are handy things to have around. If you want to see the Welcome to Netscape home page, you can simply click on the Home button on the toolbar. If you want to view the document you were looking at just a second ago, you can click on the Back button on the toolbar, and so on.

If, however, you'd rather give the Web document you're viewing more room to breathe, you can turn off the Navigation toolbar, the Location toolbar, and the Personal toolbar, in any combination, including all three (see Figure 11.6). Get this: you don't lose anything by turning them off; all their functions are still available on Communicator's menu bar.

The Navigation, Location, and Personal toolbars can be controlled by the Hide or Show selections from Communicator's View menu. When you choose the Hide option from the menu, the item disappears from view; to restore the option, click on View from the menu bar and select Show. Fiddle around with these options as you like to see what works for you.

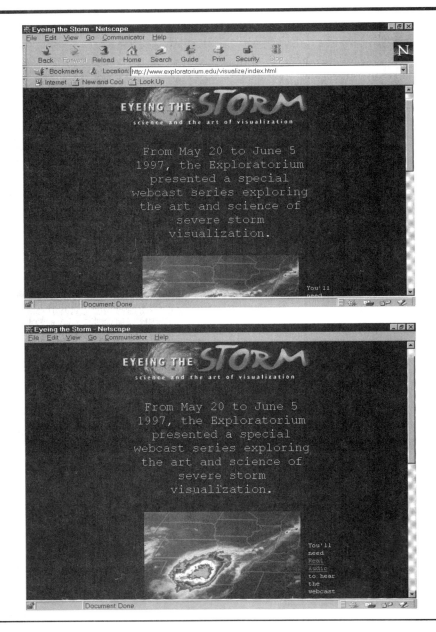

Figure 11.6:   The Communicator window above has the Navigation toolbar, the Location toolbar, and Personal toolbar turned on. The window below has all three turned off, making the viewing area a lot bigger.

You can also toggle the toolbars on and off by clicking the panels on the far left of the window. Clicking on the little panels, called *tabs* (shown in Figure 11.7), makes the toolbars collapse and expand so you can have more or less room for the page on display.

Click here to expand the Location toolbar.

Figure 11.7:   Toolbars can be toggled off and on by clicking on the tabs on the left.

Communicator has changed the way toolbars are displayed from version 3. The View menu now lists three toolbars:

◆ The Navigation toolbar, showing the command icons.

◆ The Location toolbar featuring the Bookmarks QuickFile menu and icon, and the Location text box. See Chapter 4 for detailed instructions on working with Bookmarks.

◆ The Personal toolbar, showing the items on the Bookmarks menu as buttons. For a detailed description of working with the Personal toolbar, see Chapter 4.

When you've got Communicator's "face" configured to reflect your preferences, that becomes the default configuration, and requires no special save action to remain available to you next time you run the program.

◆ Setting Up Conference

Netscape Conference is installed automatically with the standard version of Netscape Communicator. You'll need some hardware in order to make full use of Conference. The hardware you should have to use Conference is

◆ A sound card (it's possible to use Conference's non-audio tools without one, but what fun is that?)

◆ A microphone

◆ Speakers

Don't bother shelling out for a special microphone or speakers for the sake of your Conference experience; expensive equipment doesn't improve Conference's performance. The primary problem for most of us in using this sort of thing is still bandwidth, not the hardware on our desks. Go for economy in this case, and spend your money on memory and a good sound card.

The first time you start up Conference, you'll have to do a bit of setup. Not to worry, you'll be in the sure hands of the Setup Wizard, which will lead you through the process. Here are the steps to follow:

1. From the Windows 95 Start menu, select Programs ➤ Netscape Communicator ➤ Netscape Conference. The Welcome to Netscape Conference dialog box will appear.

 If for any reason starting Conference doesn't invoke the Setup Wizard, from the menu select Help ➤ Setup Wizard. Go on to step 3; you'll be fine.

2. Click on the Next button. The Welcome dialog box will be replaced by the About the Netscape Conference Setup Wizard dialog box.

3. Click on Next to continue. The About dialog box will be replaced by the Setting Up Your Business Card dialog box.

4. In the Setting Up Your Business Card dialog box, fill in the text boxes with information about yourself. The text boxes for you to fill in are:

- ◆ Name
- ◆ Email
- ◆ Photo
- ◆ Company
- ◆ Title
- ◆ Address
- ◆ Phone
- ◆ Fax

You must fill in the Name and Email text boxes. All of the other fields are optional and you can leave them blank if you wish.

5. Click on the Next button. The Setting Up Your Business Card dialog box will close and the Setting Your Directory Preferences dialog box will appear.

6. A Conference Directory is a listing of all the hip, happenin' people who use Netscape Conference. You can use this directory to look up who's online—that's how other people might find you. The Directory Preferences dialog box allows you to choose a directory server. The default server is dls.netscape.com. Unless you have some compelling reason to change this, leave it alone. You can also choose whether or not you want your own listing to appear in the directory server. If you want to do so, leave the *List my name in the phone book* box checked. If you don't, deselect the box by unchecking it.

7. Once you are done, click on Next to continue. A dialog box will appear requesting information about the speed of your connection to the Internet. Click on the radio button next to your type of Internet connection. Your options are

- ◆ 14400bps modem
- ◆ 28800bps modem or higher
- ◆ ISDN line
- ◆ LAN

8. Click on Next to continue. The Detecting Your Sound Card dialog box will appear.

9. Unless you know better, leave the default settings alone in the Detecting Your Sound Card dialog box and click on the Next button. The contents of the dialog box will change.

10. Click on Next to continue. A series of dialog boxes will appear testing various aspects of your sound system's capabilities to deliver and record sound. The messages and responses are very intuitive—just follow the Wizard as each sound test is performed, and click on Next to move on to the next one, until all of the playback and recording tests are complete.

11. When the playback and recording tests are done, a dialog box will appear informing you that the Setup Wizard has finished detecting the audio devices in your computer.

12. A dialog box will then appear congratulating you that you've set up Conference. Click on Finished. You'll be returned to the Conference window.

If your sound card didn't come with what's called a *full-duplex* driver, or if you didn't install one when you put your sound card in, you may want to check with your card's vendor to see whether such a driver is available. Having one of these babies will improve your sound card's performance significantly, so it's probably worth asking the question.

What's Out There

If you have one of the popular SoundBlaster boards and don't happen to have a full-duplex driver, you can download one from Creative Labs' Web site. Check out http://www.creaf.com.

 To modify your Conference options once you've got the program up and running, open Conference and from the menu bar select Call ➤ Preferences. You can use the Preferences dialog box that appears to change whatever you'd like. If you want to change nearly everything, or if you want to check the diagnostic parts again, just select Help ➤ Setup Wizard to re-run the Setup Wizard.

It's time to do the Internet equivalent of dropping that dime. You can learn all about running Conference in Chapter 6.

◆ Quitting Netscape Communicator

This is a handy piece of information that we don't want to neglect. When you're done with your travels for the day, simply do the following:

1. From the menu bar, select File ➤ Exit. This will quit the component you have open, but if you happen to have your connection going, it will leave you connected to your Internet service provider, so in that case...

2. Switch to your connection software—Windows 95 Dial-Up Networking, for example—and disconnect from the Internet. The way

you sever your Internet connection will depend on the method and software you use to connect.

 Selecting Exit from the File menu will close all of the Communicator components that you currently have open. If you wish to close only the current Communicator component (say, a Navigator window) select File ➤ Close. This will close the current component while leaving Communicator running.

You'll be disconnected from your Internet service provider and free now to plant hydrangeas, tap dance 'til dawn, or whatever.

You're Set to Go

Bingo. You're all set up. You've installed your Internet connection software and Communicator, you know how to start Communicator and make it look the way you want, and you can access mail and news servers. If you like, you can turn to Chapter 1 for useful background information or to Chapter 3 to get started navigating with Netscape.

What's on the CD

The CD-ROM that comes with this book contains tools and software that will get you started surfing the Internet. You'll get

♦ A customized What's Out There page linking you to millions of entertaining and useful Web sites, along with an online glossary

♦ A number of popular connectivity options that will make getting online a simple and convenient process

♦ Several software tools that enhance your surfing experience or help you add content to your own Web pages

Some of the software programs on the CD are demo or trial versions of a full product. You can find out more about the software, including how to obtain a full, registered copy of any trial software, by visiting the company's Web site. Let's take a look at each of these items in turn.

◆ The What's Out There Page

All of the many, many Internet sites discussed in this book (and then some) are linked to a customized Web page included on the CD. We call it the What's Out There page, because, obviously, it links you to all the great stuff we've pointed out in the What's Out There boxes throughout this book. It also links you to an online glossary and a bonus index of sites, called "Spots on the Web You Won't Want to Miss," to get you started on your Web travels.

You can make the What's Out There page the start-up home page you'll see when you start Navigator, or you can keep it nearby for convenient reference. In either case, you'll get quick access to a wide array of Internet resources, including

◆ Search tools and directories—such as AltaVista, HotBot, Excite, Infoseek, and Yahoo—that will enable you to find what you seek on the Internet in a jiffy and be your entry point to literally millions of Web pages

◆ Sources of free and inexpensive software that will enhance your Internet capabilities

◆ Publishing tools and resources that will get you started and help you to refine and even publicize your own Web publications

◆ Hand-selected sites on topics such as Arts and Entertainment, Computers and the Net, Personal Finance, Sports, Travel, Zines, and more

 You can quickly find terms that are defined in the online glossary by selecting Edit ➤ Find from Navigator's menu bar and typing the term of interest into the dialog box that appears.

The What's Out There home page takes advantage of Navigator's frames capability, providing easy navigation and a lot of information packed into a comprehensive layout (see Figure App.1).

The What's Out There page actually (and technically) consists of several interlinked HTML files that are stored in a single folder on the disk. All you have to do is copy the folder to your hard drive (a simple task with Windows 95) and launch Navigator, and then you can view the page. Read on for easy instructions.

What's Out There

You can always find the latest version of the What's Out There page on the Web, at http://www.dnai.com/~vox/netscape/wot/homepage.html.

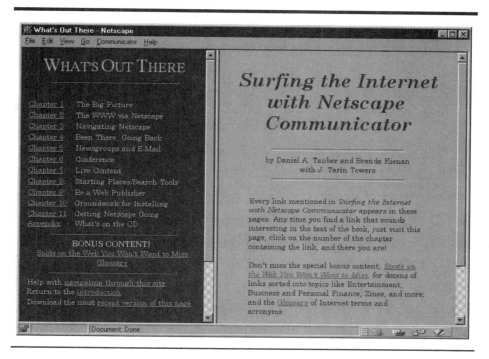

Figure App.1:   The What's Out There page makes exploring the Internet easy.

Copying the Home Page onto Your Hard Drive

The first part of this process is to copy the home page folder to your hard drive:

1. Insert the CD into your CD-ROM drive.

2. From your Desktop, double-click on the My Computer icon to display your computer's hard disk and drives.

3. Double-click on the CD-ROM drive icon to display the contents of the What's Out There CD. You'll see a folder named "wot."

4. Copy the WOT folder to your hard drive by clicking on it and dragging it to the drive C icon.

That's all there is to it. Now let's take a look at your new home page.

Launching Navigator and Looking at the Page

Now that the files are stored on your hard drive, you can use Navigator to view the What's Out There page.

Although you don't have to be connected to the Internet to view the page, you do need to be connected to follow many of its hyperlinks, because they point to sites all over the Net.

1. Launch Navigator. (See Chapter 3 if you need more details.)

2. From the menu bar, select File ➤ Open Page. The Open Page dialog box will appear.

3. Click on Choose File. The Open dialog box will appear.

4. Click on the Look In pull-down list and select your hard drive (in our case, it's drive C) to make its contents visible in the dialog box's big text area (see Figure App.2).

4. Double-click on the wot folder to open it.

5. Double-click on homepage.htm (see Figure App.3). The Netscape N icon will become animated, and the What's Out There page will appear on your screen.

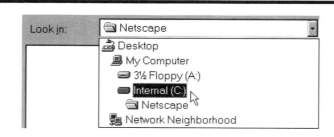

Figure App.2:   Select your hard drive from the pull-down list.

   If you open the page using a browser that doesn't support frames (or a version of Netscape Navigator earlier than 2.0), you won't be able to see the thing. Instead, a message will appear saying that the page is viewable only using a frames-capable browser such as Netscape Navigator version 2 or later.

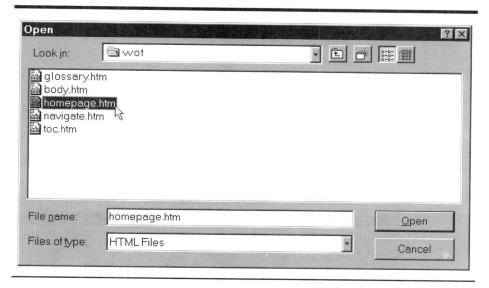

Figure App.3:   Double-click on the file named homepage.htm to open the What's Out There page.

Navigating the Page

The What's Out There page takes advantage of frames, a terrific design effect instituted by Netscape. Each frame is actually the result of a distinct HTML file; both frames are displayed in one viewing window—it's as if several Web pages were combined into one screen. In fact, it isn't *like* that—it *is* that. Pages that use frames present new options for navigating around. For helpful information about how to get around this particular page, click on the How to Navigate link in the page's left frame.

Making the What's Out There Page Your Home Page

You can keep the What's Out There page on your hard disk and open it, whenever you like, to use as a reference source, while retaining some other page as your start-up home page. Or you can make the What's Out There page your start-up home page—that is, the page that automatically appears each and every time you launch Navigator. We went over this in Chapter 3, but let's take a quick look at the process again:

1. Launch Navigator.

2. Open the What's Out There page using the instructions in the "Launching Navigator and Looking at the Page" section earlier in this appendix.

3. A URL beginning with the phrase `file:///` will be visible in the Location text box near the top of the Navigator viewing window (see Figure App.4). Click on the URL to highlight it.

Figure App.4:   Here you can see the location of the file for the What's Out There page, appearing in the familiar format of a URL.

4. From the menu bar, select Edit ➤ Copy (or press Ctrl+C) to copy the page's location to the Clipboard (the page location will remain stored there until you are ready to use it in step 7).

5. Select Edit ➤ Preferences. The Preferences dialog box will appear.

6. In the Category box that appears on the left side of the Preferences dialog box, click on Browser. The dialog box will change to make that set of preferences visible (see Figure App.5).

7. In the Home Page section of the dialog box, click in the Home Page Location text box, and then press Ctrl+V to paste in the location of the What's Out There page (you copied it to the Clipboard in step 4, remember?). It'll look like Figure App.6 when you're done.

8. Click on the OK button at the bottom of the Preferences dialog box. You'll return to the Navigator window.

9. To check that Navigator saved your changes, click on the Navigation toolbar's Home icon. The Netscape N will become animated, and in a few seconds, the What's Out There page will appear.

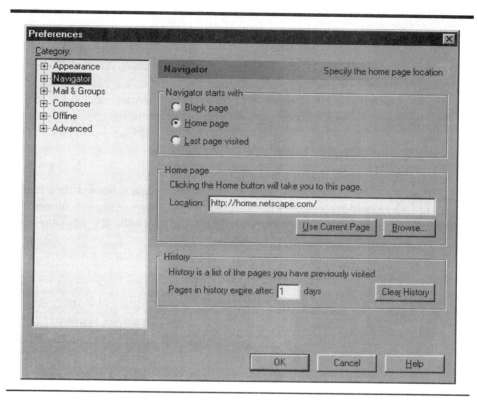

Figure App.5: The Preferences dialog box

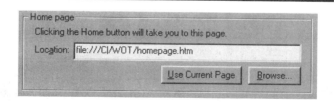

Figure App.6: Paste in the location of the What's Out There page.

Now, each and every time you start Navigator, the What's Out There page will be your launch point. You can access it at any time by clicking on the Navigation toolbar's Home icon.

You can add your favorite links to the What's Out There page using the HTML skills you learned in Chapter 9. Read on to find out more.

Adding Your Own Links to the Page

As your Web exploration expands, you may want to add your own newly discovered hyperlinks to the What's Out There page. You can keep adding stuff and expanding the page all you like, customizing it for your own purposes. All you need is some basic Web page construction know-how (which you have if you've gone through the exercises in Chapter 9 of this book). The home page files are fully customizable, and you can make any changes to them you want.

 The What's Out There home page is a document whose copyright is held by Sybex. You can copy and customize the document for your own use, but you may not copy or distribute the document for the use of others.

 It's always a good idea to make changes to your important files on *copies*, not on the original files. If you make a mistake—say, erasing all the links on a certain page—you can always reinstall the original What's Out There page from the CD. It won't have your changes, but it will have all the original links.

The HTML files that contains the hyperlinks to Internet sites are called ch1.htm, ch2.htm, etc. These pages are stored on your hard drive in the wot folder. To add your own links, simply open any of the ch*.htm files using Composer. Add hyperlinks where you would like them to appear in the page (see Chapter 9 for details), and then save and close the document. The next time you open the What's Out There page using Navigator, your links will appear.

Of course, making more sophisticated changes in the home page requires more Web page construction expertise—that's the sort of thing you'll want to get into if you have, or want, some serious HTML experience.

 You can get an updated version of the What's Out There page by clicking on the <u>Download the latest version</u> link.

◆ America Online

America Online (also known as AOL) is a suite of Internet access software and services from America Online, a well-known online service that offers Internet access via local phone numbers in most of the big U.S. cities. America Online, designed to work with Windows 95 and 3.1, provides an easy point-and-click interface that makes surfing the Internet a breeze.

If your Internet connection is through a modem, make sure that your modem is plugged in and you are not currently dialed in to the Internet before you install America Online. The installation is easy:

1. Open the aol31 or aol95 folder on the CD, depending on what version of the Windows operating system you're running, and double-click on setup.exe or setup95.exe. This will launch the AOL installation program.

2. The AOL installation program will check to make sure you have a modem and the necessary disk space to install the software. When the software is ready to continue, an Install dialog box will appear.

3. Click on Install to commence with the installation. The program will install itself; during the process a series of dialog boxes will open and close as various files are copied to your machine.

4. When installation is complete, a Setup dialog box will appear. Click on OK to close the installation program.

5. To begin using AOL, click on the AOL & Internet FREE Trial! icon. If you want to begin using AOL later, you can use the Windows 95 Start Menu and select Programs ➤ America Online ➤ AOL & Internet FREE Trial!. In either case, the sign-up procedure will be launched automatically. Get out your credit card and follow the simple steps laid out before you to register for America Online's services.

6. When prompted for a registration number and password, refer the AOL card enclosed with the CD.

This is all very easy—when you're done, turn to Chapters 10 and 11 to learn how to set up and use Netscape Communicator with America Online.

 America Online provides a copy of Microsoft Internet Explorer, another Web browser, as part of its software. You don't need to install Internet Explorer in order to use Netscape Communicator with AOL.

What's Out There

America Online's home page contains information about all of its services; visit it at http://www.aol.com.

◆ NETCOM's NETCOMplete

NETCOMplete is a suite of Internet access software and services from NETCOM Communications, a well-known Internet service provider that offers access via local phone numbers in most of the big U.S. cities. NET-COMplete, designed to work with (and *only* with) Windows 95, provides an easy point-and-click interface that makes surfing the Internet a breeze.

To install NETCOMplete, open the netcruz folder on the CD and double-click on setup.exe. The program will install itself; during the process a series of dialog boxes will open and close as various files are copied to your machine. When installation is complete, a sign-up procedure will be launched automatically. Get out your credit card and follow the simple steps laid out before you to register for NETCOM's NETCOMplete service.

You're asked for a registration code. Type **91975**.

This is all very easy—when you're done, turn to Chapters 10 and 11 to learn how to set up and use Netscape Communicator with NETCOMplete.

What's Out There

NETCOM's home page contains information about all of its services; visit it at http://www.netcom.com.

◆ Marimba's Castanet Software

Castanet is a software package that uses Java technology to broadcast select bits of news, entertainment, information, games, and even software over the Internet to your computer—you tell the Tuner what you like, and it goes and gets it. Content is delivered in customizable "channels" using Castanet's Tuner, while the Castanet Transmitter can be used to broadcast content from computers connected directly to the Internet. The full version of Castanet Tuner and the demo version of the Castanet Transmitter are both included on the CD.

The Castanet Tuner lets you choose custom content to be delivered to your Web browser in the form of Java applets and Web pages. To install the Castanet Tuner on your computer, open the castanet folder on the CD and double-click on turner.exe. As files are copied to your machine, a series of dialog boxes will appear and then close. Then you'll be stepped through the installation process. When you run the Castanet Tuner for the first time, you'll be asked to customize the channels that control the information the Tuner delivers. You must be online to customize and use the Castanet Tuner.

When the Castanet Tuner needs to update its channels or software, the software will automatically download new data or components; since only new data is downloaded, this process is generally pretty speedy. Any questions you have about installing the Castanet Tuner can be answered by selecting Help from the Tuner's menu bar, or by visiting the Marimba Web site. You can run the Castanet tuner by clicking on its icon or by selecting Start ➤ Castanet Tuner ➤ Castanet Tuner.

The Castanet Transmitter lets you broadcast your own custom content to be delivered to other users by the Castanet Tuner. To install the Castanet Transmitter demo on your computer, open the castanet folder on the CD and double-click on trans.exe. As files are copied to your machine, a series of dialog boxes will appear and then close. When the installation is complete, you can run the Castanet Transmitter from the Start Menu by selecting Programs ➤ Castanet Transmitter ➤ Castanet Transmitter. You must be using a machine with a *direct* connection to the Internet to transmit content.

> ## What's Out There
>
> Find out more about Marimba Software and the Castanet program via the Web at `http://www.marimba.com/`. That's also where you'll find information about Bongo, described below.

◆ Marimba's Bongo Demo

Bongo is a software creation tool you can use to create user interfaces called *presentations,* the content that is sent by the Marimba transmitter and played by the Marimba Tuner. A presentation can take on the form of a simple page—much like a Web page that includes static information—to full-scale interactive applications like a financial planner or a video game. Bongo presentations can incorporate Java applets and can also be used with Castanet to broadcast information to other Internet users.

To install the Bongo demo on your computer, open the castanet folder on the CD and double-click on bongo.exe. As files are copied to your machine, a series of dialog boxes will appear and then close.

After installation, you may find it helpful to run the Bongo tutorial by launching Bongo and, from the menu bar, selecting Help ➤ Index. Click on Tutorial to walk through a demonstration of how to create content using Bongo.

◆ Intermind Communicator

Intermind Communicator is a customizable Web browsing tool that uses Navigator as its interface. Register your preferences as an Intermind Communicator user, and it will direct you to news updates and Web pages that you want to read regularly. You can use Intermind Communicator's publishing tool to create your own custom content to deliver to other Internet users.

Intermind Communicator will only run on Windows 95 and NT. Before you install Intermind Communicator, close Navigator or any other Web browser you have running. To begin the Intermind Communicator installation, open the intermind folder on the CD and double-click on imc32.exe. As files are copied to your machine, a series of dialog boxes will appear and close, and you will be stepped through the setup process. When the installation is complete, Navigator will be launched, and you'll be asked to register Intermind Communicator and customize both the interface and the channel choices to your liking. Intermind Communicator runs not as a distinct program but as a customized Navigator interface.

What's Out There

Intermind's Web site offers information about Intermind Communicator, including a directory of channels. Visit http://www.intermind.com/.

◆ JetEffects

JetEffects, from Peak Technologies, is a Java authoring tool that lets you create simple animations that you can insert into Web pages. Using a drag-and-drop interface, you can animate text or images and save your creations as Java files, without any programming.

To begin the JetEffects trial version installation, open the jeteffec folder on the CD and double-click on jetfx25w.exe. As files are copied to your machine, a series of dialog boxes will appear and close, and you will be stepped through the setup process. After the installation is complete, you can start JetEffects by clicking on its icon on the Desktop.

What's Out There

Find out more about JetEffects, PeakJet, and Peak Technologies' other software by visiting http://www.peak-media.com/.

◆ PeakJet

PeakJet is a software utility that speeds your Web browsing by using intelligent caching. PeakJet pre-caches the links on Web pages you visit and "learns" your browsing habits to figure out what to keep in the cache and what pages to cache before you even visit them.

Before you install PeakJet, close Navigator or any other Web browsers you may be running. To begin the PeakJet trial version installation, open the peakjet folder on the CD and double-click on pj15I__2.exe. As files are copied to your machine, a series of dialog boxes will appear and close, and you will be stepped through the setup process.

After you install PeakJet, you must restart your computer. To use the software, start PeakJet by clicking on its icon. You can use PeakJet, rather than Dial-Up Networking, to dial into the Internet. After you've started PeakJet and connected to the Internet, start your Web browser, and PeakJet will get to work.

◆ WebPrinter

WebPrinter is a software tool that digests Web pages into booklets and prints them for you. This demo version of WebPrinter is good for four booklets.

Before you install WebPrinter, close Navigator or any other Web browsers you may be running. To begin the WebPrinter trial version installation, open the webprint folder on the CD and double-click on wp4packs.exe. When the installer launches, click on the Free 4-Pack button to commence the installation. You will then be stepped through the setup process. After you install WebPrinter, you must restart your computer. Read the WebPrinter help file, called readme.wri, for more information on setting up WebPrinter to work with the printer you have.

Surf's Up!

You've got everything you need to surf the Internet with Netscape Navigator. You've got the skills, the software, and even the convenient What's Out There page. You're on your way....

Index

Note to the Reader: Throughout this index, **boldface** page numbers indicate primary discussions of a topic. *Italic* page numbers indicate illustrations.

◆ Surf Savvy with the What's Out There CD

It's easy to find what's out there on the Net with the help of this book and its companion CD. Sure, the book shows you how to get and use Netscape Communicator, but it also shows you what's out there that can add dimension to your Internet experience. On the CD you'll find an easy-to-use Web site with tons of links to

- ◆ Directories and search tools—such as AltaVista, Excite, and Yahoo!—that provide an entry point to literally millions of Web pages
- ◆ Sources of free and inexpensive software that will enhance your time online
- ◆ Publishing tools and resources that will get you started and help you to refine and even publicize your own Web publications
- ◆ Hand-selected sites on topics such as Arts, Business, Sports, Travel, and Zines

You'll also find software on the CD that will help you speed up your surf time and create your own Java applets.

There's connect time on the CD, too! You'll find two of the most popular connectivity options: America Online and NETCOMplete—so you can get online and start surfing in a snap.

With this book/CD combo, you'll get quick access to thousands of rich Internet resources. See the Appendix for easy installation instructions for the What's Out There CD.

Customer Service and Support

For Netscape Communicator technical support, call 800/320-2099 or send e-mail to client@netscape.com.

SYBEX

© 1997 SYBEX Inc.